Defoe Abbott Marx Hardy Montaigne Machiavelli Chesterton Cooper Emerson Haggard Joyce Austen Hugo Eliot Grimm
Melville Stoker Carroll Christie Maupassant Byron Engels Molière Schiller Smith Kafka
Wilde Garnett Einstein Fitzgerald Hawthorne Dostoyevsky Hall
Goethe Cotton Kipling Doyle Willis
Baum Henry Nietzsche Balzac
Leslie Dumas Flaubert Turgenev Crane Verne
Stockton Vatsyayana Vinci
Burroughs Gogol Busch
Curtis Tocqueville Whitman
Homer Widger Tolstoy Twain Scott Plato Harte
Darwin Thoreau
Potter Freud Zola Lawrence Dickens Burton Hesse
Kant Jowett Stevenson Cervantes
Andersen Voltaire Cooke
Poe Aristotle London Descartes Wells
Hale James Hastings Irving
Bunner Shakespeare Chambers
Richter Dante da Benedict Alcott
Doré Swift Chekhov Shaw Pushkin
Wodehouse Newton

 **tredition®**

tredition was established in 2006 by Sandra Latusseck and Soenke Schulz. Based in Hamburg, Germany, tredition offers publishing solutions to authors and publishing houses, combined with world-wide distribution of printed and digital book content. tredition is uniquely positioned to enable authors and publishing houses to create books on their own terms and without conventional manufacturing risks.

For more information please visit: www.tredition.com

TREDITION CLASSICS

This book is part of the TREDITION CLASSICS series. The creators of this series are united by passion for literature and driven by the intention of making all public domain books available in printed format again - worldwide. Most TREDITION CLASSICS titles have been out of print and off the bookstore shelves for decades. At tredition we believe that a great book never goes out of style and that its value is eternal. Several mostly non-profit literature projects provide content to tredition. To support their good work, tredition donates a portion of the proceeds from each sold copy. As a reader of a TREDITION CLASSICS book, you support our mission to save many of the amazing works of world literature from oblivion. See all available books at www.tredition.com.

Project Gutenberg

The content for this book has been graciously provided by Project Gutenberg. Project Gutenberg is a non-profit organization founded by Michael Hart in 1971 at the University of Illinois. The mission of Project Gutenberg is simple: To encourage the creation and distribution of eBooks. Project Gutenberg is the first and largest collection of public domain eBooks.

Pedagogics as a System

Karl Rosenkranz

Imprint

This book is part of TREDITION CLASSICS

Author: Karl Rosenkranz
Cover design: Buchgut, Berlin – Germany

Publisher: tredition GmbH, Hamburg - Germany
ISBN: 978-3-8472-2043-5

www.tredition.com
www.tredition.de

PEDAGOGICS AS A SYSTEM.

[Inquiries from teachers in different sections of the country as to the sources of information on the subject of Teaching as a Science have led me to believe that a translation of Rosenkranz's Pedagogics may be widely acceptable and useful. It is very certain that too much of our teaching is simply empirical, and as Germany has, more than any other country, endeavored to found it upon universal truths, it is to that country that we must at present look for a remedy for this empiricism.

Based as this is upon the profoundest system of German Philosophy, no more suggestive treatise on Education can perhaps be found. In his third part, as will be readily seen, Rosenkranz follows the classification of National ideas given in Hegel's Philosophy of History. The word "Pedagogics," though it has unfortunately acquired a somewhat unpleasant meaning in English — thanks to the writers who have made the word "pedagogue" so odious — deserves to be redeemed for future use. I have, therefore, retained it in the translation.

In order that the reader may see the general scope of the work, I append in tabular form the table of contents, giving however, under the first and second parts, only the main divisions. The minor heads can, of course, as they appear in the translation, be easily located. — *Tr.*]

INTRODUCTION.

1. The science of Pedagogics cannot be derived from a simple principle with such exactness as Logic and Ethics. It is rather a mixed science which has its presuppositions in many others. In this respect it resembles Medicine, with which it has this also in common, that it must make a distinction between a sound and an unhealthy system of education, and must devise means to prevent or to cure the latter. It may therefore have, like Medicine, the three departments of Physiology, Pathology, and Therapeutics.

2. Since Pedagogics is capable of no such exact definitions of its principle and no such logical deduction as other sciences, the treatises written upon it abound more in shallowness than any other literature. Short-sightedness and arrogance find in it a most congenial atmosphere, and criticism *Pedagogics as a System.* 6 and declamatory bombast flourish in perfection as nowhere else. The literature of religious tracts might be considered to rival that of Pedagogics in its superficiality and assurance, if it did not for the most part seem itself to belong, through its ascetic nature, to Pedagogics. But teachers as persons should be treated in their weaknesses and failures with the utmost consideration, because they are most of them sincere in contributing their mite for the improvement of education, and all their pedagogic practice inclines them towards administering reproof and giving advice.

3. The charlatanism of educational literature is also fostered by the fact that teaching has become one of the most profitable employments, and the competition in it tends to increase self-glorification.

—When "Boz" in his "Nicholas Nickleby" exposed the horrible mysteries of an English boarding-school, many teachers of such schools were, as he assures us, so accurately described that they openly complained he had aimed his caricatures directly at them.—

4. In the system of the sciences, Pedagogics belongs to the Philosophy of Spirit,—and in this, to the department of Practical Philosophy, the problem of which is the comprehension of the necessity of freedom; for education is the conscious working of one will on an-

other so as to produce itself in it according to a determinate aim. The idea of subjective spirit, as well as that of Art, Science, and Religion, forms the essential condition for Pedagogics, but does not contain its principle. If one thinks out a complete statement of Practical Philosophy (Ethics), Pedagogics may be distributed among all its grades. But the point at which Pedagogics itself becomes organic is the idea of the Family, because in the family the difference between the adults and the minors enters directly through the naturalness of spirit, and the right of the children to an education and the duty of parents towards them in this respect is incontestable. All other spheres of education, in order to succeed, must presuppose a true family life. They may extend and complement the business of teaching, but cannot be its original foundation.

—In our systematic exposition of Education, we must not allow ourselves to be led into error by those theories which *Pedagogics as a System.* 7 do not recognize the family, and which limit the relation of husband and wife to the producing of children. The Platonic Philosophy is the most worthy representative of this class. Later writers who take great pleasure in seeing the world full of children, but who would subtract from the love to a wife all truth and from that to children all care, exhibit in their doctrine of the anarchy of love only a sickly (but yet how prevalent an) imitation of the Platonic state. —

5. Much confusion also arises from the fact that many do not clearly enough draw the distinction between Pedagogics as a science and Pedagogics as an art. As a science it busies itself with developing ☐*riori* the idea of Education in the universality and necessity of that idea, but as an art it is the concrete individualizing of this abstract idea in any given case. And in any such given case, the peculiarities of the person who is to be educated and all the previously existing circumstances necessitate a modification of the universal aims and ends, which modification cannot be provided for beforehand, but must rather test the ready tact of the educator who knows how to make the existing conditions fulfil his desired end. It is exactly in doing this that the educator may show himself inventive and creative, and that pedagogic talent can distinguish itself. The word "art" is here used in the same way as it is used when

we say, the art of war, the art of government, &c.; and rightly, for we are talking about the possibility of the realization of the idea.

—The educator must adapt himself to the pupil, but not to such a degree as to imply that the pupil is incapable of change, and he must also be sure that the pupil shall learn through his experience the independence of the object studied, which remains uninfluenced by his variable personal moods, and the adaptation on the teacher's part must never compromise this independence.—

6. If conditions which are local, temporal, and individual, are fixed as constant rules, and carried beyond their proper limits, are systematized as a valuable formalistic code, unavoidable error arises. The formul栯f teaching are admirable material for the science, but are not the science itself.

7. Pedagogics as a science must (1) unfold the general idea of Education; (2) must exhibit the particular phases into *Pedagogics as a System.* 8 which the general work of Education divides itself, and (3) must describe the particular standpoint upon which the general idea realizes itself, or should become real in its special processes at any particular time.

8. The treatment of the first part offers no difficulty. It is logically too evident. But it would not do to substitute for it the history of Pedagogics, simply because all the conceptions of it which appear in systematic treatises can be found there.

—Into this error G. Thaulow has fallen in his pamphlet on Pedagogics as a Philosophical Science.—

9. The second division unfolds the subject of the physical, intellectual and practical culture of the human race, and constitutes the main part of all books on Pedagogy. Here arises the greatest difficulty as to the limitations, partly because of the undefined nature of the ideas, partly because of the degree of amplification which the details demand. Here is the field of the widest possible differences. If e.g. one studies out the conception of the school with reference to the qualitative specialities which one may consider, it is evident that he can extend his remarks indefinitely; he may speak thus of technological schools of all kinds, to teach mining, navigation, war, art, &c.

10. The third division distinguishes between the different standpoints which are possible in the working out of the conception of Education in its special elements, and which therefore produce different systems of Education wherein the general and the particular are individualized in a special manner. In every system the general tendencies of the idea of education, and the difference between the physical, intellectual and practical culture of man, must be formally recognized, and will appear. The How is decided by the standpoint which reduces that formalism to a special system. Thus it becomes possible to discover the essential contents of the history of Pedagogics from its idea, since this can furnish not an indefinite but a certain number of Pedagogic systems.

— The lower standpoint merges always into the higher, and in so doing first attains its full meaning, e.g.: Education for the sake of the nation is set aside for higher standpoints, e.g. that of Christianity; but we must not suppose that the national *Pedagogics as a System.* 9 phase of Education was counted as nought from the Christian standpoint. Rather it itself had outgrown the limits which, though suitable enough for its early stage, could no longer contain its true idea. This is sure to be the case in the fact that the national individualities become indestructible by being incorporated into Christianity — a fact that contradicts the abstract seizing of such relations. —

11. The last system must be that of the present, and since this is certainly on one side the result of all the past, while on the other seized in its possibilities it is determined by the Future, the business of Pedagogics cannot pause till it reaches its ideal of the general and special determinations, so that looked at in this way the Science of Pedagogics at its end returns to its beginning. The first and second divisions already contain the idea of the system necessary for the Present.

FIRST PART.
The General Idea of Education.

12. The idea of Pedagogics in general must distinguish,

(1) The nature of Education in general;
(2) Its form;
(3) Its limits.

I.

13. The nature of Education is determined by the nature of mind — that it can develop whatever it really is only by its own activity. Mind is in itself free; but if it does not actualize this possibility, it is in no true sense free, either for itself or for another. Education is the influencing of man by man, and it has for its end to lead him to actualize himself through his own efforts. The attainment of perfect manhood as the actualization of the Freedom necessary to mind constitutes the nature of Education in general.

— The completely isolated man does not become man. Solitary human beings who have been found in forests, like the wild girl of the forest of Ardennes, sufficiently prove the fact that the truly human qualities in man cannot be developed without reciprocal action with human beings. Caspar Hauser in his subterranean prison is an illustration of what man *Pedagogics as a System.* 10 would be by himself. The first cry of the child expresses in its appeals to others this helplessness of spirituality on the side of nature. —

14. Man, therefore, is the only fit subject for education. We often speak, it is true, of the education of plants and animals; but even when we do so, we apply, unconsciously perhaps, other expressions, as "raising" and "training," in order to distinguish these. "Breaking" consists in producing in an animal, either by pain or pleasure of the senses, an activity of which, it is true, he is capable, but which he never would have developed if left to himself. On the other hand, it is the nature of Education only to assist in the producing of that which the subject would strive most earnestly to develop for himself if he had a clear idea of himself. We speak of raising trees and animals, but not of raising men; and it is only a planter who looks to his slaves only for an increase in their number.

— The education of men is quite often enough, unfortunately, only a "breaking," and here and there still may be found examples where one tries to teach mechanically, not through the understanding power of the creative WORD, but through the powerless and fruitless appeal to physical pain. —

15. The idea of Education may be more or less comprehensive. We use it in the widest sense when we speak of the Education of the race, for we understand by this expression the connection which the

acts and situations of different nations have to each other, as different steps towards self-conscious freedom. In this the world-spirit is the teacher.

16. In a more restricted sense we mean by Education the shaping of the individual life by the forces of nature, the rhythmical movement of national customs, and the might of destiny in which each one finds limits set to his arbitrary will. These often mould him into a man without his knowledge. For he cannot act in opposition to nature, nor offend the ethical sense of the people among whom he dwells, nor despise the leading of destiny without discovering through experience that before the Nemesis of these substantial elements his subjective power can dash itself only to be shattered. If he perversely and persistently rejects all our admonitions, we leave him, as a last resort, to destiny, whose iron rule must *Pedagogics as a System.* 11 educate him, and reveal to him the God whom he has misunderstood.

—It is, of course, sometimes not only possible, but necessary for one, moved by the highest sense of morality, to act in opposition to the laws of nature, to offend the ethical sense of the people that surround him, and to brave the blows of destiny; but such a one is a sublime reformer or martyr, and we are not now speaking of such, but of the perverse, the frivolous, and the conceited. —

17. In the narrowest sense, which however is the usual one, we mean by Education the influence which one mind exerts on another in order to cultivate the latter in some understood and methodical way, either generally or with reference to some special aim. The educator must, therefore, be relatively finished in his own education, and the pupil must possess unlimited confidence in him. If authority be wanting on the one side, or respect and obedience on the other, this ethical basis of development must fail, and it demands in the very highest degree, talent, knowledge, skill, and prudence.

—Education takes on this form only under the culture which has been developed through the influence of city life. Up to that time we have the na جمي period of education, which holds to the general powers of nature, of national customs, and of destiny, and which lasts for a long time among the rural populations. But in the city a greater complication of events, an uncertainty of the results of reflection, a working out of individuality, and a need of the possession of many arts and trades, make their appearance and render it impossible for men longer to be ruled by mere custom. The Telemachus of Fenelon was educated to rule himself by means of reflection; the actual Telemachus in the heroic age lived simply according to custom. —

18. The general problem of Education is the development of the theoretical and practical reason in the individual. If we say that to educate one means to fashion him into morality, we do not make our definition sufficiently comprehensive, because we say nothing of intelligence, and thus confound education and ethics. A man is not merely a human being, but as a reasonable being he is a peculiar individual, and different from all others of the race.

Pedagogics as a System. 12

19. Education must lead the pupil by an interconnected series of efforts previously foreseen and arranged by the teacher to a definite end; but the particular form which this shall take must be determined by the peculiar character of the pupil's mind and the situation in which he is found. Hasty and inconsiderate work may accomplish much, but only *systematic* work can advance and fashion him in conformity with his nature, and the former does not belong to education, for this includes in itself the idea of an end, and that of the technical means for its attainment.

20. But as culture comes to mean more and more, there becomes necessary a division of the business of teaching among different persons, with reference to capabilities and knowledge, because as the arts and sciences are continually increasing in number, one can become learned in any one branch only by devoting himself exclusively to it, and hence becoming one-sided. A difficulty hence arises which is also one for the pupil, of preserving, in spite of this unavoidable one-sidedness, the unity and wholeness which are necessary to humanity.

—The naجمى dignity of the happy savage, and the agreeable simplicity of country people, appear to very great advantage when contrasted on this side with the often unlimited narrowness of a special trade, and the endless curtailing of the wholeness of man by the pruning processes of city life. Thus the often abused savage has his hut, his family, his cocoa tree, his weapons, his passions; he fishes, hunts, plays, fights, adorns himself, and enjoys the consciousness that he is the centre of a whole, while a modern citizen is often only an abstract expression of culture. —

21. As it becomes necessary to divide the work of teaching, a difference between general and special schools arises also, from the needs of growing culture. The former present in different compass all the sciences and arts which are included in the term "general education," and which were classified by the Greeks under the general name of Encyclop梗a. The latter are known as special schools, suited to particular needs or talents.

— As those who live in the country are relatively isolated, it is often necessary, or at least desirable, that one man should *Pedagogics as a System.* 13 be trained equally on many different sides. The poor tutor is required not only to instruct in all the sciences, he must also speak French and be able to play the piano. —

22. For any single person, the relation of his actual education to its infinite possibilities can only be approximately determined, and it can be considered as only relatively finished on any one side. Education is impossible to him who is born an idiot, since the want of the power of generalizing and of ideality of conscious personality leaves to such an unfortunate only the possibility of a mechanical training.

— S隩rt, the teacher of the deaf mutes in Berlin, has made laudable efforts to educate idiots, but the account as given in his publication, "Cure of Idiots by an Intellectual Method, Berlin, 1846," shows that the result obtained was only external; and though we do not desire to be understood as denying or refusing to this class the possession of a mind *in potentia*, it appears in them to be confined to an embryonic state. —

II.

The Form of Education.

23. The general form of Education is determined by the nature of the mind, that it really is nothing but what it makes itself to be. The

mind is (1) immediate (or potential), but (2) it must estrange itself from itself as it were, so that it may place itself over against itself as a special object of attention; (3) this estrangement is finally removed through a further acquaintance with the object—it feels itself at home in that on which it looks, and returns again enriched to the form of immediateness. That which at first appeared to be another than itself is now seen to be itself. Education cannot create; it can only help to develop to reality the previously existent possibility; it can only help to bring forth to light the hidden life.

24. All culture, whatever may be its special purport, must pass through these two stages—of estrangement, and its removal. Culture must hold fast to the distinction between the subject and the object considered immediately, though it has again to absorb this distinction into itself, in order that the union of the two may be more complete and lasting. The subject recognizes then all the more certainly that what at *Pedagogics as a System.* 14 first appeared to it as a foreign existence, belongs to it as its own property, and that it holds it as its own all the more by means of culture.

—Plato, as is known, calls the feeling with which knowledge must begin, wonder; but this can serve as a beginning only, for wonder itself can only express the tension between the subject and the object at their first encounter—a tension which would be impossible if they were not in themselves identical. Children have a longing for the far-off, the strange, and the wonderful, as if they hoped to find in these an explanation of themselves. They want the object to be a genuine object. That to which they are accustomed, which they see around them every day, seems to have no longer any objective energy for them; but an alarm of fire, banditti life, wild animals, gray old ruins, the robin's songs, and far-off happy islands, &c.— everything high-colored and dazzling—leads them irresistibly on. The necessity of the mind's making itself foreign to itself is that which makes children prefer to hear of the adventurous journeys of Sinbad than news of their own city or the history of their nation, and in youth this same necessity manifests itself in their desire of travelling.—

25. This activity of the mind in allowing itself to be absorbed, and consciously so, in an object with the purpose of making it his own,

or of producing it, is *Work*. But when the mind gives itself up to its objects as chance may present them or through arbitrariness, careless as to whether they have any result, such activity is *Play*. Work is laid out for the pupil by his teacher by authority, but in his play he is left to himself.

26. Thus work and play must be sharply distinguished from each other. If one has not respect for work as an important and substantial activity, he not only spoils play for his pupil, for this loses all its charm when deprived of the antithesis of an earnest, set task, but he undermines his respect for real existence. On the other hand, if he does not give him space, time, and opportunity, for play, he prevents the peculiarities of his pupil from developing freely through the exercise of his creative ingenuity. Play sends the pupil back refreshed to his work, since in play he forgets himself *Pedagogics as a System*. 15 in his own way, while in work he is required to forget himself in a manner prescribed for him by another.

—Play is of great importance in helping one to discover the true individualities of children, because in play they may betray thoughtlessly their inclinations. This antithesis of work and play runs through the entire life. Children anticipate in their play the earnest work of after life; thus the little girl plays with her doll, and the boy pretends he is a soldier and in battle.—

27. Work should never be treated as if it were play, nor play as if it were work. In general, the arts, the sciences, and productions, stand in this relation to each other: the accumulation of stores of knowledge is the recreation of the mind which is engaged in independent creation, and the practice of arts fills the same office to those whose work is to collect knowledge.

28. Education seeks to transform every particular condition so that it shall no longer seem strange to the mind or in anywise foreign to its own nature. This identity of consciousness, and the special character of anything done or endured by it, we call Habit [habitual conduct or behavior]. It conditions formally all progress; for that which is not yet become habit, but which we perform with design and an exercise of our will, is not yet a part of ourselves.

29. As to Habit, we have to say next that it is at first indifferent as to what it relates. But that which is to be considered as indifferent or

neutral cannot be defined in the abstract, but only in the concrete, because anything that is indifferent as to whether it shall act on these particular men, or in this special situation, is capable of another or even of the opposite meaning for another man or men for the same men or in other circumstances. Here, then, appeal must be made to the individual conscience in order to be able from the depths of individuality to separate what we can permit to ourselves from that which we must deny ourselves. The aim of Education must be to arouse in the pupil this spiritual and ethical sensitiveness which does not recognize anything as *merely* indifferent, but rather knows how to seize in everything, even in the seemingly small, its universal human significance. But in relation to the highest problems he *Pedagogics as a System.* 16 must learn that what concerns his own immediate personality is entirely indifferent.

30. Habit lays aside its indifference to an external action through reflection on the advantage or disadvantage of the same. Whatever tends as a harmonious means to the realization of an end is advantageous, but that is disadvantageous which, by contradicting its idea, hinders or destroys it. Advantage and disadvantage being then only *relative* terms, a habit which is advantageous for one man in one case may be disadvantageous for another man, or even for the same man, under different circumstances. Education must, therefore, accustom the youth to judge as to the expediency or inexpediency of any action in its relation to the essential vocation of his life, so that he shall avoid that which does not promote its success.

31. But the *absolute* distinction of habit is the moral distinction between the good and the bad. For from this standpoint alone can we finally decide what is allowable and what is forbidden, what is advantageous and what is disadvantageous.

32. As relates to form, habit may be either passive or active. The passive is that which teaches us to bear the vicissitudes of nature as well as of history with such composure that we shall hold our ground against them, being always equal to ourselves, and that we shall not allow our power of acting to be paralyzed through any mutations of fortune. Passive habit is not to be confounded with obtuseness in receiving impressions, a blank abstraction from the affair in hand which at bottom is found to be nothing more than a

selfishness which desires to be left undisturbed: it is simply composure of mind in view of changes over which we have no control.
While we vividly experience joy and sorrow, pain and pleasure —
inwoven as these are with the change of seasons, of the weather,
&c. — with the alternation of life and death, of happiness and misery, we ought nevertheless to harden ourselves against them so that
at the same time in our consciousness of the supreme worth of the
mind we shall build up the inaccessible stronghold of Freedom in
ourselves. — Active habit [or behavior] is found realized in a wide
range of activity which appears in manifold forms, such as skill,
Formation of Habits. 17 dexterity, readiness of information, &c. It is a
steeling of the internal for action upon the external, as the Passive is
a steeling of the internal against the influences of the external.

33. Habit is the general form which instruction takes. For since it
reduces a condition or an activity within ourselves to an instinctive
use and wont, it is necessary for any thorough instruction. But as,
according to its content, it may be either proper or improper, advantageous or disadvantageous, good or bad, and according to its form
may be the assimilation of the external by the internal, or the impress of the internal upon the external, Education must procure for
the pupil the power of being able to free himself from one habit and
to adopt another. Through his freedom he must be able not only to
renounce any habit formed, but to form a new one; and he must so
govern his system of habits that it shall exhibit a constant progress
of development into greater freedom. We must discipline ourselves,
as a means toward the ever-changing realization of the Good in us,
constantly to form and to break habits.

— We must characterize those habits as bad which relate only to
our convenience or our enjoyment. They are often not blamable in
themselves, but there lies in them a hidden danger that they may
allure us into luxury or effeminacy. But it is a false and mechanical
way of looking at the affair if we suppose that a habit which has
been formed by a certain number of repetitions can be broken by an
equal number of denials. We can never renounce a habit utterly
except through a clearness of judgment which decides it to be undesirable, and through firmness of will. —

34. Education comprehends also the reciprocal action of the opposites, authority and obedience, rationality and individuality, work and play, habit and spontaneity. If we imagine that these can be reconciled by rules, it will be in vain that we try to restrain the youth in these relations. But a failure in education in this particular is very possible through the freedom of the pupil, through special circumstances, or through the errors of the educator himself. And for this very reason any theory of Education must take into account in the beginning this negative possibility. It must consider beforehand the dangers which threaten the pupil in all possible *Protection against Temptation.* 18 ways even before they surround him, and fortify him against them. Intentionally to expose him to temptation in order to prove his strength, is devilish; and, on the other hand, to guard him against the chance of dangerous temptation, to wrap him in cotton (as the proverb says), is womanish, ridiculous, fruitless, and much more dangerous; for temptation comes not alone from without, but quite as often from within, and secret inclination seeks and creates for itself the opportunity for its gratification, often perhaps an unnatural one. The truly preventive activity consists not in an abstract seclusion from the world, all of whose elements are innate in each individual, but in the activity of knowledge and discipline, modified according to age and culture.

—If one endeavors to deprive the youth of all free and individual intercourse with the world, one only falls into a continual watching of him, and the consciousness that he is watched destroys in him all elasticity of spirit, all confidence, all originality. The police shadow of control obscures all independence and systematically accustoms him to dependence. As the tragi-comic story of Peter Schlemihl shows, one cannot lose his own shadow without falling into the saddest fatalities; but the shadow of a constant companion, as in the pedagogical system of the Jesuits, undermines all naturalness. And if one endeavors too strictly to guard against that which is evil and forbidden, the intelligence of the pupils reacts in deceit against such efforts, till the educators are amazed that such crimes as come often to light can have arisen under such careful control.—

35. If there should appear in the youth any decided moral deformity which is opposed to the ideal of his education, the instructor must at once make inquiry as to the history of its origin, because

the negative and the positive are very closely connected in his being, so that what appears to be negligence, rudeness, immorality,
foolishness, or oddity, may arise from some real needs of the youth
which in their development have only taken a wrong direction.

36. If it should appear on such examination that the negative action was only a product of wilful ignorance, of caprice, or of arbitrariness on the part of the youth, then this calls for a simple prohibition on the part of the educator, no *Reproof and Punishment.* 19
reason being assigned. His authority must be sufficient to the pupil
without any reason. Only when this has happened more than once,
and the youth is old enough to understand, should the prohibition,
together with the reason therefor, be given.

— This should, however, be brief; the explanation must retain its
disciplinary character, and must not become extended into a doctrinal essay, for in such a case the youth easily forgets that it was his
own misbehavior which was the occasion of the explanation. The
statement of the reason must be honest, and it must present to the
youth the point most easy for him to seize. False reasons are morally blamable in themselves, and they tend only to confuse. It is a
great mistake to unfold to the youth the broadening consequences
which his act may bring. These uncertain possibilities seem to him
too powerless to affect him particularly. The severe lecture wearies
him, especially if it be stereotyped, as is apt to be the case with fault-
finding and talkative instructors. But more unfortunate is it if the
painting of the gloomy background to which the consequences of
the wrong-doing of the youth may lead, should fill his feelings and
imagination prematurely with gloomy fancies, because then the
representation has led him one step toward a state of wretchedness
which in the future man may become fearful depression and degradation. —

37. If the censure is accompanied with a threat of punishment,
then we have the same kind of reproof which in daily life we call
"scolding;" but if reproof is given, the pupil must be made to feel
that it is in earnest.

38. Only when all other efforts have failed, is punishment, which
is the real negation of the error, the transgression, or the vice, justifiable. Punishment inflicts intentionally pain on the pupil, and its

object is, by means of this sensation, to bring him to reason, a result which neither our simple prohibition, our explanation, nor our threat of punishment, has been able to reach. But the punishment, as such, must not refer to the subjective totality of the youth, or his disposition in general, but only to the act which, as result, is a manifestation of the disposition. It acts mediately on the disposition, but leaves the inner being untouched directly; and *Correction* versus *Satisfaction of Justice.* 20 this is not only demanded by justice, but on account of the sophistry that is inherent in human nature, which desires to assign to a deed many motives, it is even necessary.

39. Punishment as an educational means is nevertheless essentially corrective, since, by leading the youth to a proper estimation of his fault and a positive change in his behavior, it seeks to improve him. At the same time it stands as a sad indication of the insufficiency of the means previously used. On no account should the youth be frightened from the commission of a misdemeanor, or from the repetition of his negative deed through fear of punishment—a system which leads always to terrorism: but, although it may have this effect, it should, before all things, impress upon him the recognition of the fact that the negative is not allowed to act as it will without limitation, but rather that the Good and the True have the absolute power in the world, and that they are never without the means of overcoming anything that contradicts them.

—In the statute-laws, punishment has the opposite office. It must first of all satisfy justice, and only after this is done can it attempt to improve the guilty. If a government should proceed on the same basis as the educator it would mistake its task, because it has to deal with adults, whom it elevates to the honorable position of responsibility for their own acts. The state must not go back to the psychological ethical genesis of a negative deed. It must assign to a secondary rank of importance the biographical moment which contains the deed in process and the circumstances of a mitigating character, and it must consider first of all the deed in itself. It is quite otherwise with the educator; for he deals with human beings who are relatively undeveloped, and who are only growing toward responsibility. So long as they are still under the care of a teacher, the responsibility of their deed belongs in part to him. If we confound the standpoint in which punishment is administered in the state with that in education, we work much evil. —

40. Punishment as a negation of a negation, considered as an educational means, cannot be determined ☐*riori*, but must always be modified by the peculiarities of the individual offender and by the peculiar circumstances. Its administration *Three Kinds of Punishment.* 21 calls for the exercise of the ingenuity and tact of the educator.

41. Generally speaking, we must make a distinction between the sexes, as well as between the different periods of youth; (1) some kind of corporal punishment is most suitable for children, (2) isolation for older boys and girls, and (3) punishment based on the sense of honor for young men and women.

42. (1) Corporal punishment is the production of physical pain. The youth is generally whipped, and this kind of punishment, provided always that it is not too often administered or with undue severity, is the proper way of dealing with wilful defiance, with obstinate carelessness, or with a really perverted will, so long or so often as the higher perception is closed against appeal. The imposing of other physical punishment, e.g. that of depriving the pupil of food, partakes of cruelty. The view which sees in the rod the panacea for all the teacher's embarrassments is censurable, but equally undesirable is the false sentimentality which assumes that the dignity of humanity is affected by a blow given to a child, and confounds self-conscious humanity with child-humanity, to which a blow is the most natural form of reaction, in which all other forms of influence at last end.

— The fully-grown man ought never to be whipped, because this kind of punishment reduces him to the level of the child, and, when it becomes barbarous, to that of a brute animal, and so is absolutely degrading to him. In the English schools the rod is much used. If a pupil of the first class be put back into the second at Eton, he, although before exempt from flogging, becomes liable to it. But however necessary this system of flogging of the English aristocracy may be in the discipline of their schools, flogging in the English army is a shameful thing for the free people of Great Britain. —

43. (2) By Isolation we remove the offender temporarily from the society of his fellows. The boy left alone, cut off from all compan-

ionship, and left absolutely to himself, suffers from a sense of helplessness. The time passes heavily, and soon he is very anxious to be allowed to return to the company of parents, brothers and sisters, teachers and fellow-pupils.

Sense of Honor in the Pupil. 22

—To leave a child entirely to himself without any supervision, even if one shuts him up in a dark room, is as mistaken a practice as to leave a few together without supervision, as is too often done where they are kept after school, when they give the freest rein to their childish wantonness and commit the wildest pranks.—

44. (3) This way of isolating a child does not touch his sense of honor at all, and is soon forgotten because it relates to only one side of his conduct. It is quite different from punishment based on the sense of honor, which, in a formal manner, shuts the youth out from companionship because he has attacked the principle which holds society together, and for this reason can no longer be considered as belonging to it. Honor is the recognition of one individual by others as their equal. Through his error, or it may be his crime, he has simply made himself unequal to them, and in so far has separated himself from them, so that his banishment from their society is only the outward expression of the real isolation which he himself has brought to pass in his inner nature, and which he by means of his negative act only betrayed to the outer world. Since the punishment founded on the sense of honor affects the whole ethical man and makes a lasting impression upon his memory, extreme caution is necessary in its application lest a permanent injury be inflicted upon the character. The idea of his perpetual continuance in disgrace, destroys in a man all aspiration for improvement

—Within the family this feeling of honor cannot be so actively developed, because every member of it is bound to every other immediately by natural ties, and hence is equal to every other. Within its sacred circle, he who has isolated himself is still beloved, though it may be through tears. However bad may be the deed he has committed, he is never given up, but the deepest sympathy is felt for him because he is still brother, father, &c. But first in the contact of one family with another, and still more in the contact of an individual with any institution which is founded not on natural ties, but is set over against him as a distinct object, this feeling of honor appears. In the school, and in the matter of ranks and classes in a school, this is very important. —

45. It is important to consider well this gradation of punishment (which, starting with sensuous physical pain, passes through the external teleology of temporary isolation up to the idealism of the sense of honor), both in relation to the different ages at which they are appropriate and to the training which they bring with them. Every punishment must be considered merely as a means to some end, and, in so far, as transitory. The pupil must always be deeply conscious that it is very painful to his instructor to be obliged to punish him. This pathos of another's sorrow for the sake of his cure which he perceives in the mien, in the tone of the voice, in the delay with which the punishment is administered, will become a purifying fire for his soul.

III.

The Limits of Education.

46. The form of Education reaches its limits with the idea of punishment, because this is the attempt to subsume the negative reality and to make it conformable to its positive idea. But the limits of Education are found in the idea of its nature, which is to fashion the individual into theoretical and practical rationality. The authority of the Educator at last becomes imperceptible, and it passes over into advice and example, and obedience changes from blind conformity to free gratitude and attachment. Individuality wears off its rough edges, and is transfigured into the universality and necessity of Reason without losing in this process its identity. Work becomes enjoyment, and he finds his play in a change of activity. The youth takes possession of himself, and can be left to himself.

—There are two widely differing views with regard to the limits of Education. One lays great stress on the weakness of the pupil and the power of the teacher. According to this view, Education has for its province the entire formation of the youth. The despotism of this view often manifests itself where large numbers are to be educated together, and with very undesirable results, because it assumes that the individual pupil is only a specimen of the whole, as if the school were a great factory where each piece of goods is to be stamped exactly like all the rest. Individuality is reduced *The Limits of Individuality.* 24 by the tyranny of such despotism to cne uniform level till all originality is destroyed, as in cloisters, barracks, and orphan asylums, where only one individual seems to exist. There is a kind of Pedagogy also which fancies that one can thrust into or out of the individual pupil what one will. This may be called a superstitious belief in the power of Education. — The opposite extreme disbelieves this, and advances the policy which lets alone and does nothing, urging that individuality is unconquerable, and that often the most careful and far-sighted education fails of reaching its aim in so far as it is opposed to the nature of the youth, and that this individuality has made of no avail all efforts toward the obtaining of any end which was opposed to it. This representation of the fruitlessness of all pedagogical efforts engenders an indifference towards it which would leave, as a result, only a sort of vegetation of individuality growing at hap-hazard. —

47. *The limit of Education is* (1) *a Subjective one,* a limit made by the individuality of the youth. This is a definite limit. Whatever does not exist in this individuality as a possibility cannot be developed from it. Education can only lead and assist; it cannot create. What Nature has denied to a man, Education cannot give him any more than it is able, on the other hand, to annihilate entirely his original gifts, although it is true that his talents may be suppressed, distorted, and measurably destroyed. But the decision of the question in what the real essence of any one's individuality consists can never be made with certainty till he has left behind him his years of development, because it is then only that he first arrives at the consciousness of his entire self; besides, at this critical time, in the first place, much knowledge only superficially acquired will drop off; and again, talents, long slumbering and unsuspected, may first make their appearance. Whatever has been forced upon a child in opposition to his individuality, whatever has been only driven into him and has lacked receptivity on his side, or a rational ground on the side of culture, remains attached to his being only as an external ornament, a foreign outgrowth which enfeebles his own proper character.

—We must distinguish from that affectation which arises through a misunderstanding of the limit of individuality, the *Limit in the Means of Education.* 25 way which many children and young persons have of supposing when they see models finished and complete in grown persons, that they themselves are endowed by Nature with the power to develop into the same. When they see a reality which corresponds to their own possibility, the presentiment of a like or a similar attainment moves them to an imitation of it as a model personality. This may be sometimes carried so far as to be disagreeable or ridiculous, but should not be too strongly censured, because it springs from a positive striving after culture, and needs only proper direction. —

48. (2) *The Objective limit of Education* lies in the means which can be appropriated for it. That the talent for a certain culture shall be present is certainly the first thing; but the cultivation of this talent is the second, and no less necessary. But how much cultivation can be given to it extensively and intensively depends upon the means used, and these again are conditioned by the material resources of the family to which each one belongs. The greater and more valuable the means of culture which are found in a family are, the greater is the immediate advantage which the culture of each one has at the start. With regard to many of the arts and sciences this limit of education is of great significance. But the means alone are of no avail. The finest educational apparatus will produce no fruit where corresponding talent is wanting, while on the other hand talent often accomplishes incredible feats with very limited means, and, if the way is only once open, makes of itself a centre of attraction which draws to itself with magnetic power the necessary means. The moral culture of each one is however, fortunately from its very nature, out of the reach of such dependence.

—In considering the limit made by individuality we recognize the side of truth in that indifference which considers Education entirely superfluous, and in considering the means of culture we find the truth in the other extreme of pedagogical despotism, which fancies that it can command whatever culture it chooses for any one without regard to his individuality. —

49. (3) *The Absolute limit of Education* is the time when the youth has apprehended the problem which he has to *Arrival at the age of Majority.* 26 solve, has learned to know the means at his disposal, and has acquired a certain facility in using them. The end and aim of Education is the emancipation of the youth. It strives to make him self-dependent, and as soon as he has become so it wishes to retire and to be able to leave him to the sole responsibility of his actions. To treat the youth after he has passed this point of time still as a youth, contradicts the very idea of Education, which idea finds its fulfilment in the attainment of majority by the pupil. Since the accomplishment of education cancels the original inequality between the educator and the pupil, nothing is more oppressing, nay, revolting to the latter than to be prevented by a continued dependence from the enjoyment of the freedom which he has earned.

—The opposite extreme of the protracting of Education beyond its proper time is necessarily the undue hastening of the Emancipation.—The question whether one is prepared for freedom has been often opened in politics. When any people have gone so far as to ask this question themselves, it is no longer a question whether that people are prepared for it, for without the consciousness of freedom this question would never have occurred to them.—

50. Although educators must now leave the youth free, the necessity of further culture for him is still imperative. But it will no longer come directly through them. Their pre-arranged, pattern-making work is now supplanted by self-education. Each sketches for himself an ideal to which in his life he seeks to approximate every day.

—In the work of self-culture one friend can help another by advice and example; but he cannot educate, for education presupposes inequality.—The necessities of human nature produce societies in which equals seek to influence each other in a pedagogical way, since they establish by certain steps of culture different classes. They presuppose Education in the ordinary sense. But they wish to bring about Education in a higher sense, and therefore they veil the last form of their ideal in the mystery of secrecy.—To one who lives on contented with himself and without the impulse toward self-culture, unless his unconcern springs from his belonging to a savage state of society, the Germans give the name of Philistine, and he is always repulsive to the student who is intoxicated with an ideal.—

27

SECOND PART.
The Special Elements of Education.

51. Education in general consists in the development in man of his inborn theoretical and practical rationality; it takes on the form of labor, which changes that state or condition, which appears at first only as a mere conception, into a fixed habit, and transfigures individuality into a worthy humanity. Education ends in that emancipation of the youth which places him on his own feet. The special elements which form the concrete content of all Education in general are the Life, Cognition, and Will of man. Without life mind has no phenomenal reality; without cognition, no genuine, i.e. conscious, will; and without will, no self-assurance of life and of cognition. It is true that these three elements are in real existence inseparable, and that consequently in the dialectic they continually pass over into one another. But none the less on this account do they themselves prescribe their own succession, and they have a relative and periodical ascendancy over each other. In Infancy, up to the fifth or sixth year, the purely physical development takes the precedence; Childhood is the time of learning, in a proper sense, an act by which the child gains for himself the picture of the world such as mature minds, through experience and insight, have painted it; and, finally, Youth is the transition period to practical activity, to which the self-determination of the will must give the first impulse.

52. The classification of the special elements of Pedagogics is hence very simple: (1) the Physical, (2) the Intellectual, (3) the Practical. (We sometimes apply to these the words Orthobiotics, Didactics, and Pragmatics.)

— Ythetic training constitutes only an element of the education of Intellectual Education, just as social, moral, and religious training form elements of Practical Education. But because these latter elements concern themselves with what *Physical Education.* 28 is external, the name "Pragmatics" is appropriate. In this sphere, Pedagogics should coincide with Politics, Ethics, and Religion; but it is distinguished from them through the aptitude which it brings with it of putting into practice the problems of the other three. The scientific arrangement of these ideas must therefore show that the former, as the more abstract, constitutes the conditions, and the latter, as the more concrete, the ground of the former, which are presupposed; and in consequence of this it is itself their principal teleological presupposition, just as in man the will presupposes the cognition, and cognition life; while, at the same time, life, in a deeper sense, must presuppose cognition, and cognition will. —

First Division.
PHYSICAL EDUCATION.

53. The art of living rightly is based upon a comprehension of the process of Life. Life is the restless dialectic which ceaselessly transforms the inorganic into the organic, but at the same time creates out of itself another inorganic, in which it separates from itself whatever part of the inorganic has not been assimilated, which it took up as a stimulant, and that which has become dead and burned out. The organism is healthy when its reality corresponds to this idea of the dialectic, of a life which moves up and down, to and fro; of formation and re-formation, of organizing and disorganizing. All the rules for Physical Education, or of Hygiene, are derived from this conception.

54. It follows from this that the change of the inorganic to the organic is going on not only in the organism as a whole, but also in its every organ and in every part of every organ; and that the organic as soon as it has attained its highest point of energy, is again degraded to the inorganic and thrown out. Every cell has its history. Activity is, therefore, not contradictory to the organism, but favors in it the natural progressive and regressive metamorphosis. This process can go on harmoniously; that is, the organism can be in health only when not only the whole organism, but each special organ, is allowed, after its productive activity, the corresponding rest and recreation necessary for its self-renewal. We have this periodicity exemplified in waking *Dietetics.* 29 and sleeping, also in exhalation and inhalation, excretion and taking in of material. When we have discovered the relative antagonism of the organs and their periodicity, we have found the secret of the perennial renewal of life.

55. Fatigue makes its appearance when any organ, or the organism in general, is denied time for the return movement into itself and for renovation. It is possible for some one organ, as if isolated, to exercise a great and long-continued activity, even to the point of fatigue, while the other organs rest; as e.g. the lungs, in speaking, while the other parts are quiet; on the other hand, it is not well to speak and run at the same time. The idea that one can keep the organism in better condition by inactivity, is an error which rests upon a mechanical apprehension of life. Equally false is the idea that health depends upon the quantity and excellence of the food; without the force to assimilate it, it acts fatally rather than stimulatingly. *True strength arises only from activity.*

—The later physiologists will gradually destroy, in the system of culture of modern people, the preconceived notion which recommended for the indolent and lovers of pleasure powerful stimulants, very fat food, &c. Excellent works exist on this question.—

56. Physical Education, as it concerns the repairing, the motor, or the nervous, activities, is divided into (1) Dietetics, (2) Gymnastics, (3) Sexual Education. In real life these activities are scarcely separable, but for the sake of exposition we must consider them apart. In the regular development of the human being, moreover, the repairing system has a relative precedence to the motor system, and the latter to the sexual maturity. But Pedagogics can treat of these ideas only with reference to the infant, the child, and the youth.

FIRST CHAPTER.
Dietetics.

57. Dietetics is the art of sustaining the normal repair of the organism. Since this organism is, in the concrete, an individual one, the general principles of dietetics must, in their manner of application, vary with the sex, the age, the temperament, the occupation, and the other conditions, of the individual. Pedagogics as a science can only go over its general *Dietetics.* 30 principles, and these can be named briefly. It we attempt to speak of details, we fall easily into triviality. So very important to the whole life of man is the proper care of his physical nature during the first stages of its development, that the science of Pedagogics must not omit to consider the different systems which different people, according to their time, locality,

and culture, have made for themselves; many, it is true, embracing some preposterous ideas, but in general never devoid of justification in their time.

58. The infant's first nourishment must be the milk of its mother. The substitution of a nurse should be only an exception justified alone by the illness of the mother; as a rule, as happens in France, it is simply bad, because a foreign physical and moral element is introduced into the family through the nurse. The milk of an animal can never be as good for a child.

59. When the teeth appear, the child is first able to eat solid food; but, until the second teeth come, he should be fed principally on light, fluid nourishment, and on vegetable diet.

60. When the second teeth are fully formed, the human being is ready for animal as well as vegetable food. Too much meat is not good; but it is an anatomical error to suppose that man, by the structure of his stomach, was originally formed to live alone on vegetable diet, and that animal food is a sign of his degeneracy.

—The Hindoos, who subsist principally on vegetable diet, are not, as has been often asserted, a very gentle race: a glance into their history, or into their erotic poetry, shows them to be quite as passionate as other peoples. —

61. Man is omnivorous. Children have therefore a natural desire to taste of everything. For them eating and drinking possess a kind of poetry; there is a theoretic ingredient blended with the material enjoyment. They have, on this account, a proneness to indulge, which is deserving of punishment only when it is combined with disobedience and secrecy, or when it betrays cunning and greediness.

62. Children need much sleep, because they are undergoing the most active progressive metamorphosis. In after-life sleep and waking should be subjected to periodical regulation, but not too exactly.

Gymnastics. 31

63. The clothing of children should be adapted to them; i.e. it should be cut according to the shape of the body, and it must be loose enough to allow free play to their desire for movement.

—With regard to this as well as to the sleeping arrangements for children, less in regard to food—which is often too highly spiced and too liberal in tea, coffee, &c.—our age has become accustomed to a very rational system. The clothing of children must be not only comfortable, but it should be made of simple and cheap material, so that the free enjoyment of the child may not be marred by the constant internal anxiety that a rent or a spot may bring him a fault-finding or angry word. From too great care as to clothing, may arise a meanness of mind which at last pays too great respect to it, or an empty frivolity. This last may be induced by dressing children too conspicuously.—

64. Cleanliness is a virtue to which children should be accustomed for the sake of their physical well-being, as well as because, in a moral point of view, it is of the greatest significance. Cleanliness will not endure that things shall be deprived of their proper individuality through the elemental chaos. It retains each as distinguished from every other. While it makes necessary to man pure air, cleanliness of surroundings, of clothing, and of his body, it develops in him a sense by which he perceives accurately the particular limits of being in general.

SECOND CHAPTER.
Gymnastics.

65. Gymnastics is the art of systematic training of the muscular system. The action of the voluntary muscles, which are regulated by the nerves of the brain, in distinction from the involuntary automatic muscles depending on the spinal cord, while they are the means of man's intercourse with the external world, at the same time re-act upon the automatic muscles in digestion and sensation. Since the movement of the muscular fibres consists in the change of contraction and expansion, it follows that Gymnastics must bring about a change of movement which shall both contract and expand the muscles.

Gymnastics. 32

66. The system of gymnastic exercise of any nation corresponds always to its way of fighting. So long as this consists in the personal struggle of a hand-to-hand contest, Gymnastics will seek to increase as much as possible individual strength and adroitness. As soon as

the far-reaching missiles projected from fire-arms become the centre of all the operations of war, the individual is lost in a body of men, out of which he emerges only relatively in sharp-shooting, in the charge, in single contests, and in the retreat. Because of this incorporation of the individual in the one great whole, and because of the resulting unimportance of personal bravery, modern Gymnastics can never be the same as it was in ancient times, even putting out of view the fact that the subjectiveness of the modern spirit is too great to allow it to devote so much attention to the care of the body, and the admiration of its beauty, as was given by the Greeks.

—The Turners' unions and halls in Germany belong to the period of subjective enthusiasm of the German student population, and had a political significance. At present, they have been brought back to their proper place as an Educational means, and they are of great value, especially in large cities. Among the mountains, and even in the country towns, a special institution for bodily exercise is less necessary, for the matter takes care of itself. The attractions of the situation and the games help to foster it. In great cities, however, the houses are often destitute of halls or open places where the children can take exercise in their leisure moments. In these cities, therefore, there must be some gymnastic hall where the sense of fellowship may be developed. Gymnastics are not so essential for girls. In its place, dancing is sufficient, and gymnastics should be employed for them only where there exists any special weakness or deformity, when they may be used as a restorative or preservative. They are not to become Amazons. The boy, on the contrary, needs to acquire the feeling of good-fellowship. It is true that the school develops this in a measure, but not fully, because it determines the standing of the boy through his intellectual ambition. The academical youth will not take much interest in special gymnastics unless he can gain pre웜nence therein. Running, leaping, climbing, and lifting, are too meaningless *Gymnastics.* 33 for their more mature spirits. They can take a lively interest only in the exercises which have a warlike character. With the Prussians, and some other German states, the art of Gymnastics identifies itself with military concerns.—

67. The real idea of Gymnastics must always be that the spirit shall rule over its naturalness, and shall make this an energetic and docile servant of its will. Strength and adroitness must unite and

become confident skill. Strength, carried to its extreme produces the athlete; adroitness, to its extreme, the acrobat. Pedagogics must avoid both. All immense force, fit only for display, must be held as far away as the idea of teaching Gymnastics with the motive of utility; e.g. that by swimming one may save his life when he falls into the water, &c. Among other things, this may also be a consequence; but the principle in general must always remain: the necessity of the spirit of subjecting its organism of the body to the condition of a perfect means, so that it may never find itself limited by it.

68. Gymnastic exercises form a series from simple to compound. There appears to be so much arbitrariness in them that it is always very agreeable to the mind to find, on nearer inspection, some reason. The movements are (1) of the lower, (2) of the upper extremities; (3) of the whole body, with relative striking out, now of the upper, now of the lower extremities. We distinguish, therefore, foot, arm, and trunk movements.

69. (1) The first series of foot-movements is the most important, and conditions the carriage of all the rest of the body. They are (*a*) walking; (*b*) running; (*c*) leaping: each of these being capable of modifications, as the high and the low leap, the prolonged and the quick run. Sometimes we give to these different names, according to the means used, as walking on stilts; skating; leaping with a staff, or by means of the hands, as vaulting. Dancing is only the art of the graceful mingling of these movements; and balancing, only one form of walking.

70. (2) The second series embraces the arm-movements, and it repeats also the movements of the first series. It includes (*a*) lifting; (*b*) swinging; (*c*) throwing. All pole and bar practice comes under lifting, also climbing and carrying. *Gymnastics.* 34 Under throwing, come quoit and ball-throwing, and nine-pin playing. All these movements are distinguished from each other, not only quantitatively but also qualitatively, in the position of the stretched and bent muscles; e.g. running is something different from quick walking.

71. (3) The third series, or that of movements of the whole body, differs from the preceding two, which should precede it, in this, that it brings the organism into contact with a living object, which it has to overcome through its own activity. This object is sometimes an

element, sometimes an animal, sometimes a man. Our divisions then are (*a*) swimming; (*b*) riding; (*c*) fighting, or single combat. In swimming, one must conquer the yielding liquid material of water by arm and foot movements. The resistance met on account of currents and waves may be very great, but it is still that of a will-less and passive object. But in riding man has to deal with a self-willed being whose vitality calls forth not only his strength but also his intelligence and courage. The exercise is therefore very complicated, and the rider must be able perpetually to individualize it according to the necessity; at the same time, he must give attention not only to the horse, but to the nature of the ground and the entire surroundings. But it is only in the struggle with men that Gymnastics reaches its highest point, for in this man offers himself as a living antagonist to man and brings him into danger. It is no longer the spontaneous activity of an unreasoning existence; it is the resistance and attack of intelligence itself with which he has to deal. Fighting, or single combat, is the truly chivalrous exercise, and this may be combined with horsemanship.

— In the single combat there is found also a qualitative modification, whence we have three systems: (*a*) boxing and wrestling; (*b*) fencing with sticks; and (*c*) rapier and broad-sword fencing. In the first, which was cultivated to its highest point among the Greeks, direct immediateness rules. In the boxing of the English, a sailor-like propensity of this nation, fist-fighting is still retained as a custom. Fencing with a stick is found among the French mechanics, the so-called *compagnons*. Men often use the cane in their contests; it is a sort of refined club. When we use the sword or rapier, *Sexual Education*. 35 the weapon becomes deadly. The Southern Europeans excel in the use of the rapier, the Germans in that of the sword. But the art of single combat is much degenerated, and the pistol-duel, through its increasing frequency, proves this degeneration. —

THIRD CHAPTER.
Sexual Education.

Note. — The paragraphs relating to Sexual Education are designed for parents rather than for teachers, the parent being the natural educator of the family and sexual education relating to the preservation and continuance of the family. This chapter is accordingly, for the most part, omitted here. It contains judicious reflections, invaluable to parents and guardians. — *Tr.*

72. Gymnastic exercises fall naturally into a systematic arrangement determined by the chronological order of development through infancy, childhood, and youth. Walking, running, and leaping belong, to the first period; lifting, swinging, and throwing, to the second; swimming, riding, and bodily contests, to the third, and these last may also be continued into manhood. But with the arrival at youth, a new epoch makes its appearance in the organism. It prepares itself for the propagation of the species. It expands the individual through the need which he feels of uniting himself with another individual of the same species, but who is a polar opposite to him, in order to preserve the two in a new individual. The blood rushes more vigorously; the muscular strength becomes more easily roused into activity; an indefinable impulse, a sweet melancholy takes possession of the being. This period demands a special care in the educator.

73. The general preventive guards must be found in a rational system of food and exercise. By care in these directions, the development of the bones, and with them of the brain and spinal cord at this period, may be led to a proper strength, and that the easily-moulded material may not be perverted from its normal functions in the development of the body to a premature manifestation of the sexual instinct.

74. Special forethought is necessary lest the brain be too early over-strained, and lest, in consequence of such precocious and excessive action, the foundation for a morbid excitation of the whole nervous system be laid, which may easily *Intellectual Education — Psychological Faculties.* 36 lead to effeminate and voluptuous reveries, and to brooding over obscene representations. The excessive reading of novels, whose exciting pages delight in painting the love of the sexes for each other and its sensual phases, may lead to this, and then the mischief is done.

Second Division.
INTELLECTUAL EDUCATION.

80. *Mens sana in corpore sano* is correct as a pedagogical maxim, but false in the judgment of individual cases; because it is possible,

on the one hand, to have a healthy mind in an unhealthy body, and, on the other hand, an unhealthy mind in a healthy body. To strive after the harmony of soul and body is the material condition of all proper activity. The development of intelligence presupposes physical health. Here we are to speak of the science of the art of Teaching. This had its condition on the side of nature, as was before seen, in physical Education, but in the sphere of mind it is related to Psychology and Logic. It unites, in Teaching, considerations on Psychology as well as a Logical method.

FIRST CHAPTER.
The Psychological Presupposition.

81. If we would have a sound condition of Philosophy, it must, in intellectual Education, refer to the conception of mind which has been unfolded in Psychology; and it must appear as a defect in scientific method if Psychology, or at least the conception of the theoretical mind, is treated again as within Pedagogics. We must take something for granted. Psychology, then, will be consulted no further than is requisite to place on a sure basis the pedagogical function which relates to it.

82. The conception of *attention* is the most important to Pedagogics of all those derived from Psychology. Mind is essentially self-activity. Nothing exists for it which it does not itself posit as its own. We hear it not seldom implied that something from outside conditions must make an impression on the mind, but this is an error. Mind lets nothing act upon it unless it has rendered itself receptive to it. Without this preparatory self-excitation the object does not *Psychological Faculties.* 37 really penetrate it, and it passes by the object unconsciously or indifferently. The horizon of perception changes for each person with his peculiarities and culture. Attention is the adjusting of the observer to the object in order to seize it in its unity and diversity. Relatively, the observer allows, for a moment, his relation to all other surroundings to cease, so that he may establish a relation with this one. Without this essentially spontaneous activity, nothing exists for the mind. All result in teaching and learning depends upon the clearness and strength with which distinctions are made, and the saying, *bene qui distinguit bene docit,* applies as well to the pupil.

83. Attention, depending as it does on the self-determination of the observer, can therefore be improved, and the pupil made attentive, by the educator. Education must accustom him to an exact, rapid, and many-sided attention, so that at the first contact with an object he may grasp it sufficiently and truly, and that it shall not be necessary for him always to be adding to his acquisitions concerning it. The twilight and partialness of intelligence which forces us always to new corrections because a pupil at the very commencement did not give entire attention, must not be tolerated.

84. We learn from Psychology that mind does not consist of distinct faculties, but that what we choose to call so are only different activities of the same power. Each one is just as essential as the other, on which account Education must grant to each faculty its claim to the same fostering care. If we would construe correctly the axiom *a potiori fit denominatio* to mean that man is distinguished from animals by thought, and that mediated will is not the same as thought, we must not forget that feeling and representing are not less necessary to a truly complete human being. The special direction which the activity of apprehending intelligence takes are (1) Perception, (2) Conception, (3) Thinking. Dialectically, they pass over into each other; not that Perception rises into Conception, and Conception into Thinking, but that Thinking goes back into Conception, and this again into Perception. In the development of the young, the Perceptive faculty is most active in the infant, the Conceptive in the child, and the *The Intuitive Epoch.* 38 Thinking in the youth; and thus we may distinguish an intuitive, an imaginative, and a logical epoch.

—Great errors arise from the misapprehension of these different phases and of their dialectic, since the different forms which are suitable to the different grades of youth are mingled. The infant certainly thinks while he perceives, but this thinking is to him unconscious. Or, if he has acquired perceptions, he makes them into conceptions, and demonstrates his freedom in playing with them. This play must not be taken as mere amusement; it also signifies that he takes care to preserve his self-determination, and his power of idealizing, in opposition to the pleasant filling of his consciousness with material. Herein the delight of the child for fairy tales finds its reason. The fairy tale constantly destroys the limits of common actuality. The abstract understanding cannot endure this arbitrariness and want of fixed conditions, and thus would prefer that children should read, instead, home-made stories of the "Charitable Ann," of the "Heedless Frederick," of the "Inquisitive Wilhelmine," &c. Above all, it praises "Robinson Crusoe," which contains much heterogeneous matter, but nothing improbable. When the youth and maiden of necessity pass over into the earnestness of real life, the drying up of the imagination and the domination of the understanding presses in. —

I. *The Intuitive Epoch.*

85. Perception, as the beginning of intellectual culture, is the free grasping of a content immediately present to the spirit. Education can do nothing directly toward the performance of this act; it can only assist in making it easy: — (1) it can isolate the subject of consideration; (2) it can give facility in the transition to another; (3) it can promote the many-sidedness of the interest, by which means the return to a perception already obtained has always a fresh charm.

86. The immediate perception of many things is impossible, and yet the necessity for it is obvious. We must then have recourse to a mediated perception, and supply the lack of actual seeing by representations. But here the difficulty presents itself, that there are many objects which we are not *The Intuitive Epoch.* 39 able to represent of the same size as they really are, and we must have a reduced scale; and there follows a difficulty in making the representation, as neither too large nor too small. An explanation is then also necessary as a judicious supplement to the picture.

87. Pictures are extremely valuable aids to instruction when they are correct and characteristic. Correctness must be demanded in these substitutes for natural objects, historical persons and scenes. Without this correctness, the picture, if not an impediment, is, to say the least, useless.

— It is only since the last half of the seventeenth century, i.e. since the disappearance of real painting, that the picture-book has appeared as an educational means; first of all, coming from miniature painting. Up to that time, public life had plenty of pictures of arms, furniture, houses, and churches; and men, from their fondness for

constantly moving about, were more weary of immediate perception. It was only afterwards when, in the excitement of the thirty-
years' war, the arts of Sculpture and Painting and Christian and
Pagan Mythology became extinct, that there arose a greater necessity for pictured representations. The *Orbis Rerum Sensualium Pictus*,
which was also to be *janua linguarum reserata*, of Amos Comenius,
appeared first in 1658, and was reprinted in 1805. Many valuable
illustrated books followed. Since that time innumerable illustrated
Bibles and histories have appeared, but many of them look only to
the pecuniary profit of the author or the publisher. It is revolting to
see the daubs that are given to children. They are highly colored,
but as to correctness, to say nothing of character, they are good for
nothing. With a little conscientiousness and scientific knowledge
very different results could be obtained with the same outlay of
money and of strength. The uniformity which exists in the stock of
books which German book-selling has set in circulation is really
disgraceful. Everywhere we find the same types, even in ethno-
graphical pictures. In natural history, the illustrations were often
drawn from the imagination or copied from miserable models. This
has changed very much for the better. The same is true of architec-
tural drawings and landscapes, for which we have now better copies. —

The Intuitive Epoch. 40

88. Children have naturally a desire to collect things, and this
may be so guided that they shall collect and arrange plants, butter-
flies, beetles, shells, skeletons, &c., and thus gain exactness and
reality in their perception. Especially should they practise drawing,
which leads them to form exact images of objects. But drawing, as
children practise it, does not have the educational significance of
cultivating in them an appreciation of art, but rather that of educating the eye, as this must be exercised in estimating distances, sizes,
and colors. It is, moreover, a great gain in many ways, if, through a
suitable course of lessons in drawing, the child is advanced to a
knowledge of the elementary forms of nature.

— That pictures should affect children as works of art is not to be
desired. They confine themselves at first to distinguishing the out-
lines and colors, and do not yet appreciate the execution. If the chil-

dren have access to real works of art, we may safely trust in their power, and quietly await their moral or æsthetic effect. —

89. In order that looking at pictures shall not degenerate into mere diversion, explanations should accompany them. Only when the thought embodied in the illustration is pointed out, can they be useful as a means of instruction. Simply looking at them is of as little value towards this end as is water for baptism without the Holy Spirit. Our age inclines at present to the superstition that man is able, by means of simple intuition, to attain a knowledge of the essence of things, and thereby dispense with the trouble of thinking. Illustrations are the order of the day, and, in the place of enjoyable descriptions, we find miserable pictures. It is in vain to try to get behind things, or to comprehend them, except by thinking.

90. The ear as well as the eye must be cultivated. Music must be considered the first educational means to this end, but it should be music inspired by ethical purity. Hearing is the most internal of all the senses, and should on this account be treated with the greatest delicacy. Especially should the child be taught that he is not to look upon speech as merely a vehicle for communication and for gaining information; it should also give pleasure, and therefore he should be taught to speak distinctly and with a good style, *The Imaginative Epoch.* 41 and this he can do only when he carefully considers what he is going to say.

— Among the Greeks, extraordinary care was given to musical cultivation, especially in its ethical relation. Sufficient proof of this is found in the admirable detailed statements on this point in the "Republic" of Plato and in the last book of the "Politics" of Aristotle. Among modern nations, also, music holds a high place, and makes its appearance as a constant element of education. Piano-playing has become general, and singing is also taught. But the ethical significance of music is too little considered. Instruction in music often aims only to train pupils for display in society, and the tendency of the melodies which are played is restricted more and more to orchestral pieces of an exciting or bacchanalian character. The railroad-gallop-style only makes the nerves of youth vibrate with stimulating excitement. Oral speech, the highest form of the personal manifestation of mind, was also treated with great reverence by the ancients. Among us, communication is so generally carried on by writing and reading, that the art of speaking distinctly, correctly, and agreeably, has become very much neglected. Practice in declamation accomplishes, as a general thing, very little in this direction. But we may expect that the increase of public speaking occasioned by our political and religious assemblies may have a favorable influence in this particular. —

II. The Imaginative Epoch.

91. The activity of Perception results in the formation of an internal picture or image of its ideas which intelligence can call up at any time without the sensuous, immediate presence of its object, and thus, through abstraction and generalization, arises the conception. The mental image may (1) be compared with the perception from which it sprang, or (2) it may be arbitrarily altered and combined with other images, or (3) it may be held fast in the form of abstract signs or symbols which intelligence invents for it. Thus originate the functions (1) of the verification of conceptions, (2) of the creative imagination, and (3) of memory; but for their full development we must refer to Psychology.

92. (1) The mental image which we form of an object may *The Imaginative Epoch.* 42 be correct; again, it may be partly or wholly defective, if we have neglected some of the predicates of the perception which presented themselves, or in so far as we have added to it other predicates which only seemingly belonged to it, and which were attached to it only by its accidental empirical connection with other existences. Education must, therefore, foster the habit of comparing our conceptions with the perceptions from which they arose; and these perceptions, since they are liable to change by reason of their empirical connection with other objects, must be frequently compared with our conceptions previously formed by abstractions from them.

93. (2) We are thus limited in our conceptions by our perceptions, but we exercise a free control over our conceptions. We can create out of them, as simple elements, the manifold mental shapes which we do not treat as given to us, but as essentially our own work. In Pedagogics, we must not only look upon this freedom as if it were only to afford gratification, but as the reaction of the absolute ideal

native mind against the dependence in which the empirical reception of impressions from without, and their reproduction in conceptions, place it. In this process, it does not only fashion in itself the phenomenal world, but it rather fashions out of itself a world which is all its own.

94. The study of Art comes here to the aid of Pedagogics, especially with Poetry, the highest and at the same time the most easily communicated. The imagination of the pupil can be led by means of the classical works of creative imagination to the formation of a good taste both as regards ethical value and beauty of form. The proper classical works for youth are those which nations have produced in the earliest stages of their culture. These works bring children face to face with the picture which mind has sketched for itself in one of the necessary stages of its development. This is the real reason why our children never weary of reading Homer and the stories of the Old Testament. Polytheism and the heroism which belongs to it are just as substantial an element of childish conception as monotheism with its prophets and patriarchs. We stand beyond both, because we are mediated by both, and embrace both in our stand-point.

—The purest stories of literature designed for the amusement *The Imaginative Epoch.* 43 of children from their seventh to their fourteenth year, consist always of those which were honored by nations and the world at large. One has only to notice in how many thousand forms the stories of Ulysses are reproduced by the writers of children's tales. Becker's "Tales of Ancient Times," Gustav Schwab's most admirable "Sagas of Antiquity," Karl Grimm's "Tales of Olden Times," &c., what were they without the well-talking, wily favorite of Pallas, and the divine swine-herd? And just as indestructible are the stories of the Old Testament up to the separation of Judah and Israel. These patriarchs with their wives and children, these judges and prophets, these kings and priests, are by no means ideals of virtue in the notion of our modern lifeless morality, which would smooth out of its pattern-stories for the "dear children" everything that is hard and uncouth. For the very reason that the shadow-side is not wanting here, and that we find envy, vanity, evil desire, ingratitude, craftiness, and deceit, among these fathers of the race and leaders of "God's chosen people," have these stories so great an educational value. Adam, Cain, Abraham, Joseph, Samson, and David, have justly become as truly world-historical types as Achilles and Patroclus, Agamemnon and Iphigenia, Hector and Andromache, Ulysses and Penelope.—

95. There may be produced also, out of the simplest and most primitive phases of different epochs of culture of one and the same people, stories which answer to the imagination of children, and represent to them the characteristic features of the past of their people.

—The Germans possess such a collection of their stories in their popular books of the "Horny Sigfried," of the "Heymon Children," of "Beautiful *Magelone*," "Fortunatus," "The Wandering Jew," "Faust," "The Adventurous Simplicissimus," "The *Schildbrger*," "The Island of Felsenburg," "Lienhard and Gertrude," &c. Also, the art works of the great masters which possess national significance must be spoken of here, as the Don Quixote of Cervantes.—

96. The most general form in which the childish imagination finds exercise is that of fairy-tales; but Education must take care that it has these in their proper shape as national productions, and that they are not of the morbid kind *The Imaginative Epoch.* 44 which poetry so often gives us in this species of literature, and which not seldom degenerate to sentimental caricatures and silliness.

—The East Indian stories are most excellent because they have their origin with a childlike people who live wholly in the imagination. By means of the Arabian filtration, which took place in Cairo in the flourishing period of the Egyptian caliphs, all that was too characteristically Indian was excluded, and they were made in the "Tales of Scheherezade," a book for all peoples, with whose far-reaching power in child-literature, the local stories of a race, as e.g. Grimm's admirable ones of German tradition, cannot compare. Fairy-tales made to order, as we often see them, with a medi涡l Catholic tendency, or very moral and dry, are a bane to the youthful imagination in their stale sweetness. We must here add, however, that lately we have had some better success in our attempts since we have learned to distinguish between the na جمعی natural poetry, which is without reflection, and the poetry of art, which is conditioned by criticism and an ideal. This distinction has produced good fruits even in the picture-books of children. The pretensions of the gentlemen who printed illustrated books containing nothing more solid than the alphabet and the multiplication table have become less prominent since such men as Speckter, Fr□□ch, Gutsmuths, Hofman (the writer of "Slovenly Peter"), and others, have shown that seemingly trivial things can be handled with intellectual power, if one is blessed with it, and that nothing is more opposed to the child's imagination than the *childishness* with which so many writers for children have fallen when they attempted to descend with dignity from their presumably lofty stand-point. Men are beginning to understand that Christ promised the kingdom of heaven to little children on other grounds than because they had as it were the privilege of being thoughtless and foolish. —

97. For youth and maidens, especially as they approach manhood and womanhood, the cultivation of the imagination must allow the earnestness of actuality to manifest itself in its undisguised energy. This earnestness, no longer through the symbolism of play but in its objective reality, *The Imaginative Epoch.* 45 must now thoroughly penetrate the conceptions of the youth so that it shall prepare him to seize hold of the machinery of active life. Instead of the all-embracing Epos they should now read Tragedy, whose purifying process, through the alternation of fear and pity, unfolds to the youth the secret of all human destiny, sin and its expiation. The works best adapted to lead to history on this side are those of biography — of ancient times, Plutarch; of modern times, the autobiographies of Augustine, Cellini, Rousseau, Goethe, Varnhagen, Jung Stilling, Moritz, Arndt, &c. These autobiographies contain a view of the growth of individuality through its inter-action with the influences of its time, and, together with the letters and memoirs of great or at least note-worthy men, tend to produce a healthy excitement in the youth, who must learn to fight his own battles through a knowledge of the battles of others. To introduce the youth to a knowledge of Nature and Ethnography no means are better than those of books of travel which give the charm of first contact, the joy of discovery, instead of the general consciousness of the conquests of mind.

— If educative literature on the one hand broadens the field of knowledge, on the other it may also promote its elaboration into ideal forms. This happens, in a strict sense, through philosophical literature. But only two different species of this are to be recommended to youth: (1) well-written treatises which endeavor to solve a single problem with spirit and thoroughness; or, (2) when the intelligence has grown strong enough for it, the classical works of a real philosopher. German literature is fortunately very rich in treatises of this kind in the works of Lessing, Herder, Kant, Fichte, Schleiermacher, Humboldt, and Schiller. But nothing does more harm to youth than the study of works of mediocrity, or those of a still lower rank. They stupefy and narrow the mind by their empty, hollow, and constrained style. It is generally supposed that these standard works are too difficult, and that one must first seize them in this trivial and diluted form in order to understand them. This is one of the most prevalent and most dangerous errors, for these Introductions or Explanations, easily-comprehended Treatises, Summary Abstracts, are, because of their want of originality *The Imaginative Epoch.* 46 and of the acuteness which belongs to it, much more difficult to understand than the standard work itself from which they drain their supplies. Education must train the youth to the courage which will attempt standard works, and it must not allow any such miserable preconceived opinions to grow up in his mind as that his understanding is totally unable to comprehend works like Fichte's "Science of Knowledge," the "Metaphysics" of Aristotle, or Hegel's "Phenomenology." No science suffers so much as Philosophy from this false popular opinion, which understands neither itself nor its authority. The youth must *learn how to learn to understand*, and, in order to do this, he must know that one cannot immediately understand everything in its finest subdivisions, and that on this account he must have patience, and must resolve to read over and over again, and to think over what he has read. —

98. (3) Imagination returns again within itself to perception in that it replaces, for conceptions, perceptions themselves, which are to remind it of the previous conception. These perceptions may resemble in some way the perception which lies at the basis of the conception, and be thus more or less symbolical; or they may be merely arbitrary creations of the creative imagination, and are in this case pure signs. In common speech and writing, we call the free retaining of these perceptions created by imagination, and the re-

calling of the conceptions denoted by them, *Memory*. It is by no means a particular faculty of the mind, which is again subdivided into memory of persons, names, numbers, &c. As to its form, memory is the stage of the dissolution of conception; but as to its content, it arises from the interest which we take in a subject-matter. From this interest results, moreover, careful attention, and from this latter, facility in the reproductive imagination. If these acts have preceded, the fixing of a name, or of a number, in which the content interesting us is as it were summed up, is not difficult. When interest and attention animate us, it seems as if we did not need to be at all troubled about remembering anything. All the so-called mnemonic helps only serve to make more difficult the act of memory. This act is in itself a double function, consisting of, first, the fixing of the sign, and second, *The Logical Epoch.* 47 the fixing of the conception subsumed under it. Since the mnemonic technique adds to these one more conception, through whose means the things with which we have to deal are to be fixed in order to be able freely to express them in us, it trebles the functions of remembering, and forgets that the mediation of these and their relation — wholly arbitrary and highly artificial — must also be remembered. The true help of memory consists in not helping it at all, but in simply taking up the object into the ideal regions of the mind by the force of the infinite self-determination which mind possesses.

— Lists of names, as e.g. of the Roman emperors, of the popes, of the caliphs, of rivers, mountains, authors, cities, &c.; also numbers, as e.g. the multiplication table, the melting points of minerals, the dates of battles, of births and deaths, &c., must be learned without aid. All indirect means only serve to do harm here, and are required as self-discovered mediation only in case that interest or attention has become weakened. —

99. The means to be used, which result from the nature of memory itself, are on the one hand the pronouncing and writing of the names and numbers, and on the other, repetition; by these we gain distinctness and certainty.

— All artificial contrivances for quickening the memory vanish in comparison with the art of writing, in so far as this is not looked at as a means of relieving the memory. That a name or a number should be this or that, is a mere chance for the intelligence, an entirely meaningless accident to which we have unconditionally to submit ourselves as unalterable. The intelligence must be accustomed to put upon itself this constraint. In science proper, especially in Philosophy, our reason helps to produce one thought from others by means of the context, and we can discover names for the ideas from them. —

III. The Logical Epoch.

100. In Conception there is attained a universality of intellectual action in so far as the empirical details are referred to a *Schema*, as Kant called it. But the *necessity* of the connection is wanting to it. To produce this is the *The Logical Epoch.* 48 task of the thinking activity, which frees itself from all representations, and with its clearly defined determinations transcends conceptions. The Thinking activity frees itself from all sensuous representations by means of the processes of Conception and Perception. Comprehension, Judgment, and Syllogism, develop for themselves into forms which, as such, have no power of being perceived by the senses. But it does not follow from this that he who thinks cannot return out of the thinking activity and carry it with him into the sphere of Conception and Perception. The true thinking activity deprives itself of no content. The abstraction affecting a logical purism which looks down upon Conception and Perception as forms of intelligence quite inferior to itself, is a pseudo-thinking, a morbid and scholastic error. Education will be the better on its guard against this the more it has led the pupil by the legitimate road of Perception and Conception to Thinking. Memorizing especially is an excellent preparatory school for the Thinking activity, because it gives practice to the intelligence in exercising itself in abstract ideas.

101. The fostering of the Sense of Truth from the earliest years up, is the surest way of leading the pupil to gain the power of thinking. The unprejudiced, disinterested yielding to Truth, as well as the effort to shun all deception and false seeming, are of the greatest value in strengthening the power of reflection, as this considers nothing of value but the actually existing objective circumstances.

—The indulging an illusion as a pleasing recreation of the intelligence should be allowed, while lying must not be tolerated. Children have a natural inclination for mystifications, for masquerades, for raillery, and for theatrical performances, &c. This inclination to illusion is perfectly normal with them, and should be permitted. The graceful kingdom of Art is developed from it, as also the poetry of conversation in jest and wit. Although this sometimes becomes stereotyped into very prosaic conventional forms of speech, it is more tolerable than the awkward honesty which takes everything in its simple literal sense. And it is easy to discover whether children in such play, in the activity of free joyousness, incline to the side of mischief by their showing *The Logical Presupposition or Method.* 49 a desire of satisfying their selfish interest. Then they must be checked, for in that case the cheerfulness of harmless joking gives way to premeditation and dissimulation. —

102. An acquaintance with logical forms is to be recommended as a special educational help in the culture of intelligence. The study of Mathematics does not suffice, because it presupposes Logic. Mathematics is related to Logic in the same way as Grammar, the Physical Sciences, &c. The logical forms must be known explicitly in their pure independent forms, and not merely in their implicit state as immanent in objective forms.

SECOND CHAPTER.
The Logical Presupposition or Method.

103. The logical presupposition of instruction is the order in which the subject-matter develops for the consciousness. The subject, the consciousness of the pupil, and the activity of the instructor, interpenetrate each other in instruction, and constitute in actuality one whole.

104. (1) First of all, the subject which is to be learned has a specific determinateness which demands in its representation a certain fixed order. However arbitrary we may desire to be, the subject has a certain self-determination of its own which no mistreatment can wholly crush out, and this inherent immortal reason is the general foundation of instruction.

— To illustrate; however one may desire to manipulate a language in teaching it, he cannot change the words in it, or the inflections of the declensions and conjugations. And the same restriction is laid upon our inclinations in the different divisions of Natural History, in the theorems of Arithmetic, Geometry, &c. The theorem of Pascal remains still the theorem of Pascal, and will always remain so. —

105. (2) But the subject must be adapted to the consciousness of the pupil, and here the order of procedure and the exposition depend upon the stage which he has reached intellectually, for the special manner of the instruction must be conditioned by this. If he is in the stage of perception, we must use the illustrative method; if in the stage of conception, that of combination; and if in the stage of reflection *The Logical Presupposition or Method.* 50 that of demonstration. The first exhibits the object directly, or some representation of it; the second considers it according to the different possibilities which exist in it, and turns it around on all sides; the third questions the necessity of the connection in which it stands either with itself or with others. This is the natural order from the stand-point of the scientific intelligence: first, the object is presented to the perception; then combination presents its different phases; and, finally, the thinking activity circumscribes the restlessly moving reflection by the idea of necessity. Experiment in the method of combination is an excellent means for a discovery of relations, for a sharpening of the attention, for the arousing of a many-sided interest; but it is no true dialectic, though it be often denoted by that name.

—Illustration is especially necessary in the natural sciences and also in æsthetics, because in both of these departments the sensuous is an essential element of the matter dealt with. In this respect we have made great progress in charts and maps. Sydow's hand and wall maps and Berghaus's physical atlas are most excellent means of illustrative instruction; also Burmeister's zo · ·ical atlas. —

106. The demonstrative method, in order to bring about its proof of necessity, has a choice of many different ways. But we must not imagine, either that there are an unlimited number, and that it is only a chance which one we shall take; or that they have no connection among themselves, and run, as it were, side by side. It is not, however, the business of Pedagogics to develop different methods of proof; this belongs to Logic. We have only to remember that, logically taken, proof must be analytic, synthetic, or dialectic. Analysis begins with the single one, and leads out of it by induction to the general principle from which its existence results. Synthesis, on

the contrary, begins with a general which is presupposed as true, and leads from this through deduction to the special determinations which were implicit in it. The regressive search of analysis for a determining principle is *Invention*; the forward progress of synthesis from the simple elements seeking for the multiplicity of the single one is *Construction*. Each, in its result, passes over into the other; but their truth is found in the dialectic method, which in each *The Logical Presupposition or Method.* 51 phase allows unity to separate into diversity and diversity to return into unity. While in the analytic as well as in the synthetic method the mediation of the individual with the general, or of the general with the individual, lets the phase of particularity be only subjectively connected with it in the dialectic method, we have the going over of the general through the particular to the individual, or to the self-determination of the idea, and it therefore rightly claims the title of the genetic method. We can also say that while the inventive method gives us the idea (notion) and the constructive the judgment, the genetic gives us the syllogism which leads the determinations of reflection back again into substantial identity.

107. (3) The active mediation of the pupil with the content which is to be impressed upon his consciousness is the work of the teacher, whose personality creates a method adapted to the individual; for however clearly the subject may be defined, however exactly the psychological stage of the pupil may be regulated, the teacher cannot dispense with the power of his own individuality even in the most objective relations. This individuality must penetrate the whole with its own exposition, and that peculiarity which we call his *manner*, and which cannot be determined □*riori*, must appear. The teacher must place himself on the stand-point of the pupil, i.e. must adapt himself; he must see that the abstract is made clear to him in the concrete, i.e. must illustrate; he must fill up the gaps which will certainly appear, and which may mar the thorough seizing of the subject, i.e. must supply. In all these relations the pedagogical tact of the teacher may prove itself truly ingenious in varying the method according to the changefulness of the ever-varying needs, in contracting or expanding the extent, in stating, or indicating what is to be supplied. The true teacher is free from any superstitious belief in any one procedure as a sure specific which he fol-

lows always in a monotonous bondage. This can only happen when he is capable of the highest method. The teacher has arrived at the highest point of ability in teaching when he can make use of all means, from the loftiness of solemn seriousness, through smooth statement, to the play of jest—yes, even to the incentive of irony, and to humor.

The Subjects of Instruction. 52

—Pedagogics can be in nothing more specious than in its method, and it is here that charlatanism can most readily intrude itself. Every little change, every inadequate modification, is proclaimed aloud as a new or an improved method; and even the most foolish and superficial changes find at once their imitators, who themselves conceal their insolence behind some frivolous differences, and, with laughable conceit, hail themselves as inventors.—

THIRD CHAPTER.
Instruction.

108. All instruction acts upon the supposition that there is an inequality between present knowledge and power and that knowledge and power which are not yet attained. To the pupil belong the first, to the teacher the second. Education is the act which gradually cancels the original inequality of teacher and pupil, in that it converts what was at first the property of the former into the property of the latter, and this by means of his own activity.

I. *The Subjects of Instruction.*

109. The pupil is the apprentice, the teacher the master, whether in the practice of any craft or art, or in the exposition of any systematic knowledge. The pupil passes from the state of the apprentice to that of the master through that of the journeyman. The apprentice has to appropriate to himself the elements; journeymanship begins as he, by means of their possession, becomes independent; the master combines with his technical skill the freedom of production. His authority over his pupil consists only in his knowledge and power. If he has not these, no external support, no trick of false appearances which he may put on, will serve to create it for him.

110. These stages—(1) apprenticeship, (2) journeymanship, (3) mastership—are fixed limitations in the didactic process; they are

relative only in the concrete. The standard of special excellence varies with the different grades of culture, and must be varied that it may have any historical value. The master is complete only in relation to the journeyman and apprentice; to them he is superior. But on the *The Subjects of Instruction*. 53 other hand, in relation to the infinity of the problems of his art or science, he is by no means complete; to himself he must always appear as one who begins ever anew, one who is ever striving, one to whom a new problem ever rises from every achieved result. He cannot discharge himself from work, he must never desire to rest on his laurels. He is the truest master whose finished performances only force him on to never-resting progress.

111. The real possibility of culture is found in general, it is true, in every human being; nevertheless, empirically, there are distinguished: (1) Incapacity, as the want of all gifts; (2) Mediocrity; (3) Talent and Genius. It is the part of Psychology to give an account of all these. Mediocrity characterizes the great mass of mechanical intelligences, those who wait for external impulse as to what direction their endeavors shall take. Not without truth, perhaps, may we say, that hypothetically a special talent is given to each individual, but this special talent in many men never makes its appearance, because under the circumstances in which it finds itself placed it fails to find the exciting occasion which shall give him the knowledge of its existence. The majority of mankind are contented with the mechanical impulse which makes them into something and impresses upon them certain determinations. — Talent shows itself by means of the confidence in its own especial productive possibility, which manifests itself as an inclination, as a strong impulse, to occupy itself with the special object which constitutes its content. Pedagogics has no difficulty in dealing with mechanical natures, because their passivity is only too ready to follow prescribed patterns. It is more difficult to manage talent, because it lies between mediocrity and genius, and is therefore uncertain, and not only unequal to itself, but also is tossed now too low, now too high, is by turns despondent and over-excited. The general maxim for dealing with it is to remove no difficulty from the subject to which its efforts are directed. — Genius must be treated much in the same way as Talent. The difference consists only in this, that Genius, with a fore-

knowledge of its creative power, usually manifests its confidence with less doubt in a special vocation, and, with a more intense thirst *The Subjects of Instruction.* 54 for culture, subjects itself more willingly to the demands of instruction. Genius is in its nature the purest self-determination, in that it lives, in its own inner existence, the necessity which exists in the thing. But it can assign to the New, which is in it already immediately and subjectively, no value if this has not united itself to the already existing culture as its objective presupposition, and on this ground it thankfully receives instruction.

112. But Talent and Genius offer a special difficulty to education in the precocity which often accompanies them. But by precocity we do not mean that they early render themselves perceptible, since the early manifestation of gifts by talent and genius, through their intense confidence, is to be looked at as perfectly legitimate. But precocity is rather the hastening forward of the human being in feeling and moral sense, so that where in the ordinary course of nature we should have a child, we have a youth, and a man in the place of a youth. We may find precocity among those who belong to the class of mediocrity, but it is developed most readily among those possessed of talent and genius, because with them the early appearance of superior gifts may very easily bring in its train a perversion of the feelings and the moral nature. Education must deal with it in so far as it is inharmonious, so that it shall be stronger than the demands made on it from without, so that it shall not minister to vanity; and must take care, in order to accomplish this, that social naturalness and lack of affection be preserved in the pupil.

—Our age has to combat this precocity much more than others. We find e.g. authors who, at the age of thirty years, in which they publish their collected works or write their biography, are chilly with the feelings of old age. Music has been the sphere in which the earliest development of talent has shown itself, and here we find the absurdity that the cupidity of parents has so forced precocious talents that children of four or five years of age have been made to appear in public. —

113. Every sphere of culture contains a certain quantity of knowledge and ready skill which may be looked at, as it were, as

the created result of the culture. It is to be wished *The Subjects of Instruction.* 55 that every one who turns his attention to a certain line of culture could take up into himself the gathered learning which controls it. In so far as he does this, he is professional. The consciousness that one has in the usual way gone through a school of art or science, and has, with the general inheritance of acquisition, been handed over to a special department, creates externally a beneficial composure which is very favorable to internal progress. We must distinguish from the professional the amateur and the self-taught man. The amateur busies himself with an art, a science, or a trade, without having gone through any strict training in it. As a rule, he dispenses with elementary thoroughness, and hastens towards the pleasure which the joy of production gives. The conscious amateur confesses this himself, makes no pretension to mastership, and calls himself — in distinction from the professional, who subjects himself to rules — an unlearned person. But sometimes the amateur, on the contrary, covers over his weakness, cherishes in himself the self-conceit that he is equal to the heroes of his art or science, constitutes himself the first admirer of his own performances, seeks for their want of recognition in external motives, never in their own want of excellence; and, if he has money, or edits a paper, is intoxicated with being the patron of talent which produces such works as he would willingly produce or pretends to produce. The self-taught man has often true talent, or even genius, to whose development nevertheless the inherited culture has been denied, and who by good fortune has through his own strength worked his way into a field of effort. The self-taught man is distinguished from the amateur by the thoroughness and the industry with which he acts; he is not only equally unfortunate with him in the absence of school-training, but is much less endowed. Even if the self-taught man has for years studied and practised much, he is still haunted by a feeling of uncertainty as to whether he has yet reached the standpoint at which a science, an art, or a trade, will receive him publicly — of so very great consequence is it that man should be comprehended and recognized by man. The self-taught man therefore remains embarrassed, and does not free himself from the apprehension that he may expose some weak point to a professional, or he falls into the other extreme — he *The Act of Learning.* 56 becomes presumptuous, steps forth as a reformer, and, if he accomplishes nothing, or earns only ridicule, he sets himself down as an unrecognized martyr by an unappreciative and unjust world.

—It is possible that the amateur may transcend the stage of superficiality and subject himself to a thorough training; then he ceases to be an amateur. It is also possible that the self-taught man may be on the right track, and may accomplish as much or even more than one trained in the usual way. In general, however, it is very desirable that every one should go through the regular course of the inherited means of education, partly that he may be thorough in the elements, partly to free him from the anxiety which he may feel lest he in his solitary efforts spend labor on some superfluous work—superfluous because done long before, and of which he, through the accident of his want of culture, had not heard. We must all learn by ourselves, but we cannot teach ourselves. Only Genius can do this, for it must be its own leader in the new paths which it opens. Genius alone passes beyond where inherited culture ceases. It bears this in itself as of the past, and which it uses as material for its new creation; but the self-taught man, who would very willingly be a genius, puts himself in an attitude of opposition to things already accomplished, or sinks into oddity, into secret arts and sciences, &c.—

114. These ideas of the general steps of culture, of special gifts, and of the ways of culture appropriate to each, which we have above distinguished, have a manifold connection among themselves which cannot be established □riori. We can however remark that Apprenticeship, the Mechanical Intelligence, and the Professional life; secondly, Journeymanship, Talent, and Amateurship; and, finally, Mastership, Genius, and Self Education, have a relationship to each other.

II. *The Act of Learning.*

115. In the process of education the interaction between pupil and teacher must be so managed that the exposition by the teacher shall excite in the pupil the impulse to reproduction. The teacher must not treat his exposition as if it were a work of art which is its own end and aim, but he must always *The Act of Learning.* 57 bear in mind the need of the pupil. The artistic exposition, as such, will, by its completeness, produce admiration; but the didactic, on the con-

trary, will, through its perfect adaptation, call out the imitative instinct, the power of new creation.

—From this consideration we may justify the frequent statement that is made, that teachers who have really an elegant diction do not really accomplish so much as others who resemble in their statements not so much a canal flowing smoothly between straight banks, as a river which works its foaming way over rocks and between ever-winding banks. The pupil perceives that the first is considering himself when he speaks so finely, perhaps not without some self-appreciation; and that the second, in the repetitions and the sentences which are never finished, is concerning himself solely with *him*. The pupil feels that not want of facility or awkwardness, but the earnest eagerness of the *teacher*, is the principal thing, and that this latter uses rhetoric only as a means. —

116. In the act of learning there appears (1) a mechanical element, (2) a dynamic element, and (3) one in which the dynamic again mechanically strengthens itself.

117. As to the mechanical element, the right time must be chosen for each lesson, an exact arrangement observed, and the suitable apparatus, which is necessary, procured. It is in the arrangement that especially consists the educational power of the lesson. The spirit of scrupulousness, of accuracy, of neatness, is developed by the external technique, which is carefully arranged in its subordinate parts according to its content. The teacher must therefore insist upon it that work shall cease at the exact time, that the work be well done, &c., for on these little things many greater things ethically depend.

—To choose one's time for any work is often difficult because of the pressure of a multitude of demands, but in general it should be determined that the strongest and keenest energy of the thinking activity and of memory—this being demanded by the work— should have appropriated to it the first half of the day. —

118. The dynamical element consists of the previously *The Act of Learning.* 58 developed power of Attention, without which all the exposition made by the teacher to the pupil remains entirely foreign to him, all apparatus is dead, all arrangement of no avail, all teach-

ing fruitless, if the pupil does not by his free activity receive into his inner self what one teaches him, and thus make it his own property.

119. This appropriation must not limit itself, however, to the first acquisition of any knowledge or skill, but it must give free existence to whatever the pupil has learned; it must make it perfectly manageable and natural, so that it shall appear to be a part of himself. This must be brought about by means of Repetition. This will mechanically secure that which the attention first grasped.

120. The careful, persistent, living activity of the pupil in these acts we call Industry. Its negative extreme is Laziness, which is deserving of punishment inasmuch as it passes over into a want of self-determination. Man is by nature lazy. But mind, which is only in its act, must resolve upon activity. This connection of Industry with human freedom, with the very essence of mind, makes laziness appear blameworthy. The really civilized man, therefore, no longer knows that absolute inaction which is the greatest enjoyment to the barbarian, and he fills up his leisure with a variety of easier and lighter work. The positive extreme of Industry is the unreasonable activity which rushes in breathless chase from one action to another, from this to that, straining the person with the immense quantity of his work. Such an activity, going beyond itself and seldom reaching deliberation, is unworthy of a man. It destroys the agreeable quiet which in all industry should penetrate and inspire the deed. Nothing is more repulsive than the beggarly pride of such stupid laboriousness. One should not endure for a moment to have the pupil, seeking for distinction, begin to pride himself on an extra industry. Education must accustom him to use a regular assiduity. The frame of mind suitable for work often does not exist at the time when work should begin, but more frequently it makes its appearance after we have begun. The subject takes its own time to awaken us. Industry, inspired by a love and regard for work, has in its quiet uniformity a great force, without which no one can accomplish anything *The Act of Learning.* 59 essential. The world, therefore, holds Industry worthy of honor; and to the Romans, a nation of the most persistent perseverance, we owe the inspiring words, *"Incepto tantum opus est, c津ra res expediet"*; and, *"Labor improbus omnia vincit."*

—"Every one may glory in his industry!" This is a true word from the lips of a truly industrious man, who was also one of the most modest. But Lessing did not, however, mean by them to charter Pharisaical pedantry. The necessity sometimes of giving one's self to an excess of work injurious to the health, generally arises from the fact that he has not at other times made use of the requisite attention to the necessary industry, and then attempts suddenly and as by a forced march to storm his way to his end. The result of such over-exertion is naturally entire prostration. The pupil is therefore to be accustomed to a generally uniform industry, which may extend itself at regular intervals without his thereby overstraining himself. What is really gained by a young man who has hitherto neglected time and opportunity, and who, when examination presses, over-works himself, perhaps standing the test with honor, and then must rest for months afterwards from the over-effort? On all such occasions attention is not objective and dispassionate, but rather becomes, through anxiety to pass the examination, restless and corrupted by egotism; and the usual evil result of such compulsory industry is the ephemeral character of the knowledge thus gained. "Lightly come, lightly go," says the proverb. —

—A special worth is always attached to study far into the night. The student's "midnight lamp" always claims for itself a certain veneration. But this is vanity. In the first place, it is injurious to contradict Nature by working through the night, which she has ordained for sleep; secondly, the question is not as to the number of hours spent in work and their position in the twenty-four, but as to the quality of the work. With regard to the value of my work, it is of no moment whatsoever whether I have done it in the morning or in the evening, or how long I have labored, and it is of no consequence to any one except to my own very unimportant self. *The Act of Learning.* 60 Finally, the question presents itself whether these gentlemen who boast so much of their midnight work do not sleep in the daytime! —

121. But Industry has also two other extremes: seeming-laziness and seeming-industry. Seeming-laziness is the neglecting of the usual activity in one department because a man is so much more active in another. The mind possessed with the liveliest interest in one subject buries itself in it, and, because of this, cannot give itself

up to another which before had engrossed the attention. Thus it appears more idle than it is, or rather it appears to be idle just because it is more industrious. This is especially the case in passing from one subject of instruction to another. The pupil should acquire such a flexibility in his intellectual powers that the rapid relinquishment of one subject and the taking up of another should not be too difficult. Nothing is more natural than that when he is excited he should go back to the subject that has just been presented to him, and that he, feeling himself restrained, shall remain untouched by the following lesson, which may be of an entirely different nature. The young soul is brooding over what has been said, and is really exercising an intensive activity, though it appears to be idle. But in seeming-industry all the external motives of activity, all the mechanism of work, manifest themselves noisily, while there is no true energy of attention and productivity. One busies himself with all the apparatus of work; he heaps up instruments and books around him; he sketches plans; he spends many hours staring into vacancy, biting his pen, gazing at words, drawings, numbers, &c. Boys, under the protection of so great a scaffolding for work erected around them, often carry on their own amusements. Men, who arrive at no real concentration of their force, no clear defining of their vocation, no firm decision as to their action, dissipate their power in what is too often a great activity with absolutely no result. They are busy, very busy; they have hardly time to do this thing because they really wish or ought to do that; but, with all their driving, their energy is all dissipated, and nothing comes from their countless labors.

The Modality of the Process of Teaching. 61

III. *The Modality of the Process of Teaching.*

122. Now that we have learned something of the relation of the teacher to the taught, and of the process of learning itself, we must examine the mode and manner of instruction. This may have (1) the character of contingency: the way in which our immediate existence in the world, our life, teaches us; or it may be given (2) by the printed page; or (3) it may take the shape of formal oral instruction.

123. (1) For the most, the best, and the mightiest things that we know we are indebted to Life itself. The sum of perceptions which a human being absorbs into himself up to the fourth or fifth year of

his life is incalculable; and after this time we involuntarily gain by immediate contact with the world countless ideas. But especially we understand by the phrase "the School of Life," the ethical knowledge which we gain by what happens in our own lives.

—If one says, *Vit枏on schol杊iscendum est*, one can also say, *Vita docet*. Without the power exercised by the immediate world our intelligence would remain abstract and lifeless.—

124. (2) What we learn through books is the opposite of that which we learn through living. Life *forces* upon us the knowledge it has to give; the book, on the contrary, is entirely passive. It is locked up in itself; it cannot be altered; but it waits by us till we wish to use it. We can read it rapidly or slowly; we can simply turn over its leaves—what in modern times one calls reading;—we can read it from beginning to end or from end to beginning; we can stop, begin again, skip over passages, or cut them short, as we like. To this extent the book is the most *convenient* means for instruction. If we are indebted to Life for our perceptions, we must chiefly thank books for our understanding of our perceptions. We call book-instruction "dead" when it lacks, for the exposition which it gives, a foundation in our perceptions, or when we do not add to the printed description the perceptions which it implies; and the two are quite different.

125. Books, as well as life, teach us many things which we did not previously intend to learn directly from them. From foreign romances e.g. we learn, first of all, while we read them for entertainment, the foreign language, history *The Modality of the Process of Teaching.* 62 or geography, &c. We must distinguish from such books as those which bring to us, as it were accidentally, a knowledge for which we were not seeking, the books which are expressly intended to instruct. These must (*a*) in their consideration of the subject give us the principal results of any department of knowledge, and denote the points from which the next advance must be made, because every science arises at certain results which are themselves again new problems; (*b*) in the consideration of the particulars it must be exhaustive, i.e. no essential elements of a science must be omitted. But this exhaustiveness of execution has different meanings according to the stand-points of those for whom it

is made. How far we shall pass from the universality of the principal determinations into the multiplicity of the Particular, into the fulness of detail, cannot be definitely determined, and must vary, according to the aim of the book, as to whether it is intended for the apprentice, the journeyman, or the master; (*c*) the expression must be precise, i.e. the maximum of clearness must be combined with the maximum of brevity.

—The writing of a text-book is on this account one of the most difficult tasks, and it can be successfully accomplished only by those who are masters in a science or art, and who combine with great culture and talent great experience as teachers. Unfortunately many dabblers in knowledge undervalue the difficulty of writing text-books because they think that they are called upon to aid in the spread of science, and because the writing of compendiums has thus come to be an avocation, so that authors and publishers have made out of text-books a profitable business and good incomes. In all sciences and arts there exists a quantity of material which is common property, which is disposed of now in one way, now in another. The majority of compendiums can be distinguished from each other only by the kind of paper, printing, the name of the publisher or bookseller, or by arbitrary changes in the arrangement and execution. The want of principle with which this work is carried on is incredible. Many governments have on this account fixed prices for text-books, and commissioners to select them. This in itself is right and proper, but the use of any book should be left optional, so that the one-sidedness of a science patronized by *The Modality of the Process of Teaching.* 63 government as it were patented, may not be created through the pressure of such introduction. A state may through its censorship oppose poor text-books, and recommend good ones; but it may not establish as it were a state-science, a state-art, in which only the ideas, laws and forms sanctioned by it shall be allowed. The Germans are fortunate, in consequence of their philosophical criticism, in the production of better and better text-books, among which may be mentioned Koberstein's, Gervinus', and Vilmar's Histories of Literature, Ellendt's General History, Blumenbach's and Burmeister's Natural History, Marheineke's text-book on Religion, Schwegler's History of Philosophy, &c. So much the more unaccountable is it that, with such excellent books, the evil of such characterless books, partly inadequate and partly in poor style, should still exist when there is no necessity for it. The common style of paragraph-writing has become obnoxious, under the name of Compendium-style, as the most stiff and affected style of writing. —

126. A text-book must be differently written according as it is intended for a book for private study or for purposes of general circulation. If the first, it must give more, and must develop more clearly the internal relations; if the second, it should be shorter, and proceed from axiomatic and clear postulates to their signification, and these must have an epigrammatic pureness which should leave something to be guessed. Because for these a commentary is needed which it is the teacher's duty to supply, such a sketch is usually accompanied by the fuller text-book which was arranged for private study.

—It is the custom to call the proper text-book the "small" one, and that which explains and illustrates, the "large" one. Thus we have the Small and the Large Gervinus, &c. —

127. (3) The text-book which presupposes oral explanation forms the transition to Oral instruction itself. Since speech is the natural and original form in which mind manifests itself, no book can rival it. The living word is the most powerful agent of instruction. However common and cheap printing may have rendered books as the most convenient means of education—however possible may have become, through the multiplication of facilities for intercourse and *The Modality of the Process of Teaching*. 64 the rapidity of transportation, the immediate viewing of human life, the most forcible educational means, nevertheless the living word still asserts its supremacy. In two cases especially is it indispensable: one is when some knowledge is to be communicated which as yet is found in no compendium, and the other when a living language is to be taught, for in this case the printed page is entirely inadequate. One can learn from books to understand Spanish, French, English, Danish, &c., but not to speak them; to do this he must hear them, partly that his ear may become accustomed to the sounds, partly that his vocal organs may learn correctly to imitate them.

128. Life surprises and overpowers us with the knowledge which it gains; the book, impassive, waits our convenience; the teacher,

superior to us, perfectly prepared in comparison with us, consults our necessity, and with his living speech uses a gentle force to which we can yield without losing our freedom. Listening is easier than reading.

—Sovereigns e.g. seldom read themselves, but have servants who read to them.—

129. Oral instruction may (1) give the subject, which is to be learned, in a connected statement, or (2) it may unfold it by means of question and answer. The first decidedly presupposes the theoretical inequality of the teacher and the taught. Because one can speak while many can listen, this is especially adapted to the instruction of large numbers. The second method is either that of the catechism or the dialogue. The catechetical is connected with the first kind of oral instruction above designated because it makes demand upon the memory of the learner only for the answer to one question at a time, and is hence very often and very absurdly called the Socratic method. In teaching by means of the dialogue, we try, by means of a reciprocal interchange of thought, to solve in common some problem, proceeding according to the necessary forms of reason. But in this we can make a distinction. One speaker may be superior to the rest, may hold in his own hand the thread of the conversation and may guide it himself; or, those who mingle in it may be perfectly equal in intellect and culture, and may each take part in the development with equal independence. In this latter case, this *The Modality of the Process of Teaching.* 65 true reciprocity gives us the proper dramatic dialogue, which contains in itself all forms of exposition, and may pass from narration, description, and analysis, through satire and irony, to veritable humor. When it does this, the dialogue is the loftiest result of intelligence and the means of its purest enjoyment.

—This alternate teaching, in which the one who has been taught takes the teacher's place, can be used only where there is a content which admits of a mechanical treatment. The Hindoos made use of it in very ancient times. Bell and Lancaster have transplanted it for the teaching of poor children in Europe and America. For the teaching of the conventionalities—reading, writing, and arithmetic—as well as for the learning by heart of names, sentences, &c., it suffices, but not for any scientific culture. Where we have large numbers to instruct, the giving of the fully developed statement (the first form) is necessary, since the dialogue, though it may be elsewhere suitable, allows only a few to take part in it. And if we take the second form, we must, if we have a large number of pupils, make use of the catechetical method only. What is known as the conversational method has been sometimes suggested for our university instruction. Diesterweg in Berlin insists upon it. Here and there the attempt has been made, but without any result. In the university, the lecture of the teacher as a self-developing whole is contrasted with the scientific discussion of the students, in which they as equals work over with perfect freedom what they have heard. Diesterweg was wrong in considering the lecture-system as the principal cause of the lack of scientific interest which he thought he perceived in our universities. Kant, Fichte, Schelling, Schleiermacher, Wolf, Niebuhr, &c., taught by lectures and awakened the liveliest enthusiasm. But Diesterweg is quite right in saying that the students should not be degraded to writing-machines. But this is generally conceded, and a pedantic amount of copying more and more begins to be considered as out of date at our universities. Nevertheless, a new pedantry, that of the wholly extempore lecture, should not be introduced; but a brief summary of the extempore unfolding of the lecture may be dictated and serve a very important purpose, or the lecture may be copied. The *The Modality of the Process of Teaching*. 66 great efficacy of the oral exposition does not so much consist in the fact that it is perfectly free, as that it presents to immediate view a person who has made himself the bearer of a science or an art, and has found what constitutes its essence. Its power springs, above all, from the genuineness of the lecture, the originality of its content, and the elegance of its form: whether it is written or extemporized, is a matter of little moment. Niebuhr e.g. read, word for word, from his manuscript, and what a teacher was he! — The catechetical way of teaching is not demanded at the university except in special examinations; it belongs to the private work of the student, who must learn to be industrious of his own free impulse. The private tutor can best conduct reviews. — The institution which presupposing the lecture-system combines in itself original production with criticism, and the connected exposition with the conversation, is the *seminary*. It pursues a well-defined path, and confines itself to a small circle of associates whose grades of culture are very nearly the same. Here, therefore, can the dialogue be strongly developed because it has a fixed foundation, and each one can take part in the conversation; whereas, from the variety of opinions among a great number, it is easily perverted into an aimless talk, and the majority of the hearers, who have no chance to speak, become weary. —

130. As to the way in which the lecture is carried out, it may be so arranged as to give the whole stock of information acquired, or, without being so exact and so complete, it may bring to its elucidation only a relatively inexact and general information. The ancients called the first method the esoteric and the second the exoteric, as we give to such lectures now, respectively, the names *scholastic* and *popular*. The first makes use of terms which have become technical in science or art, and proceeds syllogistically to combine the isolated ideas; the second endeavors to substitute for technicalities generally understood signs, and conceals the exactness of the formal conclusion by means of a conversational style. It is possible to conceive of a perfectly methodical treatment of a science which at the same time shall be generally comprehensible if it strives to attain the transparency of real beauty. A scientific work of art may be correctly said *The Modality of the Process of Teaching.* 67 to be popular, as e.g. has happened to Herder's *Ideas on the Philosophy of the History of Mankind.*

— Beauty is the element which is comprehended by all, and as we declare our enmity to the distorted picture-books, books of amusement, and to the mischievous character of "Compendiums," so we must also oppose the popular publications which style themselves *Science made Easy*, &c., in order to attract more purchasers by this alluring title. Kant in his *Logic* calls the extreme of explanation Pedantry and Gallantry. This last expression would be very characteristic in our times, since one attains the height of popularity now if he makes himself easily intelligible to ladies—a didactic triumph which one attains only by omitting everything that is profound or complicated, and saying only what exists already in the consciousness of every one, by depriving the subject dealt with of all seriousness, and sparing neither pictures, anecdotes, jokes, nor pretty formalities of speech. Elsewhere Kant says: "In the effort to produce in our knowledge the completeness of scholarly thoroughness, and at the same time a popular character, without in the effort falling into the above-mentioned errors of an affected thoroughness or an affected popularity, we must, first of all, look out for the scholarly completeness of our scientific knowledge, the methodical form of thoroughness, and first ask how we can make really popular the knowledge methodically acquired at school, i.e. how we can make it easy and generally communicable, and yet at the same time not supplant thoroughness by popularity. For scholarly completeness must not be sacrificed to popularity to please the people, unless science is to become a plaything or trifling." It is perfectly plain that all that was said before of the psychological and the logical methods must be taken into account in the manner of the statement. —

131. It has been already remarked (21), in speaking of the nature of education, that the office of the instructor must necessarily vary with the growing culture. But attention must here again be called to the fact, that education, in whatever stage of culture, must conform to the law which, as the internal logic of Being, determines all objective developments of nature and of history. The Family gives the child his first *The Modality of the Process of Teaching.* 68 instruction; between this and the school comes the teaching of the tutor; the school stands independently as the antithesis of the family, and presents three essentially different forms according as it imparts a general preparatory instruction, or special teaching for different callings, or a universal scientific cultivation. Universality passes over through particularizing into individuality, which contains both the general and the particular freely in itself. All citizens of a state should have (1) a general education which (*a*) makes them familiar with reading, writing, and arithmetic, these being the means of all theoretical culture; then (*b*) hands over to them a picture of the world in its principal phases, so that they as citizens of the world can find their proper status on our planet; and, finally, it must (*c*) instruct him in the history of his own state, so that he may see that the circumstances in which he lives are the result of a determined past in its connection with the history of the rest of the world, and so may learn rightly to estimate the interests of his own country in view of their necessary relation to the future. This work the elementary schools have to perform. From this, through the *Realschule* (our scientific High School course) they pass into the school where some

particular branch of science is taught, and through the Gymnasium
(classical course of a High School or College) to the University.
From its general basis develop (2) the educational institutions that
work towards some special education which leads over to the exercise of some art. These we call Technological schools, where one
may learn farming, mining, a craft, a trade, navigation, war, &c.
This kind of education may be specialized indefinitely with the
growth of culture, because any one branch is capable in its negative
aspect of such educational separation, as e.g. in foundling hospitals
and orphan asylums, in blind and deaf and dumb institutions. The
abstract universality of the Elementary school and the one-sided
particularity of the Technological school, however, is subsumed
under a concrete universality, which, without aiming directly at
utility, treats science and art on all sides as their own end and aim.
Scientia est potentia, said Lord Bacon. Practical utility results indirectly through the progress which Scientific Cognition makes in this
free attitude, because it collects itself out of *The Modality of the Process of Teaching.* 69 the dissipation through manifold details into a
universal idea and attains a profounder insight thereby. This organism for the purpose of instruction is properly called a University. By
it the educational organization is perfected.

—It is essentially seen that no more than these three types of
schools can exist, and that they must all exist in a perfectly organized civilization. Their titles and the plan of their special teaching
may be very different among different nations and at different
times, but this need not prevent the recognition in them of the ideas
which determine them. Still less should the imperfect ways in which
they manifest themselves induce us to condemn them. It is the
modern tendency to undervalue the University as an institution
which we had inherited from the middle ages, and with which we
could at present dispense. This is an error. The university presents
just as necessary a form of instruction as the elementary school or
the technological school. Not the abolition of the university, but a
reform which shall adapt it to the spirit of the age, is the advance
which we have to make. That there are to be found outside of the
university men of the most thorough and elegant culture, who can
give the most excellent instruction in a science or an art, is most
certain. But it is a characteristic of the university in its teaching to do

away with contingency which is unavoidable in case of private
voluntary efforts. The university presents an organic, self-conscious,
encyclop梗c representation of all the sciences, and thus is created to
a greater or less degree an intellectual atmosphere which no other
place can give. Through this, all sciences and their aims are seen as
of equal authority—a personal stress is laid upon the connection of
the sciences. The imperfections of a university, which arise through
the rivalry of external ambition, through the necessity of financial
success, through the jealousy of different parties, through scholar-
ships, &c., are finitudes which it has in common with all human
institutions, and on whose account they are not all to be thrown
away.—Art academies are for Art what universities are for Science.
They are inferior to them in so far as they appear more under the
form of special schools, as schools of architecture, of painting, and
conservatories of music; while really it may well be supposed that
Architecture, *The Modality of the Process of Teaching* 70 Sculpture,
Painting, Music, the Orchestra, and the Drama, are, like the Sciences, bound together in a *Universitas artium*, and that by means of their
internal reciprocal action new results would follow.—Academies, as
isolated master-schools, which follow no particular line of teaching,
are entirely superfluous, and serve only as a *Prytaneum* for meritori-
ous scholars, and to reward industry through the prizes which they
offer. In their idea they belong with the university, this appearing
externally in the fact that most of their members are university professors. But as institutions for ostentation by which the ambition of
the learned was flattered, and to surround princes with scientific
glory as scientific societies attached to a court, they have lost all
significance. They ceased to flourish with the Ptolemies and the
Egyptian caliphs, and with absolute monarchical governments.—In
modern times we have passed beyond the abstract jealousy of the
so-called Humanities and the Natural Sciences, because we comprehend that each part of the totality can be realized in a proper
sense only by its development as relatively independent. Thus the
gymnasium has its place as that elementary school which through a
general culture, by means of the knowledge of the language and
history of the Greeks and Romans, prepares for the university;
while, on the other hand, the *Realschule*, by special attention to Natural Science and the living languages, constitutes the transition to
the technological schools. Nevertheless, because the university em-

braces the Science of Nature, of Technology, of Trade, of Finance, and of Statistics, the pupils who have graduated from the so-called high schools (h□□n Brgerschulen) and from the *Realschulen* will be brought together at the university. —

132. The technique of the school will be determined in its details by the peculiarity of its aim. But in general every school, no matter what it teaches, ought to have some system of rules and regulations by which the relation of the pupil to the institution, of the pupils to each other, their relation to the teacher, and that of the teachers to each other as well as to the supervisory authority, the programme of lessons, the apparatus, of the changes of work and recreation, shall be clearly set forth. The course of study must be arranged so *The Modality of the Process of Teaching.* 71 as to avoid two extremes: on the one hand, it has to keep in view the special aim of the school, and according to this it tends to contract itself. But, on the other hand, it must consider the relative dependence of one specialty to other specialties and to general culture. It must leave the transition free, and in this it tends to expand itself. The difficulty is here so to assign the limits that the special task of the school shall not be sacrificed and deprived of the means of performance which it (since it is also always only a part of the whole culture) receives by means of its reciprocal action with other departments. The programme must assign the exact amount of time which can be appropriated to every study. It must prescribe the order in which they shall follow each other; it must, as far as possible, unite kindred subjects, so as to avoid the useless repetition which dulls the charm of study; it must, in determining the order, bear in mind at the same time the necessity imposed by the subject itself and the psychological progression of intelligence from perception, through conception, to the thinking activity which grasps all. It must periodically be submitted to revision, so that all matter which has, through the changed state of general culture, become out of date, may be rejected, and that that which has proved itself inimitable may be appropriated; in general, so that it may be kept up to the requirements of the times. And, finally, the school must, by examinations and reports, aid the pupil in the acquirement of a knowledge of his real standing. The examination lets him know what he has really learned, and what he is able to do: the report gives him an account of his culture, exhibits to

him in what he has made improvement and in what he has fallen behind, what defects he has shown, what talents he has displayed, what errors committed, and in what relation stands his theoretical development to his ethical status.

— The opposition of the *Gymnasia* to the demands of the agricultural communities is a very interesting phase of educational history. They were asked to widen their course so as to embrace Mathematics, Physics, Natural History, Geography, and the modern languages. At first they stoutly resisted; then they made some concessions; finally, the more they made the more they found themselves in contradiction *The Modality of the Process of Teaching.* 72 with their true work, and so they produced as an independent correlate the *Realschule.* After this was founded, the gymnasium returned to its old plan, and is now again able to place in the foreground the pursuit of classical literature and history. It was thus set free from demands made upon it which were entirely foreign to its nature. — The examination is, on one side, so adapted to the pupil as to make him conscious of his own condition. As to its external side, it determines whether the pupil shall pass from one class to another or from one school to another, or it decides whether the school as a whole shall give a public exhibition — an exhibition which ought to have no trace of ostentation, but which in fact is often tinctured with pedagogical charlatanism. —

133. The Direction of the school on the side of science must be held by the school itself, for the process of the intellect in acquiring science, the progress of the method, the determinations of the subject matter and the order of its development, have their own laws, to which Instruction must submit itself if it would attain its end. The school is only one part of the whole of culture. In itself it divides into manifold departments, together constituting a great organism which in manifold ways comes into contact with the organism of the state. So long as teaching is of a private character, so long as it is the reciprocal relation of one individual to another, or so long as it is shut up within the circle of the family and belongs to it alone, so long it has no objective character. It receives this first when it grows to a school. As in history, its first form must have a religious character; but this first form, in time, disappears. Religion is the absolute relation of man to God which subsumes all other relations. In so far

as Religion exists in the form of a church, those who are members of the same church may have instruction given on the nature of religion among themselves. Instruction on the subject is proper, and it is even enjoined upon them as a law—as a duty. But further than their own society they may not extend their rule. The church may exert itself to make a religious spirit felt in the school and to make it penetrate all the teaching; but it may not presume, because it has for its subject the absolute interest of men, the interest which is *The Modality of the Process of Teaching. 73* superior to all others, to determine also the other objects of Education or the method of treating them. The technical acquisitions of Reading, Writing and Arithmetic, Drawing and Music, the Natural Sciences, Mathematics, Logic, Anthropology and Psychology, the practical sciences of finance and the municipal regulations, have no direct relation to religion. If we attempt to establish one, there inevitably appears in them a morbid state which destroys them; not only so, but piety itself disappears, for these accomplishments and this knowledge are not included in its idea.

—Such treatment of Art and Science may be well-meant, but it is always an error. It may even make a ludicrous impression, which is a very dangerous thing for the authority of religion. If a church has established schools, it must see to it that all which is there taught outside of the religious instruction, i.e. all of science and art, shall have no direct connection with it as a religious institution.—

134. The Church, as the external manifestation of religion, is concerned with the absolute relation of man, the relation to God, special in itself as opposed to his other relations; the State, on the contrary, seizes the life of a nation according to its *explicit totality*. The State should conduct the education of all its citizens. To it, then, the church can appear only as a school, for the church instructs its own people concerning the nature of religion, partly by teaching proper, that of the catechism, partly in quite as edifying a way, by preaching. From this point of view, the State can look upon the church only as one of those schools which prepare for a special avocation. The church appears to the State as that school which assumes the task of educating the religious element. Just as little as the church should the state attempt to exercise any influence over Science and Art. In this they are exactly alike, and must acknowledge the neces-

sity which both Science and Art contain within themselves and by which they determine themselves. The laws of Logic, Mathematics, Astronomy, Morals, Ythetics, Physiology, &c., are entirely independent of the state. It can decree neither discoveries nor inventions. The state in its relations to science occupies the same ground as it should do with relation to the freedom of self-consciousness. It is true that the church teaches man, *The Modality of the Process of Teaching.* 74 but it demands from him at the same time belief in the truth of its dogmas. It rests, as the real church, on presupposed authority, and sinks finally all contradictions which may be found in the absolute mystery of the existence of God. The state, on the contrary, elaborates its idea into the form of laws, i.e. into general determinations, of whose necessity it convinces itself. It seeks to give to these laws the clearest possible form, so that every one may understand them. It concedes validity only to that which can be proved, and sentences the individual according to the external side of the *deed* (overt act) not, as the church does, on its internal side — that of *intention.* Finally, it demands in him consciousness of his deed, because it makes each one responsible for his own deed. It has, therefore, the same principle with science, for the proof of necessity and the unity of consciousness with its object constitute the essence of science. Since the state embraces the school as one of its educational organisms, it is from its very nature especially called upon to guide its regulation in accordance with the manifestation of consciousness.

—The church calls this "profanation." One might say that the church, with its mystery of Faith, always represents the absolute problem of science, while the state, as to its form, coincides with science. Whenever the state abandons the strictness of proof — when it begins to measure the individual citizen by his intention and not by his deed, and, in place of the clear insight of the comprehending consciousness, sets up the psychological compulsion of a hollow mechanical authority, it destroys itself. —

135. Neither the church nor the state should attempt to control the school in its internal management. Still less can the school constitute itself into a state within the state; for, while it is only one of the means which are necessary for developing citizens, the state and the church lay claim to the whole man his whole life long. The inde-

pendence of the school can then only consist in this, that it raises within the state an organ which works under its control, and which as school authority endeavors within itself to befriend the needs of the school, while externally it acts on the church and state indirectly by means of ethical powers. The emancipation of the school can never reasonably mean its abstract isolation, *The Modality of the Process of Teaching*. 75 or the absorption of the ecclesiastical and political life into the school; it can signify only the free reciprocal action of the school with state and church. It must never be forgotten that what makes the school a school is not the total process of education, for this falls also within the family, the state, and the church; but that the proper work of the school is the process of instruction, knowledge, and the acquirement, by practice, of skill.

— The confusion of the idea of Instruction with that of Education in general is a common defect in superficial treatises on these themes. The Radicals among those who are in favor of so-called "Emancipation," often erroneously appeal to "free Greece" which generally for this fond ignorance is made to stand as authority for a thousand things of which it never dreamed. In this fictitious Hellas of "free, beautiful humanity," they say the limits against which we strive to-day did not exist. The histories of Anaxagoras, Protagoras, Diagoras, Socrates, Aristotle, Theophrastus, and of others, who were all condemned on account of their "impiety," tell quite another story. —

136. The inspection of the school may be carried out in different ways, but it must be required that its special institutions shall be embraced and cared for as organized and related wholes, framed in accordance with the idea of the state, and that one division of the ministry shall occupy itself exclusively with it. The division of labor will specially affect the schools for teaching particular avocations. The prescription of the subjects to be studied in each school as appropriate to it, of the course of study, and of the object thereof, properly falls to this department of government, is its immediate work, and its theory must be changed according to the progress and needs of the time. Niemeyer, Schwarz, and others, have made out such plans for schools. Scheinert has fully painted the *Volkschule*, Mager the *Brgerschule*, Deinhard and Kapp the *Gymnasium*. But such delineations, however correct they may be, depend upon the actual

sum of culture of a people and a time, and must therefore continually modify their fundamental Ideal. The same is true of the methods
of instruction in the special arts and sciences. Niemeyer, Schwarz,
Herbart, in their sketches of Pedagogics, Beneke in *Education of the
Will.* 76 his *Doctrine of Education,* and others, have set forth in detail
the method of teaching Reading, Writing and Arithmetic, Languages, Natural Science, Geography, History, &c. Such directions
are, however, ephemeral in value, and only relatively useful, and
must, in order to be truly practical, be always newly laid out in
accordance with universal educational principles, and with the
progress of science and art.

—The idea that the State has the right to oversee the school lies in
the very idea of the State, which is authorized, and under obliga-
tion, to secure the education of its citizens, and cannot leave their
fashioning to chance. The emancipation of the school from the State,
the abstracting of it, would lead to the destruction of the school.
There is no difficulty in Protestant States in the free inter-action of
school and church, for Protestantism has consciously accepted as its
peculiar principle individual freedom as Christianity has presented
it. For Catholic States, however, a difficulty exists. The Protestant
clergyman can with propriety oversee the *Volkschule,* for here he
works as teacher, not as priest. In the Protestant church there are
really no Laity according to the original meaning of the term. On the
contrary, Catholic clergymen are essentially priests, and as such, on
account of the unconditional obedience which, according to their
church, they have to demand, they usurp the authority of the State.
From this circumstance arise, at present, numberless collisions in
the department of school supervision.—

Third Division.
PRAGMATICS (EDUCATION OF THE WILL).

137. Both Physical and Intellectual Education are in the highest
degree practical. The first reduces the merely natural to a tool which
mind shall use for its own ends; the second guides the intelligence,
by ways conformable to its nature, to the necessary method of the
act of teaching and learning, which finally branches out into an
objective national life, into a system of mutually dependent school
organizations. But in a narrower sense we mean by practical educa-

tion the methodical development of the Will. This phrase more clearly expresses the topic to be considered in this division than others sometimes used in Pedagogics [*Bestrebungs verm*☐☐, *Social Culture*. 77 conative power]. The will is already the subject of a science of its own, i.e. of Ethics; and if Pedagogics would proceed in anywise scientifically, it must recognize and presuppose the idea and the existence of this science. It should not restate in full the doctrines of freedom of duty, of virtue, and of conscience, although we have often seen this done in empirical works on Pedagogics. Pedagogics has to deal with the idea of freedom and morality only so far as it fixes the technique of their process, and at the same time it confesses itself to be weakest just here, where nothing is of any worth without a pure self-determination.

138. The pupil must (1) become civilized; i.e. he must learn to govern, as a thing external to him, his natural egotism, and to make the forms which civilized society has adopted his own. (2) He must become imbued with morality; i.e. he must learn to determine his actions, not only with reference to what is agreeable and useful, but according to the principle of the Good; he must become virtually free, form a character, and must habitually look upon the necessity of freedom as the absolute measure of his actions. (3) He must become religious; i.e. he must discern that the world, with all its changes, himself included, is only phenomenal; the affirmative side of this insight into the emptiness of the finite and transitory, which man would so willingly make everlasting, is the consciousness of the *absolute* existing in and for itself, which, in its certainty of its truth, not torn asunder through the process of manifestation, constitutes no part of its changes, but, while it actually presents them, permeates them all, and freely distinguishes itself from them. In so far as man relates himself to God, he cancels all finitude and transitoriness, and by this feeling frees himself from the externality of phenomena. Virtue on the side of civilization is Politeness; on that of morality, Conscientiousness; and on that of religion, Humility.

FIRST CHAPTER.
Social Culture.

139. The social development of man makes the beginning of practical education. It is not necessary to suppose a special social in-

stinct. The inclination of man to the society of *Social Culture. 78* men does not arise only from the identity of their nature, but is also in certain cases affected by particular relations. The natural starting-point of social culture is the Family. But this educates the child for Society, and by means of Society the individual passes over into relations with the world at large. Natural sympathy changes to polite behavior, and this to the dexterous and circumspect deportment, whose truth nevertheless is first the ethical purity which combines with the wisdom of the serpent the harmlessness of the dove.

140. (1) The Family is the natural social circle to which man primarily belongs. In it all the immediate differences which exist are compensated by the equally immediate unity cf the relationship. The subordination of the wife to the husband, of the children to their parents, of the younger children to their elder brothers and sisters, ceases to be subordination, through the intimacy of love. The child learns obedience to authority, and in this it gives free personal satisfaction to its parents and enjoys the same. All the relations in which he finds himself there are penetrated by the warmth of implicit confidence, which can be replaced for the child by nothing else. In this sacred circle the tenderest emotions of the heart are developed by the personal interest of all its members in what happens to any one, and thus the foundation is laid of a susceptibility to all genuine or real friendship.

— Nothing more unreasonable or inhuman could exist than those modern theories which would destroy the family and would leave the children, the offspring of the anarchy of free-love, to grow up in public nurseries. This would appear to be very humanitarian; indeed these socialists talk of nothing but the interests of humanity — they are never weary of uttering their insipid jests on the institution of the family, as if it were the principle of all narrow-mindedness. Have these fanatics, who are seeking after an abstraction of humanity, ever examined our foundling-hospitals, orphan asylums, barracks, and prisons, to discover in some degree to what an atomic state of barren cleverness a human being grows who has never formed a part of a family? The Family is only one phase in the grand order of the ethical organization; but it is the substantial phase from which man passively *Social Culture. 79* proceeds, but into which, as he founds a family of his own, he actively returns. The child lives in the Family in the common joy and grief of sympathy for all, and, in the emotion with which he sees his parents approach death while he is hastening towards the full enjoyment of existence, experiences the finer feelings which are so powerful in creating in him a deeper and more tender understanding of everything human. —

141. (2) The Family rears the children not for itself but for the civil society. In this we have a system of morals producing externally a social technique, a circle of fixed forms of society. This technique endeavors to subdue the natural roughness of man, at least as far as it manifests itself externally. Because he is spirit, man is not to yield himself to his immediateness; he is to exhibit to man his naturalness as under the control of spirit. The etiquette of propriety on the one hand facilitates the manifestation of individuality by means of which the individual becomes interesting to others, and on the other hand, since its forms are alike for all, it makes us recognize the likeness of the individual to all others and so makes their intercourse easier.

— The conventional form is no mere constraint; but essentially a protection not only for the freedom of the individual, but much more the protection of the individual against the rude impetuosity of his own naturalness. Savages and peasants for this reason are, in their relations to each other, by no means as unconstrained as one often represents them, but hold closely to a ceremonious behavior. There is in one of Immerman's stories, "The Village Justice," a very excellent picture of the conventional forms with which the peasant loves to surround himself. The scene in which the townsman who thinks that he can dispense with forms among the peasants is very entertainingly taught better, is exceedingly valuable in an educational point of view. The feeling of shame which man has in regard to his mere naturalness is often extended to relations where it has no direct significance, since this sense of shame is appealed to in children in reference to things which are really perfectly indifferent externalities. —

142. Education with regard to social culture has two *Social Culture.* 80 extremes to avoid: the youth may, in his effort to prove his

individuality, become vain and conceited, and fall into an attempt to appear interesting; or he may become slavishly dependent on conventional forms, a kind of social pedant. This state of nullity which contents itself with the mechanical polish of social formalism is ethically more dangerous than the tendency to a marked individuality, for it betrays emptiness; while the effort towards a peculiar differentiation from others, to become interesting to others, indicates power.

143. When we have a harmony of the manifestation of the individual with the expression of the recognition of the equality of others we have what is called deportment or politeness, which combines dignity and grace, self-respect and modesty. We call it when fully complete, Urbanity. It treats the conventional forms with irony, since, at the same time that it yields to them, it allows the productivity of spirit to shine through them in little deviation from them, as if it were fully able to make others in their place.

— True politeness shows that it remains master of forms. It is very necessary to accustom children to courtesy and to bring them up in the etiquette of the prevailing social custom; but they must be prevented from falling into an absurd formality which makes the triumph of a polite behavior to consist in a blind following of the dictates of the last fashion-journal, and in the exact copying of the phraseology and directions of some book on manners. One can best teach and practise politeness when he does not merely copy the social technique, but comprehends its original idea. —

144. (3) But to fully initiate the youth into the institutions of civilization one must not only call out the feelings of his heart in the bosom of the family, not only give to him the formal refinement necessary to his intercourse with society; it must also perform to him the painful duty of making him acquainted with the mysteries of the ways of the world. This is a painful duty, for the child naturally feels an unlimited confidence in all men. This confidence must not be destroyed, but it must be tempered. The mystery of the way of the world is the deceit which springs from selfishness. We must provide against it by a proper degree of distrust. We must teach the youth that he may be imposed upon by deceit, dissimulation, *Moral Culture.* 81 and hypocrisy, and that therefore he must not give his

confidence lightly and credulously. He himself must learn how he can, without deceit, gain his own ends in the midst of the throng of opposing interests.

—Kant in his Pedagogics calls that worldly-wise behavior by which the individual is to demean himself in opposition to others, Impenetrability. By its means man learns how to "manage men." In Lord Chesterfield's letters to his son, we have pointed out the true value of egotism in its relation to morals. All his words amount to this, that we are to consider every man to be an egotist, and to convert his very egotism into a means of finding out his weak side; i.e. to flatter him by exciting his vanity, and by means of such flattery to ascertain his limits. In common life, the expression "having had experiences" means about the same thing as having been deceived and betrayed.—

SECOND CHAPTER.
Moral Culture.

145. The truth of social culture lies in moral culture. Without this latter, every art of behavior remains worthless, and can never attain the clearness of Humility and Dignity which are possible to it in its unity with morality. For the better determination of this idea Pedagogics must refer to Ethics itself, and can here give the part of its content which relates to Education only in the form of educational maxims. The principal categories of Ethics in the domain of morality are the ideas of Duty, Virtue, and Conscience. Education must lay stress on the truth that nothing in the world has any absolute value except will guided by the right.

146. Thence follows (1) the maxim relating to the idea of Duty, that we must accustom the pupil to unconditional obedience to it, so that he shall perform it for no other reason than that it is duty. It is true that the performance of a duty may bring with it externally a result agreeable or disagreeable, useful or harmful; but the consideration of such connection ought never to determine us. This moral demand, though it may appear to be excessive severity, is the absolute foundation of all genuine ethical practice. All "highest *Moral Culture.* 82 happiness theories," however finely spun they may be, when taken as a guide for life, lead at last to Sophistry, and this to contradictions which ruin the life.

147. (2) Virtue must make actual what duty commands, or, rather, the actualizing of duty is Virtue. And here we must say next, then, that the principal things to be considered under Virtue are (*a*) the dialectic of particular virtues, (*b*) renunciation, and (*c*) character.

148. (*a*) From the dialectic of particular virtues there follows the educational maxim that we must practise all virtues with equal faithfulness, for all together constitute an ethical system complete in itself, in which no one is indifferent to another.

—Morality should recognize no distinction of superiority among the different virtues. They reciprocally determine each other. There is no such thing as one virtue which shines out above the others, and still less should we have any special gift for virtue. The pupil must be taught to recognize no great and no small in the virtues, for that one which may at first sight seem small is inseparably connected with that which is seemingly the greatest. Many virtues are attractive by reason of their external consequences, as e.g. industry because of success in business, worthy conduct because of the respect paid to it, charity because of the pleasure attending it; but man should not practise these virtues because he enjoys them: he must devote the same amount of self-sacrifice and of assiduity to those virtues which (as Christ said) are to be performed in secret.—

—It is especially valuable, in an educational respect, to gain an insight, into the transition of which each virtue is empirically capable, into a negative as well as into a positive extreme. The differences between the extremes and the golden mean are differences in quality, although they arrive at this difference in quality by means of difference in quantity. Kant has, as is well known, attacked the Aristotelian doctrine of the ethical μεσοτες, since he was considering the qualitative difference of the mind as differentiating principle; this was correct for the subject with which he dealt, but in the objective development we do arrive on *Moral Culture.* 83 the other hand at the determination of a quantitative limit; e.g. a man, with the most earnest intention of doing right, may be in doubt whether he has not, in any task, done more or less than was fitting for him.—

—As no virtue can cease its demands for us, no one can permit any exceptions or any provisional circumstances to come in the way of his duties. Our moral culture will always certainly manifest itself in very unequal phases if we, out of narrowness and weakness, neglect entirely one virtue while we diligently cultivate another. If we are forced into such unequal action, we are not responsible for the result; but it is dangerous and deserves punishment if we voluntarily encourage it. The pupil must be warned against a certain moral negligence which consists in yielding to certain weaknesses, faults, or crimes, a little longer and a little longer, because he has fixed a certain time after which he intends to do better. Up to that time he allows himself to be a loiterer in ethics. Perhaps he will assert that his companions, his surroundings, his position, &c., must be changed before he can alter his internal conduct. Wherever education or temperament favors sentimentality, we shall find birthdays, new-year's day, confirmation day, &c., selected as these turning points. It is not to be denied that man proceeds in his internal life from epoch to epoch, and renews himself in his most internal nature, nor can we deny that moments like those mentioned are especially favorable in man to an effort towards self-transformation because they invite introspection; but it is not to be endured that the youth, while looking forward to such a moment, should consciously persist in his evil-doing. If he does, we shall have as consequences that when the solemn moment which he has set at last arrives, at the stirring of the first emotion he perceives with terror that he has changed nothing in himself, that the same temptations are present to him, the same weakness takes possession of him, &c. In our business, in our theoretical endeavors, &c., it may certainly happen that, on account of want of time, or means, or humor, we may put off some work to another time; but morality stands on a higher plane than these, because it, as the concrete absoluteness of the will, makes unceasing demand on the whole and undivided man. In morality there are no vacations, no *Moral Culture.* 84 interims. As we in ascending a flight of stairs take good care not to make a single mis-step, and give our conscious attention to every step, so we must not allow any exceptions in moral affairs, must not appoint given times for better conduct, but must await these last as natural crises, and must seek to live in time as in Eternity. —

149. (*b*) From Renunciation springs the injunction of self-government. The action of education on the will to form habits in it, is discipline or training in a narrower sense. Renunciation teaches

us to know the relation in which we in fact, as historical persons, stand to the idea of the Good. From our empirical knowledge of ourselves we derive the idea of our limits; from the absolute knowledge of ourselves on the other hand, which presents to us the nature of Freedom as our own actuality, we derive the conception of the resistless might of the genuine will for the good. But to actualize this conception we must have practice. This practice is the proper renunciation. Every man must devise for himself some special set of rules, which shall be determined by his peculiarities and his resulting temptations. These rules must have as their innermost essence the subduing of self, the vanquishing of his negative arbitrariness by means of the universality and necessity of the will.

—In order to make this easy, the youth may be practised in renouncing for himself even the arbitrariness which is permitted to him. One often speaks of renunciation as if it belonged especially to the middle ages and to Catholicism; but this is an error. Renunciation in its one-sided form as relying on works, and for the purpose of mortification, is asceticism, and belongs to them; but Renunciation in general is a necessary determination of morals. The keeping of a journal is said to assist in the practice of virtue, but its value depends on how it is kept. To one it may be a curse, to another a blessing. Fichte, G□□, Byron, and others, have kept journals and have been assisted thereby; while others, as Lavater, have been thwarted by them. Vain people will every evening record with pen and ink their admiration of the correct course of life which they have led in the day devoted to their pleasure.—

150. (c) The result of the practice in virtue, or, as it is *Moral Culture.* 85 commonly expressed, of the individual actualization of freedom, is the methodical determinateness of the individual will as Character. This conception of character is formal, for it contains only the identity which is implied in the ruling of a will on its external side as constant. As there are good, strong and beautiful characters, so there are also bad, weak, and detestable ones. When in Pedagogics, therefore, we speak so much of the building up of a character, we mean the making permanent of a direction of the individual will towards the actualization of the Good. Freedom ought to be the character of character. Education must therefore observe closely the inter-action of the factors which go to form character, viz., (α) the

temperament, as the natural character of the man; (β) external events, the historical element; (γ) the energy of the Will, by which, in its limits of nature and history, it realizes the idea of the Good in and for itself as the proper ethical character. Temperament determines the Rhythm of our external manifestation of ourselves; the events in which we live assign to us the ethical problem, but the Will in its sovereignty stamps its seal on the form given by these potentialities. Pedagogics aims at accustoming the youth to freedom, so that he shall always measure his deed by the idea of the Good. It does not desire a formal independence, which may also be called character, but a real independence resting upon the conception of freedom as that which is absolutely necessary. The pedagogical maxim is then: Be independent, but be so through doing Good.

— According to preconceived opinion, stubbornness and obstinacy claim that they are the foundation of character. But they may spring from weakness and indeterminateness, on which account one needs to be well on his guard. A gentle disposition, through enthusiasm for the Good, may attain to quite as great a firmness of will. Coarseness and meanness are on no account to be tolerated. —

151. (3) We pass from the consideration of the culture of character to that of conscience. This is the relation which the moral agent makes between himself as manifestation and himself as idea. It compares itself, in its past or future, with its nature, and judges itself accordingly as good or bad. This independence of the ethical judgment is the soul proper of *Religious Culture.* 86 all morality, the negation of all self-deception and of all deception through another. The pedagogical maxim is: Be conscientious. Be in the last instance dependent only upon the conception which thou thyself hast of the idea of the Good!

— The self-criticism prompted by conscience hovers over all our historical actuality, and is the ground of all our rational progress. Fichte's stern words remain, therefore, eternally true: "He who has a bad character, must absolutely create for himself a better one." —

THIRD CHAPTER.
Religious Culture.

152. Social culture contains the formal phase, moral culture the real phase, of the practical mind. Conscience forms the transition to

religious culture. In its apodeictic nature, it is the absoluteness of spirit. The individual discerns in the depths of its own consciousness the determinations of universality and of necessity to which it has to subject itself. They appear to it as the voice of God. Religion makes its appearance as soon as the individual distinguishes the Absolute from himself as personal, as a subject existing for itself and therefore for him. The atheist remains at the stage of insight into the absoluteness of the logical and physical, æsthetic and practical categories. He may, therefore, be perfectly moral. He lacks religion, though he loves to characterize his uprightness by this name, and to transfer the dogmatic determinations of positive religion into the ethical sphere. It belongs to the province of religion that I demean myself towards the Absolute not only as toward that which is my own substance, and that in relation to it not I alone am the subject, but that to me also the substance in itself is a personal subject for itself. If I look upon myself as the only absolute, I make myself devoid of spiritual essence. I am only absolute self-consciousness, for which, because it as idea relates only to itself, there remains only the impulse to a persistent conflict with every self-consciousness not identical with it. Were this the case, such a self-consciousness would be only theoretical irony. In religion I know the Absolute as essence, when I am known by him. Everything else, *Religious Culture.* 87 myself included, is finite and transitory, however significant it may be, however relatively and momentarily the Infinite may exist in it. As existence even, it is transitory. The Absolute, positing itself, distinguishing itself from itself in unity with itself, is always like to itself, and takes up all the unrest of the phenomenal world back again into its simple essence.

153. This process of the individual spirit, in which it rises out of the multiplicity of all relations into union with the Absolute as the substantial subject, and in which nature and history are united, we may call, in a restricted sense, a change of heart [Gemuth]. In a wider sense of the word we give this name to a certain sentimental cheerfulness (light-heartedness), a sense of comfort — of little significance. The highest emotions of the heart culminate in religion, whose warmth is inspired by practical activity and conscientiousness.

154. Education has to fit man for religion. (1) It gives him the conception of it; (2) it endeavors to have this conception actualized in him; (3) it subordinates the theoretical and practical process in fashioning him to a determinate stand-point of religious culture.

— In the *working out* or detailed treatment of Pedagogics, the position which the conception of religion occupies is very uncertain. Many writers on Education place it at the beginning, while others reserve it for the end. Others naجميly bring it forward in the midst of heterogeneous surroundings, but know how to say very little concerning it, and urge teachers to kindle the fire of religious feeling in their pupils by teaching them to fear God. Through all their writing, we hear the cry that in Education nothing is so important as Religion. Rightly understood, this saying is quite true. The religious spirit, the consciousness of the Absolute, and the reverence for it, should permeate all. Not unfrequently, however, we find that what is meant by religion is theology, or the church ceremonial, and these are only one-sided phases of the total religious process. The Anglican High-Church presents in the colleges and universities of England a sad example of this error. What can be more deadening to the spirit, more foreign to religion, than the morning and evening *Theoretical Process of Religious Culture.* 88 prayers as they are carried on at Oxford and Cambridge with machine-like regularity! But also to England belongs the credit of the sad fact, that, according to Kohl's report, there live in Manchester, Liverpool, Birmingham, and London, thousands of men who have never enjoyed any teaching in religion, have never been baptized, who live absolutely without religion in brutal stupidity. Religion must form the culminating point of Education. It takes up into itself the didactical and practical elements, and rises through the force of its content to universality. —

I. *The Theoretical Process of Religious Culture.*

155. Religion, in common with every content of the spirit, must pass through three stages of feeling, conception, and comprehension. Whatever may be the special character of any religion it cannot avoid this psychological necessity, either in its general history or in the history of the individual consciousness. The teacher must understand this process, partly in order that he may make it easier to the youth, partly that he may guard against the malformation of the

religious feeling which may arise through the fact of the youth's remaining in one stage after he is ready for another and needs it. Pedagogics must therefore lay out beforehand the philosophy of religion, on which alone can be found the complete discussion of this idea.

156. (1) Religion exists first as religious feeling. The person is still immediately identical with the Divine, does not yet distinguish himself from the absoluteness of his being, and is in so far determined by it. In so far as he feels the divine, he is a mystery to himself. This beginning is necessary. Religion cannot be produced in men from the external side; its genesis belongs rather to the primitive depths in which God himself and the individual soul are essentially one.

—The educator must not allow himself to suppose that he is able to make a religion. Religion dwells originally in every individual soul, for every one is born of God. Education can only aid the religious feeling in its development. As far as regards the psychological form, it was quite correct for Schleiermacher and his followers to characterize the absoluteness *Theoretical Process of Religious Culture.* 89 of the religious feeling as the feeling of dependence, for feeling is determined by that which it feels; it depends upon its content. But in so far as God constitutes the content of the feeling, there appears the opposite of all dependence or absolute emancipation. I maintain this in opposition to Schleiermacher. Religion lifts man above the finite, temporal and transitory, and frees him from the control of the phenomenal world. Even the lowest form of religion does this; and when it is said that Schleiermacher has been unjustly criticized for this expression of dependence, this distinction is overlooked.—

157. But religious feeling as such rises into something higher when the spirit distinguishes the content of this religious feeling from any other content which it also feels, represents it clearly to itself, and places itself over against it formally as a free individual.

—But we must not understand that the religious feeling is destroyed in this process; in rising to the form of distinct representation, it remains at the same time as a necessary form of the Intelligence.—

158. If the spirit is held back and prevented from passing out of the simplicity of feeling into the act of distinguishing the perception from what it becomes, the conception—if its efforts towards the forming of this conception are continually re-dissolved into feeling, then feeling, which was as the first step perfectly healthy and correct, will become morbid and degenerate into a wretched mysticism. Education must, therefore, make sure that this feeling is not destroyed by the progress of its content into perception and conception on the side of psychological form, but rather that it attains truth thereby.

159. (2) Conception as the ideally transformed perception dissects the religious content on its different sides, and follows each of these to its consequence. Imagination controls the individual conceptions, but by no means with that absoluteness which is often supposed; for each picture has in itself its logical consequence to which imagination must yield; e.g. if a religion represents God as an animal, or as half animal and half man, or as man, each of these conceptions has in its development its consequences for the imagination.

Theoretical Process of Religious Culture. 90

160. We rise out of the stage of Conception when the spirit tries to determine the universality of its content according to its necessity, i.e. when it begins to think. The necessity of its pictures is a mere presupposition for the imagination. The thinking activity, however, recognizes not only the contradiction which exists between the sensuous, limited form of the individual conception, and the absolute nature of its content, but also the contradiction in which the conceptions find themselves with respect to each other.

161. If the spirit is prevented from passing out of the varied pictures of conception to the supersensuous clearness and simplicity of the thinking activity—if the content which it already begins to seize as idea is again dissolved into the confusion of the picture-world, then the religion of imagination, which was a perfectly proper form as the second step, becomes perverted into some form of idolatry, either coarse or refined. Education must therefore not oppose the thinking activity if the latter undertakes to criticize religious conceptions; on the contrary, it must guide this so that the discovery of the contradictions which unavoidably adhere to sensuous form shall

not mislead the youth into the folly of throwing away, with the relative untruth of the form, also the religious content in general.

—It is an error for educators to desire to keep the imagination apart from religious feeling, but it is also an error to detain the mind, which is on its formal side the activity of knowing, in the stage of imagination, and to desire to condemn it thence into the service of canonical allegories. The more, in opposition to this, it is possessed with the charm of thinking, the more is it in danger of condemning the content of religion itself as a mere fictitious conception. As a transition-stage the religion of imagination is perfectly normal, and it does not in the least impair freedom if, for example, one has personified evil as a living Devil. The error does not lie in this, but in the making absolute these determinate, æsthetic forms of religion. The reaction of the thinking activity against such æsthetic absolutism then undertakes in its negative absolutism to despise the content also, as if it were a mere conception. —

162. (3) In the thinking activity the spirit attains that *Theoretical Process of Religious Culture.* 91 form of the religious content which is identical with that of its simple consciousness, and above which there is no other for the intelligence as theoretical. But we distinguish three varieties in this thinking activity: the abstract, the reflective, and the speculative. The Abstract gives us the religious content of consciousness in the form of abstractions or dogmas, i.e. propositions which set up a definition as a universal, and add to it another as the reason for its necessity. The Reflective stage busies itself with the relation of dogmas to each other, and with the search for the grounds on which their necessity must rest. It is essentially critical, and hence skeptical. The explanation of the dogmas, which is carried on in this process of reasoning and skeptical investigation, is completed alone in speculative thinking, which recognizes the free unity of the content and its form as its own proper self-determination of the content, creating its own differences. Education must know this stage of the intelligence, partly that it may in advance preserve, in the midst of its changes, that repose which it brings into the consciousness; partly that it may be able to lead to the process of change itself, in accordance with the organic connection of its phases. We should prevent the criticism of the abstract understanding by the reflective stage as little as we should that of

the imagination by the thinking activity. But the stage of reflection is not the last possibility of the thinking activity, although, in the variety of its skepticism it often takes itself for such, and, with the emptiness of mere negation to which it holds, often brings itself forward into undesirable prominence. It becomes evident, in this view, how very necessary for man, with respect to religion, is a genuine philosophical culture, so that he may not lose the certainty of the existence of the Absolute in the midst of the obstinacy of dogmas and the changes of opinions.

163. Education must then not fear the descent into dogmatic abstraction, since this is an indispensable means for theoretical culture in its totality, and the consciousness cannot dispense with it in its history. But Education has, in the concrete, carefully to discern in which of these stages of culture any particular consciousness may be. For if for mankind as a race the fostering of philosophy is absolutely *Practical Process of Religious Culture.* 92 necessary, it by no means follows that this necessity exists for each individual. To children, to women, e.g. for all kinds of simple and limited lives, the form of the religion of the imagination is well suited, and the form of comprehension can come only relatively to them. Education must not, then, desire powerfully and prematurely to develop the thinking activity before the intelligence is really fully grown.

—The superficial thinking which many teachers demand in the sphere of religion is no less impractical than the want of all guidance into rightly ordered meditations on religious subjects. It is natural that the lower form of intelligence should, in contrast with the higher, appear to be frivolous, because it has no need of change of form as the higher has, and on this account it looks upon the destruction of the form of a picture or a dogma as the destruction of religion itself. In our time the idea is very prevalent that the content itself must change with the changing of the psychological form, and that therefore a religion in the stage of feeling, of conception, and of comprehension, can no longer be the same in its essence. These suppositions, which are so popular, and are considered to be high philosophy, spring from the superficiality of psychological inquiry.—

164. The theoretical culture of the religious feeling endeavors therefore with the freedom of philosophical criticism to elevate the presupposition of Reason in the religious content to self-assured insight by means of the proof of the necessity of its determinations. This is the only reasonable pedagogical way not only to prevent the degeneration of the religious consciousness into a miserable mysticism or into frivolity, but also to remove these if they are already existent.

—External seclusion avails nothing. The crises of the world-historical changes in the religious consciousness find their way through the thickest cloister walls; the philosopher Reinhold was a pupil of the Jesuits, the philosopher Schad of the Benedictines.—

II. *The Practical Process of Religious Culture.*

165. The theoretical culture is truly practical, for it gives man definite conceptions and thoughts of the Divine and his *Practical Process of Religious Culture.* 93 relation to him. But in a narrower sense that culture is practical which relates to the Will as such. Education has in this respect to distinguish (1) consecration—religious feeling in general,—(2) the induction of the youth into the forms of a positive religion, and (3) his reconciliation with his lot.

166. (1) Religious feeling presupposes morality as an indispensable condition without which it cannot inculcate its ideas. But if man from a merely moral stand-point places himself in relation to the idea of Duty as such, the ethical religious stand-point differs from it in this, that it places the necessity of the Good as the self-determination of the divine Will and thus makes of practice a personal relation to God, changing the Good to the Holy and the Evil to Sin. Education must therefore first accustom the youth to the idea, that in doing the Good he unites himself with God as with the absolute Person, but that in doing Evil he separates himself from him. The feeling that he through his deed comes into contact with God himself, positively or negatively, deepens the moral conduct to an intense sensibility of the heart.

167. (2) The religious sense which grows in the child that he has an uninterrupted personal relation to the Absolute as a person, constitutes the beginning of the practical forming of religion. The second step is the induction of the child into the objective forms of

worship established in some positive religion. Through religious training the child learns to renounce his egotism; through attendance on religious services he learns to give expression to his religious feeling in prayer, in the use of symbols, and in church festivals. Education must, however, endeavor to retain freedom with regard to these forms, so that they shall not be confounded with Religion itself. Religion displays itself in these ceremonies, but they as mere forms are of value only in so far as they, while externalities, are manifestations of the spirit which produces them.

— If the mechanism of ceremonial forms is taken as religion itself, the service of God degenerates into the false service of religion, as Kant has designated it in *Religion within the Limits of Pure Reason*. Nothing is more destructive to the sensibility to all real religious culture than the want of earnestness with which prayers, readings from the Bible, *Practical Process of Religious Culture.* 94 attendance on church, the communion, &c., are often practised by teachers. But one must not conclude from this extreme that an ignorance of all sacred forms in general would be more desirable for the child. —

168. (3) It is possible that a man on the stand-point of ecclesiastical religious observances may be fully contented; he may be fully occupied in them, and perfect his life thereby in perfect content. But by far the greater number of men will see themselves forced to experience the truth of religion in the hard vicissitudes of their lot, since they carry on some business, and with that business create for themselves a past whose consequences condition their future. They limit themselves through their deeds, whose involuntary-voluntary authors they become; involuntary in so far as they are challenged to the deeds from the totality of events, voluntary in so far as they undertake them and bring about an actual change in the world. The history of the individual man appears therefore on the one hand, if we consider its material, as the work of circumstances; but on the other hand, if we reflect on the form, as the act of a self-determining actor. Want of freedom (the being determined through the given situation) and freedom (the determination to the act) are united in actual life as something which is exactly so, and cannot become anything else as final. The essence of the spiritual being stands always over against this unavoidable limitation as that which is in itself infinite, which is beyond all history, because the absolute spir-

it, in and for itself, has no history. That which one calls his history is only the manifesting of himself, and his everlasting return out of this manifestation into himself an act which in absolute spirit coincides with the transcending of all manifestation. From the nature which belongs to him there arises for the individual spirit the impulse towards a holy life, i.e. the being freed from his history even in the midst of its process. He gratifies this impulse negatively through the considering of what has happened as past and gone, as that which lives now only ideally in the recollection; and positively through the positing of a new actual existence in which he strives to realize the idea of freedom which constitutes his necessity, as purer and higher than before. This constant new-birth out of the grave of the past *Practical Process of Religious Culture.* 95 to the life of a more beautiful future is the genuine reconciliation with destiny. The false reconciliation may assume different forms. It may abstain from all action because man through this limits himself and becomes responsible. This is to despair of freedom, which condemns the spirit to the loss of itself since its nature demands activity. The abstract quietism of the Indian penitents, of the Buddhists, of the fanatical ascetics, of the Protestant recluses, &c., is an error of this kind. The man may become indifferent about the ethical determinateness of his deeds. In this case he acts; but because he has no faith in the necessary connection of his deeds through the means of freedom, a connection which he would willingly ascribe to mere chance, he loses his spiritual essence. This is the error of indifference and of its frivolity, which denies the open mystery of the ruling of destiny. Education must therefore imbue man with respect for external movements of history and with confidence in the inexhaustibleness of the progressive human spirit, since only by producing better things can he affirmatively elevate himself above his past. This active acknowledgment of the necessity of freedom as the determining principle of destiny gives the highest satisfaction to which practical religious feeling may arrive, for blessedness develops itself in it— that blessedness which does not know that it is circumscribed by finitude and transitoriness, and which possesses the immortal courage to strive always anew for perfection with free resignation at its non-realization, so that happiness and misery, pleasure and pain, are conquered by the power of disinterested self-sacrifice.

— The escape from action in an artificial absence of all events in life, which often sinks to a veritable brutalizing of man, is the distinguishing feature of all monkish pedagogics. In our time there is especial need of a reconciliation between man and destiny, for all the world is discontented. The worst form of discontent is when one is, as the French say, *blas語>; though the word is not, as many fancy, derived originally from the French, but from the Greek βλαζειν, to wither. It is true that all culture passes through phases, each of which becomes momentarily and relatively wearisome, and that in so far one may be blas語> in any age. But in modern times Absolute Process of Religious Culture. 96 this state of feeling has increased to that of thorough disgust — disgust which nevertheless at the same time demands enjoyment. The one who is blas語> has enjoyed everything, felt everything, mocked at everything. He has passed from the enjoyment of pleasure to sentimentality, i.e. to rioting in feeling; from sentimentality to irony with regard to feeling, and from this to the torment of feeling his entire weakness and emptiness as opposed to these. He ridicules this also, as if it were a consolation to him to fling away the universe like a squeezed lemon, and to be able to assert that in pure nothingness lies the truth of all things. And yet nevertheless this irony furnishes the point on which Education can fasten, in order to kindle anew in him the religious feeling, and to lead him back to a loving recognition of actuality, to a respect for his own history. The greatest difficulty which Education has to encounter here is the coquetry, the miserable eminence and self-satisfaction which have undermined the man and made him incapable of all simple and natural enjoyment. It is not too much to assert that many pupils of our Gymnasia are affected with this malady. Our literature is full of its products. It inveighs against its dissipation, and nevertheless at the same time cannot resist a certain kind of pleasure in it. Diabolical sentimentality! —*

III. The Absolute Process of Religious Culture.

169. In comparing the stages of the theoretical and practical culture of the religious feeling their internal correspondence appears. Feeling, as immediate knowledge, and the consecration of the sense by means of piety; imagination with all its images, and the church services with their ceremonial observances; finally, the comprehending of religion as the reconciliation with destiny, as the internal emancipation from the dominion of external events — all these correspond to each other. If we seize this parallelism all together, we have the progress which religion must make in its historical process, in which it (1) begins as natural; (2) goes on to historical precision, and (3) elevates this to a rational faith. These stages await every man in as far as he lives through a complete religious culture, but this may be for the individual a question of chance.

Absolute Process of Religious Culture. 97

170. (1) A child has as yet no definite religious feeling. He is still only a possibility capable of manifold determinations. But, since he is a spirit, the essence of religion is active in him, though as yet in an unconscious form. The substance of spirit attests its presence in every individual, through his mysterious impulse toward the absolute and towards intercourse with God. This is the initiatory stage of natural religion, which must not be confounded with the religion which makes nature the object of worship (fetichism, &c.)

171. (2) But while the child lives into this in his internal life, he comes in contact with definite forms of religion, and will naturally, through the mediation of the family, be introduced to some one of them. His religious feeling takes now a particular direction, and he accepts religion in one of its historical forms. This positive religion meets the precise want of the child, because it brings into his consciousness, by means of teaching and sacred rites, the principal elements which are found in the nature of religion.

172. (3) In contradistinction to the natural basis of religious feeling, all historical religions rest on the authoritative basis of revelation from God to man. They address themselves to the imagination, and offer a system of objective forms of worship and ceremonies. But spirit, as eternal, as self-identical, cannot forbear as thinking activity to subject the traditional religion to criticism and to compare it as a phenomenal existence. From this criticism arises a religion which satisfies the demands of the reason, and which, by means of insight into the necessity of the historical process, leads to the exercise of a genuine toleration towards its many-sided forms. This religion mediates between the unity of the thinking consciousness and the religious content, while this content, in the history of religious feeling, appears theoretically as dogma, and practically as the command of an absolute and incomprehensible authority. It is just as simple as the unsophisticated natural religious feeling, but its simplicity is at the same time master of itself. It is just as specific in its determinations as the historical religion, but its determinateness is at the same time universal, since it is worked out by the thinking reason.

Absolute Process of Religious Culture. 98

*173. Education must superintend the development of the religious con-
sciousness towards an insight into the necessary consequence of its different stages. Nothing is more absurd than for the educator to desire to avoid
the introduction of a positive religion, or a definite creed, as a middle stage
between the natural beginning of religious feeling and its end in philosophical culture. Only when a man has lived through the entire range of one-
sided phases — through the crudeness of such a concrete individualizing of
religion, and has come to recognize the universal nature of religion in a
special form of it which excludes other forms — only when the spirit of a
congregation has taken him into its number, is he ripe to criticize religion
in a conciliatory spirit, because he has then gained a religious character
through that historical experience. The self-comprehending universality
must have such a solid basis as this in the life of the man; it can never form
the beginning of one's culture, but it may constitute the end which turns
back again to the beginning. Most men remain at the historical stand-
point. The religion of reason, as that of the minority, constitutes in the
different religions the invisible church, which seeks by progressive reform
to purify these religions from superstition and unbelief. It is the duty of the
state, by making all churches equal in the sight of the law, to guard religion
from the temptation of impure motives, and, through the granting of such
freedom to religious individuality, to help forward the unity of a rational
insight into religion which is distinct from the religious feeling only in its
form, not in its content. Not a philosopher, but Jesus of Nazareth freed the
world from all selfishness and all bondage.*

*174. With this highest theoretical and practical emancipation, the gen-
eral work of education ends. It remains now to be shown how the general
idea of Education shapes its special elements into their appropriate forms.
From the nature of Pedagogics, which concerns itself with man in his en-
tirety, this exposition belongs partly to the history of culture in general,
partly to the history of religion, partly to the philosophy of history. The
pedagogical element in it always lies in the ideal which the spirit of a nation or of an age creates out of itself, and which it seeks to realize in its
youth.*

Particular Systems of Education. 99

THIRD PART.
Particular Systems of Education.

*175. The definite actuality of Education originates in the fact that its
general idea is individualized, according to its special elements, in a specif-*

ic statement which we call a pedagogical principle. The number of these principles is not unlimited, but from the idea of Education contains only a certain number. If we derive them therefore, we derive at the same time the history of Pedagogics, which can from its very nature do nothing else than make actual in itself the possibilities involved in the idea of Education. Such a derivation may be called an a priori construction of history, but it is different from what is generally denoted by this term in not pretending to deduce single events and characters. All empirical details are confirmation or illustration for it, but it does not attempt to seek this empirical element a priori.

— The history of Pedagogics is still in the stage of infancy. At one time it is taken up into the sphere of Politics; at another, into that of the history of Culture. The productions of some of the most distinguished writers on the subject are now antiquated. Cramer of Stralsund made, in 1832, an excellent beginning in a comprehensive and thorough history of Pedagogy; but in the beginning of his second part he dwelt too long upon the Greeks, and lost himself in too wide an exposition of practical Philosophy in general. Alexander Kapp has given us excellent treatises on the Pedagogics of Aristotle and Plato. But with regard to modern Pedagogics we have relatively very little. Karl v. Raumer, in 1843, began to publish a history of Pedagogics since the time of the revival of classical studies, and has accomplished much of value on the biographical side. But the idea of the general connection and dependence of the several manifestations has not received much attention, and since the time of Pestalozzi books have assumed the character of biographical confessions. Particular Systems of Education. 100 Strmpell, in 1843, developed the Pedagogics of Kant, Fichte, and Herbart. —

176. Man is educated by man for humanity. This is the fundamental idea of all Pedagogics. But in the shaping of Pedagogics we cannot begin with the idea of humanity as such, but only with the natural form in which it primarily manifests itself — that of the nation. But the naturalness of this principle disappears in its development, since nations appear in interaction on each other and begin dimly to perceive their unity of species. The freedom of spirit over nature makes its appearance, but to the spirit explicitly in the transcendent form of abstract theistic religion, in which God appears as the ruler over Nature as merely dependent; and His chosen people plant the root of their nationality no longer in the earth, but in this belief. The unity of the abstractly natural and abstractly spiritual determinateness is the concrete unity of the spirit with nature, in which it recognizes nature

as its necessary organ, and itself as in its nature divine. Spirit in this stage, as the internal presupposition of the two previously named, takes up into itself on one hand the phase of nationality, since this is the form of its immediate individualization; but it no longer distinguishes between nations as if they were abstractly severed the one from the other, as the Greeks shut out all other nations under the name of barbarians. It also takes up into itself the phase of spirituality, since it knows itself as spirit, and knows itself to be free from nature, and yet it does not estrange itself as the Jews did in their representation of pure spirit, in reference to which nature seems to be only the work of its caprice. Humanity knows nature as its own, because it knows the Divine spirit and its creative energy manifesting itself in nature and history, as also the essence of its own spirit. Education can be complete only with Christianity as the religion of humanity.

177. We have thus three different systems of religion — (1) the National; (2) the Theocratic; and (3) the Humanitarian. The first works in harmony with nature since it educates the individual as a type of his species. The original nationality endeavors sharply to distinguish itself from others, and to impress on each person the stamp of its uniform type. System of National Education. 101 One individual is like every other, or at least should be so. The second system in its manner of manifestation is identical with the first. It even marks the national difference more emphatically; but the ground of the uniformity of the individuals is with it not merely the natural common interest, but it is the consequence of the spiritual unity, which abstracts from nature, and as history, satisfied with no present, hovers continually outside of itself between past and future. The theocratic system educates the individual as the servant of God. He is the true Jew only in so far as he is this; the genealogical identity with the father Abraham is a condition but not the principle of the nationality. The third system liberates the individual to the enjoyment of freedom as his essence, and educates the human being within national limits which no longer separate but unite, and, in the consciousness that each individual, without any kind of mediation, has a direct relation to God, makes of him a man who knows himself to be a member of the spiritual world of humanity. We can have no fourth system beyond this. From the side of the State-Pedagogics we might characterize these systems as that of the nation-State, the God-State, and the humanity-State. From the time of the establishment of the last, no one nation can attain to any sovereignty over the others. By means of the world-religion of Christianity, the education of nations has come to the point of taking for its ideal, man as determining himself according to the demands of reason.

First Division.

THE SYSTEM OF NATIONAL EDUCATION.

178. The National is the primitive system of education, since the family is the organic starting-point of all education, and is in its enlargement the basis of nationality.

— Education is always education of the mind. Even unorganized nations, those in a state of nature, the so-called savage nations, are possessed of something more than a mere education of the body; for, though they set much value upon gymnastic and warlike practice and give much time to them, they inculcate also respect for parents, for the aged, and for the decrees of the community. Education with them is essentially family training, and its content is natural love System of National Education. 102 and reverence. We cannot deny that the finer forms of those to which we are accustomed are wanting. Besides, education among all these people of nature is very simple and much the same, though great differences in its management may exist arising from differences of situation or from temperament of race. —

179. National Education is divided into three special systems: (1) Passive, (2) Active, (3) Individual. It begins with the humility of an abstract subjection to nature, and ends with the arrogance of an abstract rejection of nature.

180. Man yields at first to the natural authority of the family; he obeys unconditionally its behests. Then he substitutes for the family, as he goes on his culture, the artificial family of his caste, to whose rules he again unconditionally yields. To dispense with this artificialty and this tyranny, at last he abstracts himself from the family and from culture. He flees from both, and becoming a monk he again subjects himself to the tyranny of his order. The monks presents to us the mere type of his species.

181. This absolute abstraction from nature and from culture, this quietism of spiritual isolation, is the ultimate result of the Passive system. In opposition to this, the Active system seeks the positive vanquishing of naturalness. Its people are courageous. They attack other nations in order to rule over them as conquerors. They live for the continuation of their life after death, and build for themselves on this account tombs of granite. They brave the dangers of the sea. The abstract prose of the patriarchal-state, the fantastic chimeras of the caste-state, the ascetic self-renunciation of the cloister-state, yield gradually to the recognition of actuality; and the fundamental principle of Persian education consisted in the inculcation of veracity.

182. But the nationality which is occupied with simple, natural elements — other nations, death, the mystery of the ocean — may revert to the abstractions of the previous stage, which in education often take on cruel forms — nay, often truly horrible. First, when the spirit begins not only to suspect its true nature, but rather to recognize itself as the true essence; and when the God of Light places as the motto on his temple the command to self-knowledge, the natural individuality System of Passive Education. 103 becomes free. Neither the passive nor the active system understands the free self-distinction of the individual from the rest. In them, to be an individuality is a betrayal of the very idea of their existence, and even the suspicion of such a charge suffices utterly and mercilessly to destroy the one to whom it refers. Even the solitary individuality of the despot is not the one-ness of free individuality: he is only an example of his kind; only in his kind is he singular. Nationality rises to individuality through the free dialectic of its race, wherein it dissolves its own presupposition.

183. Nevertheless individuality must always proceed from naturalness. Esthetically it seeks nature, but the nature of the activity itself, in order, by penetrating it with mind, to make of it a work of art; practically it seeks it, partly to disdain it in gloomy resignation, partly to enjoy it in excessive sensual ecstasy, demoniacally to heighten the extravagance of its own internal feeling in wild revels.

— The Germans were not savage in the common signification of this term. They were men each one of whom constituted himself willingly a centre for others, or, if this was not the case, renounced them in proud self-sufficiency. All the glory and all the disgrace of our race lies in the power of individualizing which is divinely breathed into our veins. As a natural element, if this be not controlled, it degenerates easily into intractableness, into violence. The Germans need therefore, in order to be educated, severe service, the imposition of difficult tasks; and for this reason they appropriate to themselves, now the Roman law, now the Greek philology, now Gallic usages, &c., in order to work off their superfluous strength in such opposition. The natural reserve of the German found its solvent in Christianity. By itself, as the history of the German race shows, it would have been destroyed in vain distraction. First of all, the German race, in the

confidence of its immediate consciousness, ventured forth upon the sea, and managed the ship upon its waves as if they rode a charger. —

FIRST GROUP.
THE SYSTEM OF PASSIVE EDUCATION.

184. All education desires to free man from his finitude, to make him ethical, to unite him with God. It begins therefore Family Education. 104 with a negative relation to naturalness, but at once falls into a contradiction of its aim, which is to convert the opposition to nature into a natural necessity. Spirit subjects the individual (1) to the rule of the family as naturally spiritual; (2) to the rule of the caste as to a principle in itself spiritual, mediated through the division of labor, which it nevertheless, through its power of being inherited, joins again to the family; (3) to the abstract self-determination of the monkish quietism, which turns itself away as well from the family as from work, and constitutes this flight from nature and history, this absolute passivity, into an educational ideal.

—We shall not here enter into the details of this system, but simply endeavor to remove from their differences the want of clearness which is generally found involved in any mention of them, so that the phrases of hierarchical and theocratical education are used without any historical accuracy. —

I. Family Education.

185. The Family, as the organic starting-point of all education, makes the beginning. The nation looks upon itself as a family. Among all unorganized people education is family-education, though they are not conscious of its necessity. Identical in principle with these people, but distinguished from them in its consciousness of it, the Chinese nation, in their laws, regulations, and customs, have constituted the family the absolute basis of their life and the only principle of their education.

186. The natural element of the family is found in marriage and relationship; the spiritual, in love. We may call the nature of family feeling which is the immediate unity of both elements, by the name of Piety. In so far as this appears not merely as a substantial feeling but at the same time as law, there arises from it the subordination of the abstract obedience of the woman as wife to the husband, of children to the parents, of the younger children to the elder. In this obedience man first renounces his self-will and his natural roughness; he learns to master his passions, and to conduct himself with deferential gentleness.

—When the principle ruling the family is transferred to political relations, there arises the tyranny of the Chinese Caste Education. 105 state, which cannot be fully treated here. We find everywhere in it an analogical relation to that of parents and children. In China the ruler is the father and mother of the country; the civil officers are representatives of a paternal authority, &c. It follows that in school the children will be ranked according to their age. The authority of parents over children is according to the principle entirely unconditional, but in actuality very mild. The abandonment of daughters by the poorest classes in the great cities is not objected to, for the government rears the children in orphan asylums, where they are cared for by nurses appointed by the state. —

187. The distinction of these relations which are conditioned by nature takes on the external shape of a definite ceremonial, the learning of which is a chief element of education. In conformity with the naturalness of the whole principle all crimes against it are punished by whipping, which does not necessarily entail dishonor. In order to lead man to the mastery of himself and to obedience to those who are naturally set over him, education develops an endless number of fragmentary maxims to keep attention ever watchful over himself, and his behavior always fenced in by a code of prescriptions.

—We find in such moral sentences the substance of what is called, in China, Philosophy. —

188. The theoretical education includes Heading, Writing—i.e. painting the letters with a brush—Arithmetic, and the making of verses. But the ability to do these things is not looked at as means of culture but as ends in themselves, and to fit one therefore for the undertaking of state offices. The Chinese possess formally all the means for literary culture—printing, libraries, schools, and academies; but the worth of these is not great. Their value has been often over-rated because of their external resemblance to those found among us.

II. Caste Education.

189. The members of the Family are certainly immediately distinguished among each other as to sex and age, but this difference is entirely immaterial as far as the nature of their employment goes. In China, therefore, every man can attain any position; he who is of humblest birth in the great Caste Education. 106 state-family can climb to the highest honor. But the progress of spirit now becomes so mediated that the division of labor shall be made the principle on which a new distinction shall arise in the family:

each one shall perfect himself only in that labor which was allotted to him as his own through his birth into a particular family. This fatalism (caste-distinction) breaks up the life, but increases its tension, for spirit works on the one hand towards the deepening of its distinctions; on the other, towards leading them back into the unity which the natural determining directly opposes.

190. The chief work of education thus consists in teaching each one the rights and duties of his caste so that he shall act only exactly within their limits, and not pollute himself by passing beyond them. As the family-state concerns itself with fortifying the natural distinction by a far-reaching and vigorous ceremonial, so the caste-state must do the same with the distinction of class. A painful etiquette becomes more and more endless in its requisitions the higher the caste, in order to make the isolation more sharply defined and more perceptible.

— This feature penetrates all exclusively caste-education. The aristocracy exiles itself on this account from its native country, speaks a foreign language, loves its literature, adopts foreign customs, lives in foreign countries — in Italy, Paris, &c. In this way man becomes distinguished from others. But that man should strive thus to distinguish himself has its justification in the mystery of his birth, and this is assuredly always the principle of the caste-state in which it exists. The castes lead to genealogical records, which are of the greatest importance in determining the destiny of the individual. The Brahmin may strike down one of a lower caste who has defiled him by contact, without becoming thereby liable to punishment; rather would he be to blame if he did not commit the murder. Thus formerly was it with the officer who did not immediately kill the citizen or the common soldier who struck him a blow, &c. —

191. The East Indian culture is far deeper and richer than the Chinese. The theoretical culture includes Reading, Writing, and Arithmetic; but these are subordinate, as mere means for the higher activities of Poetry, Speculation, Science, Buddhistic Education. 107 and Art. The practical education limits itself strictly by the lines of caste, and since the caste system constitutes a whole in itself, and each for its permanence needs the others, it cannot forbear giving utterance suggestively to what is universally human in the free soul, in a multitude of fables (Hitopadesa) and apothegms (sentences of Bartrihari). Especially for the education of princes is a minor of the world sketched out.

— Xenophon's Cyropedia is of Greek origin, but it is Indian in its thought. —

III. Monkish Education.

192. Family Education demands unconditional obedience towards parents and towards all who stand in an analogous position. Caste Education demands unconditional obedience to the duties of the caste. The family punishes by whipping; the caste, by excommunication, by loss of honor. The opposition to nature appears in both systems in the form of a rigid ceremonial, distinguishing between the differences arising from nature. The family as well as the caste has within it a manifold fountain of activity, but it has also just as manifold a limitation of the individual. Spirit is forced, therefore, to turn against nature in general. It must become indifferent to the family. But it must also oppose history, and the fixed distinctions of division of labor as necessitated by nature. It must become indifferent to work and the pleasure derived from it. That it may not be conditioned either by nature or by history, it denies both, and makes its action to consist in producing an abstinence from all activity.

193. Such an indifference towards nature and history produces the education which we have called monkish. Those who support this sect care for food, clothing, and shelter, and for these material contributions, as the laity, receive in return from those who live this contemplative life the spiritual contribution of confidence in the blessings which wait upon ascetic contemplation. The family institution as well as the institution of human labor is subordinated to abstract isolation, in which the individual lives only for the purification of his soul. All things are justified by this end. Castes are found no more; only those are bound Buddhistic Education — System of Active Education. 108 to the observance of a special ceremonial who as nuns or monks subject themselves to the unconditional obedience to the rules of the cloister, these rules solemnly enjoining on the negative side celibacy and cessation from business, and on the positive side prayer and perfection.

194. In the school of the Chinese Tao-tse, and in the command to the Brahmin after he has established a family to become a recluse, we find the transition as it actually exists to the Buddhistic Quietism which has covered the rocky heights of Thibet with countless cloisters, and reared the people who are dependent upon it into a childlike amiability, into a contented repose. Art and Science have here no value in themselves, and are regarded only as ministering to religion. To be able to read in order to mutter over the prayers is desirable. With the premeditated effort in the state of a monk to reduce self to nothing as the highest good, the system of passive education attains its highest point. But the spirit cannot content itself in this abstract and dreamy absence of all action, though it demands a high stage of culture, and it has recourse therefore to action, partly on the positive side to conquer nature, partly to double its own existence in making history. Inspired with affirmative courage, it descends triumphantly from the mountain heights, and fears secularization no more.

SECOND GROUP.
THE SYSTEM OF ACTIVE EDUCATION.

195. Active Education elevates man from his abstract subjection to the family, the caste, asceticism, into a concrete activity with a definite aim which subjects those elements as phases of its mediation, and grants to each individual independence on the condition of his identity with it. These aims are the military state, the future after death, and industry. There is always an element of nature present from which the activity proceeds; but this no longer appears, like the family, the caste, the sensuous egotism, as immediately belonging to the individual, but as something outside of himself which limits him, and, as his future life, has an internal relation to him, yet is essential to him and assigns to him the object of his activity. The Persian has as an Military Education. 109 object of conquest, other nations; the Egyptian, death; the Phœnician, the sea.

I. Military Education.

196. That education which would emancipate a nation from the passivity of abstraction must throw it into the midst of an historical activity. A nation finds not its actual limits in its locality: it can forsake this and wander far away from it. Its true limit is made by another nation. The nation which knows itself to be actual, turns itself therefore against other nations in order to subject them and to reduce them to the condition of mere accidents of itself. It begins a system of conquest which has in itself no limitations, but goes from one nation to another, and extends its evil course indefinitely. The final result of this attack is that it finds itself attacked and conquered.

— The early history of the Persian is twofold: the patriarchal in the high valleys of Iran, and the religio-hierarchical among the Medes. We find under these circumstances a repetition of the principal characteristics of the Chinese, Indian, and Buddhist educations. In ancient Zend there were also castes. Among the Persians themselves, as they descended from their

mountains to the conquest of other nations, there was properly only a military nobility. The priesthood was subjected to the royal power which represented the absolute power of actuality. Of the Persian kings, Cyrus attacked Western Asia; Cambyses, Africa; Darius and Xerxes, Europe; until the reaction of the spiritually higher nationality did not content itself with self-preservation, but under the Macedonian Alexander made the attack on Persia itself. —

197. Education enjoined upon the Persians (1) to speak the truth; (2) to learn to ride and to use the bow and arrow. There is implied in the first command a recognition of actuality, the negation of all dreamy absorption, of all fantastical indetermination; and in this light the Persian, in distinction from the Hindoo, appears to be considerate and reasonable. In the second command is implied warlike practice, but not that of the nomadic tribes. The Persian fights on horseback, and thus appears in distinction from the Indian Priestly Education. 110 hermit seclusion and the quietism of the Lamas as restless and in constant motion.

— The Family increases in value as it rears a large number of warriors. Many children were a blessing. The king of Persia gave a premium for all children over a certain number. Nations were drawn in as nations by war; hence the immense multitude of a Persian army. Everything — family, business, possessions — must be regardlessly sacrificed to the one aim of war. Education, therefore, cultivated an unconditional, all-embracing obedience to the king, and the slightest inclination to assert an individual independence was high treason and was punished with death. In China, on the contrary, duty to the family is paramount to duty to the state, or rather is itself duty to the state. The civil officer who mourns the loss of one of his family is released during the period of mourning from the duties of his function. —

198. The theoretical education, which was limited to reading, writing, and to instruction, was, in the usages of culture, in the hands of the Magians, the number of whom was estimated at eighty thousand, and who themselves had enjoyed the advantages of a careful education, as is shown by their gradation into Herbeds, Moheds, and Destur-Moheds; i.e. into apprentices, journeymen, and masters. The very fundamental idea of their religion was military; it demanded of men to fight on the side of the king of light, and guard against the prince of darkness and evil. It gave to him thus the honor of a free position between the world-moving powers and the possibility of a self-creative destiny, by which means vigor and chivalrous feeling were developed. Religion trained the activity of man into actualiza-

tion on this planet, increasing by its means the dominion of the good, by purifying the water, by planting trees, by extirpating troublesome wild beasts. Thus it increased bodily comfort, and no longer, like the monk, treated this as a mere negative.

II. Priestly Education.

199. War has in death its force. It produces this, and by its means decides who shall serve and who obey. But the nation that finds its activity in war, though it makes death its absolute means, yet finds its own limit in death. Other Priestly Education. 111 nations are only its boundaries, which it can overpass in fighting with and conquering them. But death itself it can never escape, whether it come in the sands of the desert — which buried for Cambyses an army which he sent to the oracle of the Libyan Ammon — or in the sea, that scorns the rod of the angry despot, or by the sword of the freeman who guards his household gods. On this account, that people stands higher that in the midst of life reflects on death, or rather lives for it. The education of such a nation must be priestly because death is the means of the transition to the future life, and consequently equivalent to a new birth, and becomes a religious act. Neither the family-state, nor the caste-state, nor the monkish nor military-state, are hierarchies in the sense that the leading of the national life by a priesthood produces. But in Egypt this was actually the case, because the chief educational tribunal was the death-court which concerned only the dead, in awarding to them or denying them the honor of burial as the result of their whole life, but in its award affected also the honor of the surviving family.

200. General education here limited itself to imparting the ability to read, write, and calculate. Special education consisted properly only in an habitual living into a definite business within the circle of the Family. In this fruitful and warm land the expense of supporting children was very small. The division into classes was without the cruel features of the Indian civilization, and life itself in the narrow Nile valley was very social, very rich, very full of eating and drinking, while the familiarity with death heightened the force of enjoyment. In a stricter sense only, the warriors, the priests, and the kings, had, properly speaking, an education. The aim of life, which was to determine in death its eternal future, to secure for itself a passage into the still kingdom of Amenth, manifested itself externally in the care which they expended on the preservation of the dead shell of the immortal soul, and on this account worked itself out in building tombs which should last for ever. The Chinese builds a wall to secure his family-state from attack; the Hindoo builds pagodas for his gods; the Buddhist erects for himself monastic cells; the Persian Industrial Education. 112 constructs in Persepolis the tomb of his kings, where they may retire in the evening of their lives after they have rioted in Ecbatana, Babylon, and Susa; but the Egyptian builds his own tomb, and carries on war only to protect it.

III. Industrial Education.

201. The system of active education was to find its solution in a nation which wandered from the coast of the Red Sea to the foot of the Lebanon mountains on the Mediterranean, and ventured forth upon the sea which before that time all nations had avoided as a dangerous and destructive element. The Phœnician was industrial, and needed markets where he could dispose of the products of his skill. But while he sought for them he disdained neither force nor deceit; he planted colonies; he stipulated that he should have in the cities of other nations a portion for himself; he urged the nations to adopt his pleasures, and insensibly introduced among them his culture and even his religion. The education of such a nation must have seemed profane, because it fostered indifference towards family and one's native land, and made the restless and passionate activity subservient to gain. The understanding and usefulness rose to a higher dignity.

202. Of the education of the Phœnicians we know only so much as to enable us to conclude that it was certainly various and extensive: among the Carthaginians, at least, that their children were practised in reading, writing, and arithmetic, in religious duties; secondly, in a trade; and, finally, in the use of arms, is not improbable. Commerce became with the Phœnicians a trade, the egotism of which makes men dare to plough the inhospitable sea, and to penetrate eagerly the horror of its vast distances, but yet to conceal from other nations their discoveries and to wrap them in a veil of fable.

— It is a beautiful testimony to the disposition of the Greeks, that Plato and others assign as a cause of the low state of Arithmetic and Mathematics among the Phœnicians and Egyptians the want of a free and disinterested seizing of them. —

Individual Education — Ythetic Education. 113

THIRD GROUP.
THE SYSTEM OF INDIVIDUAL EDUCATION.

203. One-sided passivity as well as one-sided activity is subsumed under Individuality, which makes itself into its own end and aim. The Phœni-

cian made gain his aim; his activity was of a utilistic character. Individuality as a pedagogical principle is indeed egotistic in so far as it endeavors to achieve its own peculiarity, but it is at the same time noble. It desires not to have but to be. Individuality also begins as natural, but it elevates nature by means of art to ideality. The solution of beauty is found in culture, since this renounces the charm of appearance for the knowledge of the True. The æsthetic individuality is followed by the practical, which has indeed no natural basis, but proceeds from an artificial basis as a state formed for a place of refuge. In order internally to create a unity in this, is framed a definite code of laws; in order externally to assure it, the invincible warrior is demanded. Education is therefore, more exactly speaking, juristic and military practice. The morality of the state is loosened as it reduces into its mechanism one nation after another, until the individuality, become dæmonic, makes its war-hardened legions tremble with weakness. We characterize this individuality as dæmonic because it desires recognition simply for its own sake. Not for its beauty and culture, not for its knowledge of business and its bravery, only for its peculiarity as such does it claim value, and in the effort to secure this it is ready to hazard life itself. In its naturally-growing existence this individuality is deep, but at the same time without self-limit. The nations educate themselves to this individuality when they destroy the world of Roman world — that of self-limit and balance — which they find.

I. Ythetic Education.

204. The system of individual education begins with the transfiguration of the immediate individuality into beauty. On the side of nature this system is passion, for individuality is given through nature; but on the side of spirit it is active, for spirit must determine itself to restrain its measure as the essence of beauty.

Ythetic Education. 114

205. Here the individual is of value only in so far as he is beautiful. At first beauty is apprehended as natural, but then it is carried over into the realm of spirit, and the Good is posited as identical with the Beautiful. The ideal of æsthetic education remains always that there shall be also an external unity of the Good with the Beautiful, of Spirit with Nature.

— We cannot here give in detail the history of Greek Education. It is the best known among us, and the literature in which it is worked out is very widely spread. Among the common abridged accounts we mention here *only the works of Jacobs, of Cramer & Bekker's "Charinomos." We must content ourselves with mentioning the turning-points which follow from the nature of the principle. —*

206. Culture was in Greece thoroughly national. Education gave to the individual the consciousness that he was a Greek and no barbarian, a free man and so subject only to the laws of the state, and not to the caprice of any one person. Thus the nationality was freed at once from the abstract unity of the family and from the abstract distinction of caste, while it appeared with the manifold talents of individuals of different races. Thus the Dorian race held as essential, gymnastics; the Ulians, music; the Ionics, poetry. The Ulian individuality was subsumed in the history of the two others, so that these had to proceed in their development with an internal antagonism. The education of the Dorian race was national education in the fullest sense of the word; in it the education of all was the same, and was open to all, even including the young women; among the Ionic race it was also in its content truly national, but in its form it was varied and unlike, and, for those belonging to various great families, private. The former, reproducing the Oriental phase of abstract unity, educated all in one mould; the latter was the nursery of particular individualities.

207. (1) Education in the heroic age, without any systematic arrangement on the subject, left each one perfectly free. The people related the histories of the adventures of others, and through their own gave material to others again to relate stories of them.

— The Greeks began where the last stage of the active Ythetic Education. 115 system of education ended — with piracy and the seizure of women. Swimming was a universal practice among the sea-dwelling Greeks, just as in England — the mistress of the ocean — rowing is the most prominent exercise among the young men, and public regattas are held. —

208. (2) In the period of state-culture proper, education developed itself systematically; and gymnastics, music, and grammatics, or literary culture, constituted the general pedagogical elements.

209. Gymnastics aimed not alone to render the body strong and agile, but, far more, to produce in it a noble carriage, a dignified and graceful manner of appearance. Each one fashioned his body into a living, divine statue, and in the public games the nation crowned the victor.

— Their love of beautiful boys is explicable not merely by their interest in beautiful forms, but especially by their interest in individuality. The low

condition of the women could not lie at the foundation of it, for among the Spartans they were educated as nearly as possible like the men, and yet among them and the Cretans the love of boys was recognized in their legislation. To be without a beloved (ἀ.𐤁953;της), or a lover (ἐισπνηλας), was among them considered as disgraceful as the degradation of the love by unchastity was contemptible. What charm was there, then, in love? Manifestly only beauty and culture. But that a person should be attracted by one and not by another can be accounted for only by the peculiar character, and in so far the boy-love and the man-friendship which sprang from it, among the Greeks, are very characteristic and noteworthy phenomena. –

210. It was the task of Music, by its rhythm and measure, to fill the soul with well-proportioned harmony. So highly did the Greeks prize music, and so variously did they practise it, that to be a musical man meant the same with them as to be a cultivated man with us. Education in this respect was very painstaking, inasmuch as music exercises a very powerful influence in developing discreet behavior and self-possession into a graceful naturalness.

– Among the Greeks we find an unrestricted delight in nature – a listening to her manifestations, the tone of which betrays the subjectivity of things as subjectivity. In comparison - Ythetic Education. 116 with this tender sympathy with nature of the Greeks – who heard in the murmur of the fountains, in the dashing of the waves, in the rustling of the trees, and in the cry of animals, the voice of divine personality – the sight and hearing of the Eastern nations for nature is dull. –

211. The stringed instrument, the cithern, was preferred by the Greeks to all wind instruments because it was not exciting, and allowed the accompaniment of recitation or song, i.e. the contemporaneous activity of the spirit in poetry. Flute-playing was first brought from Asia Minor after the victorious progress of the Persian war, and was especially cultivated in Thebes. They sought in vain afterwards to oppose the wild excitement raised by its influence.

212. Grammar comprehended Letters (γράμματα), i.e. the elements of literary culture, reading and writing. Much attention was given to correct expression. The Fables of Yop, the Iliad, and the Odyssey, and later the tragic poets, were read, and partly learned by heart. The orators borrowed from them often the ornament of their commonplace remarks.

213. (3) The internal growth of what was peculiar to the Grecian State came to an end with the war for the Hegemony. Its dissolution began, and

the philosophical period followed the political. The beautiful ethical life was resolved into thoughts of the True, Good, and Beautiful. Individuality turned more towards the internal, and undertook to subject freedom, the existing regulations, laws and customs, to the criticism of reason as to whether these were in and for themselves universal and necessary. The Sophists, as teachers of Grammar, Rhetoric, and Philosophy, undertook to extend the cultivation of Reflection; and this introduced instability in the place of the immediate fixed state of moral customs. Among the women, the Hetære undertook the same revolution; in the place of the πότνια μήτηρ appeared the beauty, who isolated herself in the consciousness of her charms and in the perfection of her varied culture, and exhibited herself to the public admiration. The tendency to idiosyncrasy often approached wilfulness, caprice and whimsicality, and opposition to the national moral sense. A Diogenes in a tub became possible; the soulless but graceful frivolity of an Alcibiades charmed, even though it was externally condemned; a Socrates - Ythetic Education. 117 completed the break in consciousness, and urged upon the system of the old morality the pregnant question, whether Virtue could be taught? Socrates worked as a philosopher who was to educate. Pythagoras had imposed upon his pupils the abstraction of a common, exactly-defined manner of living. Socrates, on the contrary, freed his disciples — in general, those who had intercourse with him — leading them to the consciousness of their own individuality. He revolutionized the youth in that he taught them, instead of a thoughtless obedience to moral customs, to seek to comprehend their purpose in the world, and to rule their actions according to it. Outwardly he conformed in politics, and in war as at Marathon; but in the direction of his teaching he was subjective and modern.

214. This idea, that Virtue could be taught, was realized especially by Plato and Aristotle; the former inclining to Dorianism, the latter holding to the principle of individuality in nearly the modern sense. As regards the pedagogical means — Gymnastics, Music, and Grammar — both philosophers entirely agreed. But, in the seizing of the pedagogical development in general, Plato asserted that the education of the individual belonged to the state alone, because the individual was to act wholly in the state. On the other hand, Aristotle also holds that the state should conduct the education of its citizens, and that the individual should be trained for the interest of the state; but he recognizes also the family, and the peculiarity of the individual, as positive powers, to which the state must accord relative freedom. Plato sacrificed the family to the state, and must therefore have

*sacred marriages, nurseries, and common and public educational instituti-
ons. Each one shall do only that which he is fitted to do, and shall work at
this only for the sake of perfecting it: to what he shall direct his energies,
and in what he shall be instructed, shall be determined by the government,
and the individuality consequently is not left free. Aristotle also will have
for all the citizens the same education, which shall be common and public;
but he allows, at the same time, an independence to the family and self-
determination to the individual, so that a sphere of private life presents
itself within Ythetic Education. 118 the state: a difference by means of
which a much broader sway of individuality is possible.*

*— These two philosophers have come to represent two very different di-
rections in Pedagogics, which at intervals, in certain stages of culture,
reappear — the tyrannical guardianship of the state which assumes the work
of education, tyrannical to the individual, and the free development of the
liberal state-education, in opposition to idiosyncrasy and fate. —*

215. *The principle of æsthetic individuality reaches its highest manifestation when the individual, in the decay of public life, in the disappearance of
all beautiful morality, isolates himself, and seeks to gain in his isolation
such strength that he can bear the changes of external history around him
with composure — "ataraxy." The Stoics sought to attain this end by turning their attention inward into pure internality, and thus, by preserving
the self-determination of abstract thinking and willing, maintaining an
identity with themselves: the Epicureans endeavored to do the same, with
this difference however, that they strove after a positive satisfaction of the
senses by filling them with concrete pleasurable sensations. As a consequence of this, the Stoics isolated themselves in order to maintain themselves in the exclusiveness of their internal unconditioned relation to themselves, while the Epicureans lived in companies, because they achieved the
reality of their pleasure-seeking principle through harmony of feeling and
through the sweetness of friendship. In so far the Epicureans were Greeks
and the Stoics Romans. With both, however, the beauty of manifestation
was secondary to the immobility of the inner feeling. The plastic attainment of the Good and the Beautiful was cancelled in the abstraction of
thinking and feeling. This was the advent of the Roman principle among
the Greeks.*

216. *The pedagogical significance of Stoicism and Epicureanism consists
in this, that, after the moral life in public and in private were sundered
from each other, the individual began to educate himself, through philosophical culture, into stability of character, for which reason the Roman*

emperors particularly disliked the Stoics. At many times, a resignation to the Stoic philosophy was sufficient to make one suspected. Practical Education. 119 But, at last, the noble emperor, in order to win himself a hold in the chaos of things, was forced himself to become a Stoic and to flee to the inaccessible stillness of the self-thinking activity and the self-moving will. Stoics and Epicureans had both what we call an ideal. The Stoics used the expression "kingdom"; as Horace says, sarcastically, "Sapiens rex est nisi — pituita molesta est."

II. Practical Education.

217. The truth of the solution of the beautiful individuality is the promise of the activity conformable to its purpose [i.e. teleological activity], which on the one hand considers carefully end and means, and on the other hand seeks to realize the end through the corresponding means, and in this deed subjects mere beauty of form. The practical individuality is therefore externally conditioned, since it is not its own end like the Beautiful, whether Stoical or Epicurean, but has an end, and finds its satisfaction not so much in this after it is attained as in the striving for its attainment.

218. The education of this system begins with very great simplicity. But after it has attained its object, it abandons itself to using the results of æsthetic culture as a recreation without any specific object. What was to the Greeks a real delight in the Beautiful became therefore with the Romans simply an æsthetic amusement, and as such must finally be wearisome. The earnestness of individuality made itself in mysticism into a new aim, which was distinguished from the original one in that it concealed in itself a mystery and exacted a theoretically æsthetic practice.

219. (1) The first epoch of Roman education, as properly Roman, was the juristic-military education of the republic. The end and aim of the Roman was Rome; and Rome, as from the beginning an eclectic state, could endure only while its laws and external politics were conformable to some end. It bore the same contradiction within itself as in its external attitude. This forced it into robbery, and the plebeians were related to the patricians in the same way, for they robbed them gradually of all their privileges. On this account education directed itself partly to giving a knowledge of the Law, partly to communicating a capacity for war. The boys Practical Education. 120 were obliged to commit to memory and recite the laws of the twelve tables, and all the youths were subject to military service. The Roman possessed no individuality of native growth, but one mediated through the intermingling of various fugitives, which developed a very great energy. Hence from the first he was attentive to himself, he watched jealously over the limits of his rights and the rights of others, measured his strength, moderated himself, and constantly guarded himself. In contrast with the careless cheerfulness of the Greeks, he therefore appears gloomy.

— The Latin tongue is crowded with expressions which paint presence of mind, effort at reflection, a critical attitude of mind, the importance of personal control: as *gravitas morum, sui compos esse, sibi constare, austeritas, vir strenuus, vir probus, vitam honestam gerere, sibimet ipse imperare*, &c. The Etruscan element imparted to this earnestness an especially solemn character. The Roman was no more, like the Greek, unembarrassed at naturalness. He was ashamed of nakedness; *verecundia, pudor*, were genuinely Roman. *Vitam præferre pudori* was shameful. On the contrary, the Greek gave to Greeks a festival in exhibiting the splendor of his naked body, and the inhabitants of Crotona erected a statue to Philip only because he was so perfectly beautiful. Simply to be beautiful, only beautiful, was enough for the Greek. But a Roman, in order to be recognized, must have done something for Rome: *se bene de republica mereri*. —

220. In the first education of children the agency of the mother is especially influential, so that woman with the Romans took generally a more moral, a higher, and a freer position. It is worthy of remark that while, as the beautiful, she set the Greeks at variance, among the Romans, through her ethical authority, she acted as reconciler.

221. The mother of the Roman helped to form his character; the father undertook the work of instruction. When in his fifteenth year the boy exchanged the toga *prætextata* for the toga *virilis*, he was usually sent to some relative, or to some jurist, as his guardian, to learn thoroughly, under his guidance, of the laws and of the state; with the seventeenth began military service. All education was for a long time entirely a private affair. On account of the necessity of Practical Education. 121 a mechanical unity in work which war demands, the greatest stress was laid upon obedience. In its restricted sense education comprised Reading, Writing, and Arithmetic; the last being, on account of its usefulness, more esteemed by the Romans than by the Greeks, who gave more time to Geometry. The schools, very characteristically, were called *Ludi*, because their work was, in distinction from other practice, regarded simply as a recreation, as play.

— The Roman recognized with pride this distinction between the Greek and himself; Cicero's Introduction to his Essay on Oratory expresses it. To be practical was always the effort of the reflective character of the Romans, *which was always placing new ends and seeking the means for their attainment; which loved moderation, not to secure beauty thereby, but respected it as a means for a happy success (medium tenuere beati); which did not possess serene self-limitation, or σωφροσύνη, but calculation quid valeant humeri, quid ferre recusent; but which, in general, went far beyond the Greeks in persistency of will, in constantia animi. The schools were at first held publicly in shops; hence the name trivium. Very significant for the Roman is the predicate which he conferred upon theoretical subjects when he called them artes bon欠optim欠liberales, ingenu潔i>, &c., and brought forth the practical element in them. —*

222. (2) But the practical education could no longer keep its ground after it had become acquainted with the 盎hetic. The conquest of Greece, Asia Minor, and Egypt, made necessary, in a practical point of view, the acquisition of the Grecian tongue, so that these lands, so permeated with Grecian culture, might be thoroughly ruled. The Roman of family and property, therefore, took into his service Greek nurses and teachers who should give to his children, from their earliest years, Greek culture. It is, in the history of education, a great evil when a nation undertakes to teach a foreign tongue to its youth. Then the necessity of trade with the Greeks caused the study of Rhetoric, so that not only in the deliberations of the senate and people, but in law, the ends might be better attained. Whatever effort the Roman government made to prevent the invasion of the Greek rhetorician was all in vain. The Roman youth sought for this Practical Education. 122 knowledge, which was so necessary to them in foreign lands, e.g. in the flourishing school of rhetoric on the island of Rhodes. At last, even the study of Philosophy commended itself to the practical Roman, in order that he might recover for himself confidence amid the disappointments of life. When his practical life did not bring him any result, he devoted himself in his poverty to abstract contemplation. The Greeks would have Philosophy for its own sake; the ataraxy of the Stoics, Epicureans, and Skeptics even, desired the result of a necessary principle; but the Roman, on the contrary, wished to lift himself by philosophemes above trouble and misfortune.

— This direction which Philosophy took is noteworthy, not alone in Cicero and Seneca, but at the fall of the Roman empire, when Boethius wrote in his prison his immortal work on the consolations of Philosophy. —

223. The earnestness which sought a definite end degenerated in the very opposite of activity with him who had no definite aim. The idleness of the wealthy Roman, who felt himself to be the lord of a limitless world, devoted itself to dissipation and desire for enjoyment, which, in its entire want of moderation, abused nature. The finest form of the extant education was that in belles-lettres, which also for the first time came to belong to the sphere of Pedagogics. There had been a degeneration of art in India and Greece, and also an artistic trifling. But in Rome there arose a pursuit of art in order to win a certain consideration in social position, and to create for one's self a recreation in the emptiness of a soul satiated with sensual debauchery. Such a seizing of art is frivolous, for it no longer recognizes its absoluteness, and subordinates it as a means to subjective egotism. Literary salons then appear.

— In the introduction to his Cataline, Sallust has painted excellently this complete revolution in the Roman education. The younger Pliny in his letters furnishes ample material to illustrate to us this pursuit of belles-lettres. In Nero it became idiotic. We should transgress our prescribed limits did we enter here into particulars. An analysis would show the perversion of the æsthetic into the practical, the æsthetic losing thereby its proper nature. But the Roman could not Practical Education. 123 avoid this perversion, because, according to his original aim, he could not move except towards the utile et honestum. —

224. (3) But this pursuit of fine art, this aimless parade, must at last weary the Roman. He sought for himself again an object to which he could vigorously devote himself. His sovereignty was assured, and conquest as an object could no more charm him. The national religion had fallen with the destruction of the national individuality. The soul looked out over its historical life into an empty void. It sought to establish a relation between itself and the next world by means of dæmonic forces, and in place of the depreciated nationality and its religion we find the eclecticism of the mystic society. There were, it is true, in national religions certain secret signs, rites, words, and meanings; but now, for the first time in the history of the world, there appeared mysteries as pedagogical societies, which concerned themselves only with private things and were indifferent to nationality. Everything was profaned by the roughness of violence. Man believed no longer in the old gods, and the superstitious faith in ghosts became only a thing fit to frighten children with. Thus man took refuge in secrecy, which had for his satiety a piquant charm.

225. The education of the mysteries was twofold, theoretical and practical. In the theoretical we find a regular gradation of symbols and symbolical acts through which one seemed gradually to attain to the revelation of

the secret; the practical contained a regular gradation of ascetic actions alternating with an abandonment to wild orgies. Both raised one from the rank of the novice to that of the initiated. In the higher orders they formed an ethical code of laws, and this form Pedagogics has retained in all such secret culture, mutatis mutandis, down to the Illuminati.

— In the Roman empire, its Persian element was the worship of Mithras; its Egyptian, that of Isis; its Grecian, the Pythagorean doctrines. All these three, however, were much mingled with each other. The Roman legions, who really no longer had any native country, bore these artificial religions throughout the whole world. The confusion of excitement led often to Somnambulism, which was not yet understood, and to belief in miracles. Apollonius of Tyana, the Individual Education — Theocratic Education. 124 *messiah of Ethnicism, is the principal figure in this group; and, in comparison with him, Jamblichus appears only as an enthusiast and Alexander of Abonoteichos as an impostor. —*

III. Abstract Individual Education.

226. What the despair of the declining nations sought for in these mysteries was Individuality, which in its singularity is conscious of the universality of the rational spirit, as its own essence. This individuality existed more immediately in the Germanic race, which nevertheless, on account of its nature, formed first in Christianity its true actualization. It can be here only pointed out that they most thoroughly, in opposition to nature, to men, and to the gods, felt themselves to be independent; as Tacitus says, "Securi adversus homines, securi adversus Deos." This individuality, which had only itself for an end, must necessarily be destroyed, and was saved only by Christianity, which overcame and enlightened its dæmonic and defiant spirit. We cannot speak here of a system of Education. Respect for personality, the free acknowledgment of the claims of woman, the loyalty to the leader chosen by themselves, loyalty to their friends (the idea of fellowship), — these features should all be well-noted, because from them arose the feudalism of the middle ages. What Cæsar and Tacitus tell us of the education of the Germans expresses only the emancipation of individuality, which in its immediate crudeness had no other form in which to manifest itself than wars of conquest.

— To the Roman there was something dæmonic in the German. He perceived dimly in him his future, his master. When the Romans were to meet the Cimbri and Teutons in the field, their commander had first to accustom them for a whole day to the fearful sight of the wild, giant-like forms. —

227. The system of National Education founded its first stage on the substantial basis of the family-spirit; its second stage on the division of the nation by means of division of labor which it makes permanent in castes; its third stage presents the free opposition of the laity and clergy; in its System of Theocratic Education. 125 next phase it makes war, immortality, and trade, by turns, its end; thirdly, it posits beauty. patriotic youth, and the immediateness of individuality, as the essence of mankind, and at last dissolves the unity of nationality in the consciousness that all nations are really one since they are all human beings. In the intermixture of races in the Roman world arises the conception of the human race, the genus humanum. Education had become eclectic: the Roman legions levelled the national distinctions. In the wavering of all objective morality, the necessity of self-education in order to the formation of character appeared ever more and more clearly; but the conception, which lay at the foundation, was always, nevertheless, that of Roman, Greek, or German education. But in the midst of these nations another system had striven for development, and this did not base itself on the natural connection of nationality, but made this, for the first time, only a secondary thing, and made the direct relation of man to God its chief idea. In this system God himself is the teacher. He manifests to man His will as law, to which he must unconditionally conform for no other reason than that He is the Lord, and man His servant, who can have no other will than His. The obedience of man is therefore, in this system, abstract until through experience he gradually attains to the knowledge that the will of God has in it the very essence of his own will. Descent, Talent, Events, Work, Beauty, Courage, — all these are indifferent things compared with the subjection of the human to the divine will. To be well-pleasing to God is almost the same as belief in Him. Without this identity, what is natural in national descent is of no value. According to its form of manifestation, Judaism is below the Greek spirit. It is not beautiful, but rather grotesque. But in its essence, as the religion of the contradiction between the idea and its existence, it goes beyond nature, which it perceives to be established by an absolute, conscious, and reasonable Will; while the Greek concealed from himself only mythically his dependence on nature, on his mother-earth. The Jews have been preserved in the midst of all other culture by the elastic power of the thought of God as One who was free from the control of nature. The Jews have a patri-

otism in common with the Romans. *The Maccabees, System of Theocratic Education. 126 for example, were not inferior to the Romans in greatness.*

— Abraham is the genuine Jew because he is the genuinely faithful man. He does not hesitate to obey the horrible and inhuman command of his God. Circumcision was made the token of the national unity, but the nation may assimilate members to itself from other nations through this rite. The condition always lies in belief in a spiritual relation to which the relation of nationality is secondary. The Jewish nation makes proselytes, and these are widely different from the Socii of the Romans or the Metoeci of the Athenians. —

228. To the man who knows Nature to be the work of a single, incomparable, rational Creator, she loses independence. He is negatively freed from her control, and sees in her only an absolute means. As opposed to the fanciful sensuous intuitions of Ethnicism, this seems to be a backward step, but for the emancipation of man it is a progress. He no longer fears Nature but her Lord, and admires Him so much that prose rises to the dignity of poetry in his telological contemplation. Since man stands over and beyond nature, education is directed to morality as such, and spreads itself out in innumerable limitations, by means of which the distinction of man from nature is expressly asserted as a difference. The ceremonial law appears often arbitrary, but in its prescriptions it gives man the satisfaction of placing himself as will in relation to will. For example, if he is forbidden to eat any specified part of an animal, the ground of this command is not merely natural — it is the will of the Deity. Man learns therefore, in his obedience to such directions, to free himself from his self-will, from his natural desires. This exact outward conformity to subjectivity is the beginning of wisdom, the purification of the will from all individual egotism.

— The rational substance of the Law is found always in the Decalogue. Many of our modern much-admired authors exhibit a superficiality bordering on shallowness when they comment alone on the absurdity of the miracles, and abstract from the profound depth of the moral struggle, and from the practical rationality of the ten commandments. —

System of Theocratic Education. 127

229. Education in this theocratical system is on one side patriarchal. The Family is very prominent, because it is considered to be a great happiness for the individual to belong from his very earliest life to the company of those who believe in the true God. On its other side it is hierarchical, as its ceremonial law develops a special office, which is to see that obedience is paid to its multifarious regulations. And, because these are often perfectly arbitrary, Education must, above all, practise the memory in learning them all, so that they may always be remembered. The Jewish monotheism shares this necessity with the superstition of ethnicism.

230. But the technique proper of the mechanism is not the most important pedagogical element of the theocracy. We find this in its historical significance, since its history throughout has a pedagogical character. For the people of God show us always, in their changing intercourse with their God, a progress from the external to the internal, from the lower to the higher, from the past to the future. Its history, therefore, abounds in situations very interesting in a pedagogical point of view, and in characters which are eternal models.

231. (1) The will of God as the absolute authority is at first to them, as law, external. But soon God adds to the command to obedience, on one hand, the inducement of a promise of material prosperity, and on the other hand the threat of material punishment. The fulfilment of the law is also encouraged by reflection on the profit which it brings. But, since these motives are all external, they rise finally into the insight that the law is to be fulfilled, not on their account, but because it is the will of the Lord; not alone because it is conducive to our happiness, but also because it is in itself holy, and written in our hearts: in other words, man proceeds from the abstract legality, through the reflection of eud齒nism, to the internality of moral sentiment — the course of all education.

— This last stand-point is especially represented in the excellent Gnomic of Jesus Sirach — a book so rich in pedagogical insight, which paints with master-strokes the relations of husband and wife, parents and children, master and servants, - System of Theocratic Education. 128 friend and friend, enemy and enemy, and the dignity of labor as well as the necessity of its division. This priceless book forms a side-piece from the theocratic stand-point to the Republic of Plato and his laws on ethical government. —

232. (2) The progress from the lower to the higher appeared in the conquering of the natural individuality. Man, as the servant of Jehovah, must have no will of his own; but selfish naturalness arrayed itself so much the more vigorously against the abstract "Thou shalt," allowed itself to descend into an abstraction from the Law, and often reached the most unbridled extravagance. But since the Law in inexorable might always remained the same, always persistent, in distinction from the inequalities of the deed of man, it forced him to come back to it, and to conform himself to its demands. Thus he learned criticism, thus he rose from naturalness into spirit. This progress is at the same time a progress from necessity to freedom, because criticism always gradually opens a way for man into insight, so that he finds the will of God to be the truth of his own self-determination. Because God is one and absolute, there arises the expectation that His Will will become the basis for the will of all nations and men. The criticism of the understanding must recognize a contradiction in the fact that the will of the true God is the law of only one nation; feared by other nations, moreover, by reason of their very worship of God as a gloomy mystery, and detested as odium generis humani. And thus is developed the thought that the isolation of the believers will come to an end as soon as the other nations recognize their faith as the true one, and are received into it. Thus here, out of the deepest penetration of the soul into itself, as among the Romans out of the fusion of nations, we see appear the idea of the human race.

233. (3) The progress from the past to the future unfolded the ideal servant of God who fulfils all the Law, and so blots out the empirical contradiction that the "Thou shalt" of the Law attains no adequate actuality. This Prince of Peace, who shall gather all nations under his banner, can therefore have no other thing predicated of him than Holiness. He is not beautiful as the Greeks represented their ideal, not System of Humanitarian Education. 129 brave and practical as was the venerated Virtus of the Romans; he does not place an infinite value on his individuality as the German does: but he is represented as insignificant in appearance, as patient, as humble, as he who, in order to reconcile the world, takes upon himself the infirmities and disgrace of all others. The ethnical nations have only a lost Paradise behind them; the Jews have one also before them. From this belief in the Messiah who is to come, from the certainty which they have of conquering with him, from the power of esteeming all things of small importance in view of such a future, springs the indestructible nature of the Jews. They ignore the fact that Christianity is the necessary result of their own history. As the nation that is to be (des Seinsollens), they are merely a historical nation, the nation among nations, whose education — whenever the Jew has not changed and corrupted its nature through modern culture — is still always patriarchal, hierarchal, and mnemonic.

Third Division.
The System of Humanitarian Education

234. The systems of national and theocratic education came to the same result, though by different ways, and this result is the conception of a hu-

man race in the unity of which the distinctions of different nations find their Truth. But with them this result is only a conception, being a thing external to their actuality. They arrive at the painting of an ideal of the way in which the Messiah shall come. But these ideals exist only in the mind, and the actual condition of the people sometimes does not correspond to them at all, and sometimes only very relatively. The idea of spirit had in these presuppositions the possibility of its concrete actualization; one individual man must become conscious of the universality and necessity of the will as being the very essence of his own freedom, so that all heteronomy should be cancelled in the autonomy of spirit. Natural individuality appearing as national determinateness was still acknowledged, but was deprived of its abstract isolation. The divine authority of the truth of the individual will is to be recognized, but at the same time freed from its estrangement towards itself. While Christ was a Jew and obedient to the System of Humanitarian Education. 130 divine Law, he knew himself as the universal man who determines himself to his own destiny; and while only distinguishing God, as subject, from himself, yet holds fast to the unity of man and God. The system of humanitarian education began to unfold from this principle, which no longer accords the highest place to the natural unity of national individuality, nor to the abstract obedience of the command of God, but to that freedom of the soul which knows itself to be absolute necessity. Christ is not a mere ideal of the thought, but is known as a living member of actual history, whose life, sufferings and death for freedom form the security as to its absolute justification and truth. The Aesthetic, philosophical, and political ideal are all found in the universal nature of the Christian ideal, on which account no one of them appears one-sided in the life of Christ. The principle of Human Freedom excludes neither art, nor science, nor political feeling.

235. In its conception of man the humanitarian education includes both the national divisions and the subjection of all men to the divine law, but it will no longer endure that one should grow into an isolating exclusiveness, and another into a despotism which includes in it somewhat of the accidental. But this principle of humanity and human nature took root so slowly that its presuppositions were repeated within itself and were really conquered in this reproduction. These stages of culture were the Greek, the Roman, and the Protestant churches, and education was metamorphosed to suit the formation of each of these.

— For the sake of brevity we would wish to close with these general definitions; the unfolding of their details is intimately bound up with the his-

tory of politics and of civilization. We shall be contented if we give correctly the general whole. –

236. Within education we can distinguish three epochs: the monkish, the chivalric, and that education which is to fit one for civil life. Each of these endeavored to express all that belonged to humanity as such; but it was only after the recognition of the moral nature of the Family, of Labor, of Culture, and of the conscious equal title of all men to their rights, that this became really possible.

Epoch of Monkish Education. 131

I. The Epoch of Monkish Education.

237. The Greek Church seized the Christian principle still abstractly as deliverance from the world, and therefore, in the education proceeding from it, it arrived only at the negative form, positing the universality of the individual man as the renunciation of self. In the dogmatism of its teaching, as well as in the ascetic severity of its practical conduct, it was a reproduction of the theocratic principle. But when this had assumed the form of national centralization, the Greek Church dispensed with this, and, as far as regards its form, it returned again to the quietism of the Orient.

238. The monkish education is in general identical in all religions, in that, through the egotism of its way of living and the stoicism of its way of thinking, through the separation of its external existence and the mechanism of a thoughtless subjection to a general rule as well as to the special command of superiors, it fosters a spiritual and bodily dulness. The Christian monachism, therefore, as the fulfilment of monachism in general, is at the same time its absolute dissolution, because, in its merely abstracting itself from the world instead of affirmatively conquering it, it contradicts the very principle of Christianity.

239. We must notice as the fundamental error of this whole system, that it does not in free individuality seek to produce the ideal of divine-humanity, but to copy in external reproduction its historical manifestation. Each human being must individually offer up as sacrifice his own individuality. Each biography has its Bethlehem, its Tabor, and its Golgotha.

240. Monachism looks upon freedom from one's self and from the world which Christianity demands only as an abstract renunciation of self, which it seeks to compass, like Buddhism, by the vow of poverty, chastity, and obedience, which must be taken by each individual for all time.

124

— This rejection of property, of marriage, and of self-will, is at the same time the negation of work, of the family, and of responsibility for one's actions. In order to avoid the danger of avarice and covetousness, of sensuality and of nepotism, of error and of guilt, monachism seizes the convenient - Epoch of Monkish Education. 132 way of abstract severance from all the objective world without being able fully to carry out this negation. Monkish Pedagogics must, in consequence, be very particular about an external separation of their disciples from the world, so as to make the work of abstraction from the world easier and more decided. It therefore builds cloisters in the solitude of deserts, in the depth of forests, on the summits of mountains, and surrounds them with high walls having no apertures; and then, so as to carry the isolation of the individual to its farthest possible extreme it constructs, within these cloisters, cells, in imitation of the ancient hermits — a seclusion the immediate consequence of which is the most limitless and most paltry curiosity. —

241. Theoretically the monkish Pedagogics seeks, by means of the greatest possible silence, to place the soul in a state of spiritual immobility, which at last, through the want of all variety of thought, goes over into entire apathy, and antipathy towards all intellectual culture. The principal feature of the practical culture consists in the misapprehension that one should ignore Nature, instead of morally freeing himself from her control. As she, again and again asserts herself, the monkish discipline proceeds to misuse her, and strives through fasting, through sleeplessness, through voluntary self-inflicted pain and martyrdom, not only to subdue the wantonness of the flesh, but to destroy the love of life till it shall become a positive loathing of existence. In and for itself the object of the monkish vow — property, the family, and will — is not immoral. The vow is, on this account, very easy to violate. In order to prevent all temptation to this, monkish Pedagogics invents a system of supervision, partly open, partly secret, which deprives one of all freedom of action, all freshness of thinking and of willing, and all poetry of feeling, by means of the perpetual shadow of spies and informers. The monks are well versed in all police-arts, and the regular succession of the hierarchy spurs them on always to distinguish themselves in them.

242. The gloomy breath of this education penetrated all the relations of the Byzantine State. Even the education of the emperor was infected by it; and in the strife for freedom waged by the modern Greeks against the Turks, the Igumeni Epoch of Chivalric Education. 133 of the cloisters were the real leaders of the insurrection. The independence of individuality, as opposed to monkish abstraction, more or less degenerates into the crude form of soldier and pirate life. And thus it happened that this principle was not left to appear merely as an exception, but to be built up positively into humanity; and this the German world, under the guidance of the Roman Church, undertook to accomplish.

II. The Epoch of Chivalric Education.

243. The Romish Church negated the abstract substantiality of the Greeks through the practical aim which she in her sanctity in works founded, and by means of which she raised up German individuality to the idealism of chivalry, i.e. a free military service in behalf of Christendom.

244. It is evident that the system of monkish education was taken up into this epoch as one of its elements, being modified to conform to it: e.g. the Benedictines were accustomed to labor in agriculture and in the transcribing of books, and this contradicted the idea of monachism, since that in and for itself tends to an absolute forgetfulness of the world and a perfect absence of all activity in the individual. The begging orders were public preachers, and made popular the idea of love and unselfish devotion to others. They labored toward self-education, especially by means of the ideal of the life of Christ; e.g. in Tauler's classical book on the Imitation of Jesus, and in the work of Thomas-à-Kempis which resembles it. Through a fixed contemplative communion with the conception of the Christ who suffered and died for Love, they sought to find content in divine rest and self-abandonment.

245. German chivalry sprang from Feudalism. The education of those pledged to military duty had become confined to practice in the use of arms. The education of the chivalric vassals pursued the same course, refining it gradually through the influence of court society and through poetry, which devoted itself either to the relating of graceful tales which were really works of art, or to the glorification of woman. Girls were brought up without especial care. The boy until he was seven years old remained in the hands of women; Epoch of Chivalric Education. 134 then he became a lad (a young gentleman), and learned the manner of offensive and defensive warfare, on foot and on horseback; between his sixteenth and eighteenth year, through a formal ceremony (the laying on of the sword), he was duly authorized to bear arms. But whatever besides this he might wish to learn was left to his own caprice.

246. In contradistinction to the monkish education, Chivalry placed an infinite value on individuality, and this it expressed in its extreme sensibility to the feeling of honor. Education, on this account, endeavored to foster this reflection of the self upon itself by means of the social isolation in which it placed knighthood. The knight did not delight himself with common possessions, but he sought for him who had been wronged, since with him he could find enjoyment as a conqueror. He did not live in simple marriage, but strove for the piquant pleasure of making the wife of another the lady of his heart, and this often led to moral and physical infidelity. And, finally, the knight did not obey alone the general laws of knightly honor, but he strove, besides, to discover for himself strange things, which he should undertake with his sword, in defiance of all criticism, simply because it pleased his caprice so to do. He sought adventures.

247. The reaction against the innumerable number of fantastic extravagancies arising from chivalry was the idea of the spiritual chivalry which was to unite the cloister and the town, abstract self-denial and military life, separation from the world and the sovereignty of the world — an undeniable advance, but an untenable synthesis which could not prevent the dissolution of chivalry — this chivalry, which, as the rule of the stronger, induced for a long time the destruction of all regular culture founded on principles, and brought a period of absence of all education. In this perversion of chivalry to a grand vagabondism, and even to robbery, noble souls often rushed into ridiculous excesses. This decline of chivalry found its truth in Citizenship, whose education, however, did not, like the πόλις and the civitas of the ancients, limit itself to itself, but, through the presence of the principle of Christianity, accepted the whole circle of humanity as the aim of its culture.

Education of Civil Life — Civil Education. 135

III. The Epoch of Education fitting one for Civil Life.

248. The idea of the State had gradually worked itself up to a higher plane with trade and industry, and found in Protestantism its spiritual confirmation. Protestantism, as the self assurance of the individual that he was directly related to God without any dependence on the mediation of any man, rose to the truth in the autonomy of the soul, and began out of the abstract phantasmagoria of monachism and chivalry to develope Christianity, as the principle of humanitarian education, into concrete actuality. The cities were not merely, in comparison with the clergy and the nobility, the "third estate"; but the citizen who himself managed his commonwealth,

and defended its interests with arms, developed into the citizen of a state which absorbed the clergy and nobility, and the state-citizen found his ultimate ideal in pure Humanity as cognized through reason.

249. The phases of this development are (1) Civil education as such, in which we find chivalric education metamorphosed into the so-called noble, both however being controlled as to education, within Catholicism by Jesuitism, within Protestantism by Pietism. (2) Against this tendency to the church, we find reacting on the one hand the devotion to a study of antiquity, and on the other the friendly alliance to immediate actuality, i.e. with Nature. We can name these periods of Pedagogics those of its ideals of culture. (3) But the truth of all culture must forever remain moral freedom. After Education had arrived at a knowledge of the meaning of Idealism and Realism, it must seize as its absolute aim the moral emancipation of man into Humanity; and it must conform its culture by this aim, since technical dexterity, friendly adroitness, proficiency in the arts, and scientific insight, can attain to their proper rank only through moral purity.

1. Civil Education as such.

250. The one-sidedness of monkish and chivalric education was cancelled by civil education inasmuch as it destroyed the celibacy of the monk and the estrangement of the knight from his family, doing this by means of the inner Civil Education. 136 life of the family; for it substituted, in the place of the negative emptiness of the duty of holiness of the celibate, the positive morality of marriage and the family; while, instead of the abstract poverty and the idleness of the monkish piety and of knighthood, it asserted that property was the object of labor, i.e. it asserted the self-governed morality of civil society and of commerce; and, finally, instead of the servitude of the conscience in unquestioning obedience to the command of others, and instead of the freakish self-sufficiency of the caprice of the knights, it demanded obedience to the laws of the commonwealth as representing his own self-conscious, actualized, practical Reason, in which laws the individual can recognize and acknowledge himself.

— As this civil education left free the sensuous enjoyment, freedom in this was without bounds for a time, until, after men became accustomed to labor and to their freedom of action, the possibility of enjoyment created from within outward a moderation which sumptuary laws and prohibitions of gluttony, drunkenness, &c., could never create from the external side. What the monk inconsistently enjoyed with a bad conscience, the citizen and the clergyman could take possession of as a gift of God. After the first

*millennium of Christianity, when the earth had not, according to the cur-
rent prophecies, been destroyed, and after the great plague in the fourteenth
century, there was felt an immense pleasure in living, which manifested
itself externally in the fifteenth century in delicate wines, dainty food,
great eating of meat, drinking of beer, and, in the domain of dress, in pea-
ked shoes, plumes, golden chains, bells, &c. There was much venison, but,
as yet, no potatoes, tea and coffee, &c. The feeling of men was quarrelsome.
For a more exact painting of the Education of this time, very valuable
authors are Sebastian Brant, Th. Murner, Ulrich von Hutten, Fischart,
and Hans Sachs. Gervinus is almost the only one who has understood how
to make this material useful in its relation to spirit. —*

*251. In contrast with the heaven-seeking of the monks and the sentimen-
tal love-making of the knight, civil education established, as its principle,
Usefulness, which traced out in things their conformity to a proposed end
in order to gain Civil Education. 137 as great a mastery over them as possible. The understanding was trained with all exactness that it might
clearly seize all the circumstances. But since family-life did not allow the
egotism of the individual ever to become as great as was the case with the
monk and the knight, and since the cheer of a sensuous enjoyment in cellar
and kitchen, in clothing and furniture, in common games and in pictures-
que parades, penetrated the whole being with soft pleasure, there was developed with all propriety and sobriety a house-morality, and, with all the
prose of labor, a warm and kindly disposition, which left room for innocent
merriment and roguery, and found, in conformity to religious services, its
serious transfiguration. Beautiful burgher-state, thou wast weakened by
the thirty years' war, and hast been only accidentally preserved sporadical-
ly in Old England and in some places in Germany, only to be at last swept
away by the flood of modern world-pain, political sophistry, and anxiety
for the future!*

*252. The citizen paid special attention to public education, heretofore
wholly dependent upon the church and the cloister; he organized city
schools, whose teachers, it is true, for a long time compassed only accidental culture, and were often employed only for tumultuous and short terms.
The society of the brotherhood of the Hieronymites introduced a better
system of instruction before the close of the fourteenth century, but education had often to be obtained from the so-called travelling scholars (vagan-
tes, bacchantes, scholastici, goliardi). The teachers of the so-called
schol☰exteriores, in distinction from the schools of the cathedral and cloister, were called now locati, then stampuales — in German, Kinder-Meister.*

The institution of German schools soon followed the Latin city schools. In order to remove the anarchy in school matters, the citizens aided the rise of universities by donations and well-invested funds, and sustained the street-singing of the city scholars (currende), an institution which was well-meant, but which often failed of its end because on the one hand it was often misused as a mere means of subsistence, and on the other hand the sense of honor of those to whom it was devoted not unfrequently became, through their manner of living, lowered to humiliation. The defect Civil Education. 138 of the monkish method of instruction became ever more apparent, e.g. the silly tricks of their mnemotechnique, the utter lack of anything which deserved the name of any practical knowledge, &c. The necessity of instruction in the use of arms led to democratic forms. Printing favored the same. Men began to concern themselves about good text-books. Melanchthon was the hero of the Protestant world, and as a pattern was beyond his time. His Dialectics, Rhetoric, Physics, and Ethics, were reprinted innumerable times, commented upon, and imitated. After him Amos Comenius, in the seventeenth century, had the greatest influence through his Didactica Magna and his Janua Reserta. In a narrower sphere, treating of the foundation of Gymnasial Philology, the most noticeable is Sturm of Strasburg. The universities in Catholic countries limited themselves to the Scholastic Philosophy and Theology, together with which we find slowly struggling up the Roman Law and the system of Medicine from Bologna and Salerno. But Protestantism first raised the university to any real universality. Tbingen, K□□sberg, Wittenberg, Jena, Leipzic, Halle, G□□ngen, &c., were the first schools for the study of all sciences, and for their free and productive pursuit.

253. *The Commons, which at first appeared with the clergy and the nobility as the Third Estate, formed an alliance with monarchy, and both together produced a transformation of the chivalric education. Absolutism reduced the knights to mere nobles, to whom it truly conceded the prerogative of appointment as spiritual prelates as well as officers and counsellors of state, but only on the condition of the most complete submission; and then, to satisfy them, it invented the artificial drinking festivals, of a splendid life at court, and a temptingly-impressive sovereignty of beauty. In this condition, the education of the nobles was essentially changed in so far as to cease to be alone military. To the art of war, which moreover was made so very much milder by the invention of fire-arms, must be now added an activity of the mind which could no longer dispense with some knowledge of History, Heraldry, Genealogy, Literature, and Mythology. Since the*

French nation soon enough gave tone to the style of conversation, and after the time of Louis XIV. controlled Civil Education. 139 the politics of the continent, the French language, as conventional and diplomatic, became a constant element in the education of the nobility in all the other countries of Europe.

— Practically the education of the noble endeavored to make the individual quite independent, so that he should, by means of the important quality of an advantageous personal appearance and the prudence of his agreeable behavior, make himself into a ruler of all other men, capable of enjoying his own position, i.e. he should copy in miniature the manners of an absolute sovereign. To this was added an empirical knowledge of men by means of ethical maxims, so that they might discover the weak side of every man, and so be able to outwit him. Mundus vult decipi, ergo decipiatur. According to this, every man had his price. They did not believe in the Nemesis of a divine destiny; on the contrary, disbelief in the higher justice was taught. One must be so elastic as to suit himself to all situations, and, as a caricature of the ancient ataraxy, he must acquire as a second nature a manner perfectly indifferent to all changes, the impassibility of an aristocratic repose, the amphibious sang-froid of the "gentleman." The man in the world as the man of the world sought his ideal in endless dissimulation, and in this, as the flowering of his culture, he took the highest interest. Intrigue, in love as well as in politics, was the soul of the nobleman's existence. —

— They endeavored to complete the refinement of manners by sending the young man away with a travelling tutor. This was very good, but degenerated at last into the mechanism of the foolish travelling of the tourist. The noble was made a foreigner, a stranger to his own country, by means of his abode at Paris or Venice, while the citizen gradually outstripped him in genuine culture. —

254. The education of the citizen as well as that of the noble was taken possession of, in Catholic countries by the Jesuits, in Protestant countries by the Pietists: by the first, with a military strictness; by the second, in a social and effeminate form. Both, however, agreed in destroying individuality, inasmuch as the one degraded man into a will-less machine for executing the commands of others, and the other deadened him in cultivating the feeling of his sinful worthlessness.

Jesuitic Education. 140

(a) Jesuitic Education.

255. Jesuitism combined the maximum of worldly freedom with an appearance of the greatest piety. Proceeding from this stand-point, it devoted itself in education to elegance and showy knowledge, to diplomacy and what was suitable and convenient in morals. To bring the future more into its power, it adapted itself not only to youth in general, but especially to the youth of the nobler classes. To please these, the Jesuits laid great stress upon a fine deportment. In their colleges dancing and fencing were well-taught. They knew how well they should by this course content the noble, who had by preference usurped the name of Education for this technical way of giving formal expression to personality.

— In instruction they developed so exact a mechanism that they gained the reputation of having model school regulations, and even Protestants sent their children to them. From the close of the sixteenth century to the present time they have based their teaching upon the ratio et institutio Studiorum Societatis Jesu of Claudius Aquaviva, and, following that, they distinguish two courses of teaching, a higher and a lower. The lower included nothing but an external knowledge of the Latin language, and some fortuitous knowledge of History, of Antiquities, and of Mythology. The memory was cultivated as a means of keeping down free activity of thought and clearness of judgment. The higher course comprehended Dialectics, Rhetoric, Physics, and Morals. Dialectics appeared in the form of Sophistry. In Rhetoric, they favored the polemical-emphatic style of the African fathers of the Church and their pompous phraseology; in Physics, they stopped with Aristotle, and especially advised the reading of the books De Generatione et Corruptione, and De Cœlo, on which they commented after their fashion; finally, in Morals casuistic skepticism was their central point. They made much of Rhetoric on account of their sermons, giving to it much attention, and introduced especially Declamation. Contriving showy public examinations under the guise of Latin School Comedies, they thus amused the public, disposed them to approval, and at the same time quite innocently practised the pupil in dissimulation. —

— Diplomacy in behavior was made necessary to the Jesuits as well by their strict military discipline as by their system Pietistic Education. 141 of reciprocal mistrust, espionage, and informing. Abstract obedience was a reason for any act of the pupils, and they were freed from all responsibility as to its moral justification. This empirical exact following out of all commands, and refraining from any criticism as to principles, created a moral indifference, and, from the necessity of having consideration for the peculiarities and caprices of the superior on whom all others were dependent,

arose eye-service, and the coldness of isolation sprang from the necessity which each felt of being on his guard against every other as against a tale-bearer. The most deliberate hypocrisy and pleasure in intrigue merely for the sake of intrigue — this most refined poison of moral corruption — were the result. Jesuitism had not only an interest in the material profit, which, when it had corrupted souls, fell to its share, but it also had an interest in the process of corruption. With absolute indifference as to the idea of morality, and absolute indifference as to the moral quality of the means used to attain its end, it rejoiced in the superiority of secrecy, of the accomplished and calculating understanding, and in deceiving the credulous by means of its graceful, seemingly-perfect, moral language. —

— It is not necessary to speak here of the morality of the Order. It is sufficiently recognized as the contradiction, that the idea of morality insists upon the eternal necessity of every deed, but that in the realizing of the action all determinations should be made relative and should vary with the circumstances. As to discipline, they were always guided by their fundamental principle, that body and soul, as in and for themselves one, could vicariously suffer for each other. Thus penitence and contrition were transformed into a perfect materialism of outward actions, and hence arose the punishments of the Order, in which fasting, scourging, imprisonment, mortification, and death, were formed into a mechanical artificial system. —

(b) Pietistic Education.

256. Jesuitism would make machines of man, Pietism would dissolve him in the feeling of his sinfulness: either would destroy his individuality. Pietism proceeded from the principle of Protestantism, as, in the place of the Catholic Pelagianism with its sanctification by works, it offered justication Pietistic Education. 142 *by faith alone. In its tendency to internality was its just claim. It would have even the letters of the Bible translated into the vivacity of sentiment. But in its execution it fell into the error of one-sidedness in that it placed, instead of the actuality of the spirit and its freedom, the confusion of a limited personality, placing in its stead the personality of Christ in an external manner, and thus brought back into the very midst of Protestantism the principle of monachism — an abstract renunciation of the world. Since Protestantism has destroyed the idea of the cloister, it could produce estrangement from the world only by exciting public opinion against such elements of society and culture which it stigmatized as worldly for its members, e.g. card-playing, dancing, the theatre, &c. Thus it became negatively dependent upon works; for since its follo-*

wers remained in reciprocal action with the world, so that the temptation to backsliding was a permanent one, it must watch over them, exercise an indispensable moral-police control over them, and thus, by the suspicion of each other which was involved, take up into itself the Jesuitical practice, although in a very mild and affectionate way. Instead of the forbidden secrecy of the cloister, it organized a separate company, which we, in its regularly constituted assembly, call a conventicle. Instead of the cowl, it put on its youth a dress like that of the world, but scant and ashen-colored; it substituted for the tonsure closely-cut hair and shaven beard, and it often went beyond the obedience of the monks in its expression of pining humility and prudish composure. Education within such a circle could not well recognize nature and history as manifestations of God, but it must consider them to be limitations to their union with God, from which death can first then completely release them. The soul which knew that its home could be found only in the future world, must feel itself to be a stranger upon the earth, and from such an opinion there must arise an indifference and even a contempt for science and art, as well as an aversion for a life of active labor, though an unwilling and forced tribute might be paid to it. Philosophy especially was to be shunned as dangerous. Bible lectures, the catechism and the hymn-book, were the one thing needful to the "poor in spirit." Religious poetry and music were, of all the arts, the only ones deserving of any cultivation. The The Ideal of Culture. – The Humanitarian Ideal. 143 education of Pietism endeavored, by means of a carefully arranged series of representations, to create in its disciples the feeling of their absolute nothingness, vileness, godlessness, and abandonment by God, in order to displace the torment of despair as to themselves and the world by a warm, dramatic, and living relation to Christ – a relation in which all the Eroticism of the mystical passion of the begging-friars was renewed in a somewhat milder form and with a strong tendency to a sentimental sweetishness.

2. The Ideal of Culture.

257. Civil Education arose from the recognition of marriage and the family, of labor and enjoyment, of the equality of all before the Law, and of the duty of self-determination. Jesuitism in the Catholic world and Pietism in the Protestant were the reaction against this recognition – a return into the abstract asceticism of the middle ages, not however in its purity, but mixed with some regard for worldly possessions. In opposition to this reaction the commonwealth produced another, in which it undertook to deliver individuality by means of a reversed alienation. On the one hand, it absor-

bed itself in the conception of the Greek-Roman world. In the practical interests of the present, it externalized man in a past which held to the present no immediate relation, or it externalized him in the affairs which were to serve him as means of his comfort and enjoyment; it created an abstract idealism — a reproduction of the old view of the world — or an abstract Realism in a high appreciation of things which should be considered of value only as a means. In one direction, Individuality proceeded towards a dead nationality; in the other, towards an unlimited world-commonwealth. In one case, the ideal was the æsthetic republicanism of the Greeks; in the other, the utilitarian cosmopolitanism of the Romans. But, in considering the given circumstances, both united in the feeling of humanity, with its reconciliatory and pitying gentleness toward the beggar or the criminal.

(a) The Humanitarian Ideal.

258. The Oriental-theocratic education is immanent in Christian education through the Bible. Through the mediation of the Greek and Roman churches the views of the ancient The Philanthropic Ideal. 144 world were subsumed but not entirely subdued. To accomplish this was the problem of humanitarian education. It aimed to teach the Latin and Greek languages, expecting thus to secure the action of a purely humane disposition. The Greeks and Romans being sharply marked nationalities, how could one cherish such expectations? It was possible only relatively in contradiction, partly to a provincial population from whom all genuine political sense had departed, partly to a church limited by a confessional, to which the idea of humanity as such had become almost lost in dogmatic fault-findings. The spirit was refreshed in the first by the contemplation of the pure patriotism of the ancients, and in the second by the discovery of Reason among the heathen. In contrast to formlessness distracted by the want of all ideal of culture of provincialism and dogmatic confusions, we find the power of representation of ancient art. The so-called uselessness of learning dead languages imparted to the mind, it knew not how, an ideal drift. The very fact that it could not find immediate profit in its knowledge gave it the consciousness of a higher value than material profit. The ideal of the Humanities was the truth to Nature which was found in the thought-painters of the ancient world. The study of language merely with regard to its form, must lead one involuntarily to the actual seizing of its content. The Latin schools were fashioned into Gymnasia, and the universities contained not merely professors of Eloquence, but also teachers of Philology.

(b) The Philanthropic Ideal.

259. The humanitarian tendency reached its extreme in the abstract forgetting of the present, and the omitting to notice its just claim. Man discovered at last that he was not at home with himself in Rome and Athens. He spoke and wrote Latin, if not like Cicero, at least like Muretius, but he often found himself awkward in expressing his meaning in his mothertongue. He was often very learned, but he lacked judgment. He was filled with enthusiasm for the republicanism of Greece and Rome, and yet at the same time was himself exceedingly servile to his excellent and august lords. Against this gradual deadening of active individuality, the result of a perverted study of the classics, we find now reacting The Philanthropic Ideal. 145 the education of enlightenment, which we generally call the philanthropic. It sought to make men friendly to the immediate course of the world. It placed over against the learning of the ancient languages for their own sake, the acquisition of the more needful branches of Mathematics, Physics, Geography, History, and the modern languages, calling these the real studies. Nevertheless it often retained the instruction in the Latin language because the Romance languages have sprung from it, and because, through its long domination, the universal terminology of Science, Art, and Law, is rooted in it. Philanthropy desired to develope the social side of its disciple through an abstract of practical knowledge and personal accomplishments, and to lead him again, in opposition to the hermit-like sedentary life of the book-pedant, out into the fields and the woods. It desired to imitate life even in its method, and to instruct pleasantly in the way of play or by dialogue. It would add to the simple letters and names the contemplation of the object itself, or at least of its representation by pictures; and in this direction, in the conversation-literature which it prepared for children, it sometimes fell into childishness. It performed a great service when it gave to the body its due, and introduced simple, natural dress, bathing, gymnastics, pedestrian excursions, and a hardening against the influences of wind and weather. As this Pedagogics, so friendly to children, deemed that it could not soon enough begin to honor them as citizens of the world, it was guilty in general of the error of presupposing as already finished in its children much that it itself should have gradually developed; and as it wished to educate the European as such, or rather man as such, it came into an indifference concerning the concrete distinctions of nationality and religion. It coincided with the philologists in placing, in a concealed way, Socrates above Christ, because he had worked no miracles, and taught only morality. In such a dead cosmopolitanism, individuality disappeared in the indeterminateness of a general humanity, and saw itself forced to agree with the humanistic education in proclaiming the truth of Nature as the pedagogical ideal, with the distinction, that while Humanism believed this ideal realized in the Greeks and Romans, Philanthropism found itself The Philanthropic Ideal. 146 *compelled to presuppose an abstract notion, and often manifested a not unjustifiable pleasure in recognizing in the Indians of North America, or of Otaheite, the genuine man of nature. Philosophy first raised these conceptions to the idea of the State, which fashioned the cognition of Reason and of the reform which follows from its idea, into an organic element in itself.*

— The course which the developing of the philanthropic ideal has taken is as follows: (1) Rousseau in his writings, Emile and the Nouvelle Heloise, first preached the evangel of Natural Education, the abstraction from History, the negation of existing culture, and the return to the simplicity and innocence of nature. Although he often himself testified in his experience his own proneness to evil in a very discouraging way, he fixed as an almost unlimited axiom in French and German Pedagogics his principal maxim, that man is by nature good. (2) The reformatory ideas of Rousseau met with only a very infrequent and sporadic introduction among the Romanic nations, because among them education was too dependent on the church, and retained its cloister-like seclusion in seminaries, colleges, &c. In Germany, on the contrary, it was actualized, and the Philanthropia, established by Basedow in Dessau, Brunswick, and Schnepfenthal, made experiments, which nevertheless very soon departed somewhat from the ultraism of Basedow and had very excellent results. (3) Humanity existed in concreto only in the form of nations. The French nation, in their revolution, tried the experiment of abstracting from their history, of levelling all distinctions of culture, of enthroning a despotism of Reason, and of organizing itself as humanity, pure and simple. The event showed the impossibility of such a beginning. The national energy, the historical impulse, the love of art and science, came forth from the midst of the revolutionary abstraction, which was opposed to them, only the more vigorously. The grande nation, their grande arm{#/i>, and gloire — that is to say, for France — absorbed all the humanitarian phases. In Germany the philanthropic circle of education was limited to the higher ranks. There was no exclusiveness in the Philanthropia, for there nobles and citizens, Catholics and Protestants, Russians and Swiss, were mingled; but these were always the children of wealthy The Philanthropic Ideal. 147 *families, and to these the plan of education was adapted. Then appeared Pestalozzi and directed education also to the lower classes of society — those which are called, not without something approaching to a derogatory meaning, the people. From this*

*time dates popular education, the effort for the intellectual and moral eleva-
tion of the hitherto neglected atomistic human being of the non-property-
holding multitude. There shall in future be no dirty, hungry, ignorant,
awkward, thankless, and will-less mass, devoted alone to an animal existence. We can never rid ourselves of the lower classes by having the
wealthy give something, or even their all, to the poor, so as to have no
property themselves; but we can rid ourselves of it in the sense that the
possibility of culture and independent self-support shall be open to every
one, because he is a human being and a citizen of the commonwealth. Ignorance and rudeness and the vice which springs from them, and the malevo-
lent frame of mind against the human race, which are bound up with crime — these shall disappear. Education shall train man to self-conscious
obedience to law, as well as to kindly feeling towards the erring, and to an
effort not merely for their removal but for their improvement. But the more
Pestalozzi endeavored to realize his ideal of human dignity, the more he
comprehended that the isolated power of a private man could not attain it,
but that the nation itself must make their own education their first business. Fichte by his lectures first made the German nation fully accept these
thoughts, and Prussia was the first state which, by her public schools and
her conscious preparation for defence, broke the path for National Education; while among the Romanic nations, in spite of their more elaborate
political formalism, it still depends partly upon the church and partly upon
the accident of private enterprise. Pestalozzi also laid a foundation for a
national pedagogical literature by his story of Leonard and Gertrude. This
book appeared at first in 1784, i.e. in the same year in which Schiller's
Robbers and Kant's Critique of Pure Reason announced a new phase in the
Drama and in Philosophy. —*

*— The incarnation of God, which was, up to the time of the Reformation,
an esoteric mystery of the Church, has since then become continually more
and more an exoteric problem of the State. —*

Free Education. 148

3. Free Education.

*260. The ideal of culture of the humanitarian and the philanthropic edu-
cation was taken up into the conception of an education which recognizes
the Family, social caste, the Nation, and Religion, as positive elements of
the practical spirit, but which will know each of these as determined from
within through the idea of humanity, and laid open for reciprocal dialectic
with the rest. Physical development shall become the subject of a national*

*system of gymnastics fashioned for use, and including in itself the know-
ledge of the use of arms. Instruction shall, in respect to the general encyc-
lop楝c culture, be the same for all, and parallel to this shall run a system of
special schools to prepare for the special avocations of life. The method of
instruction shall be the simple representation of the special idea of the
subject, and no longer the formal breadth of an acquaintance with many
subjects which may find outside the school its opportunity, but within it
has no meaning except as the history of a science or an art. Moral culture
must be combined with family affection and the knowledge of the laws of
the commonwealth, so that the dissension between individual morality and
objective legality may ever more and more disappear. Education shall,
without estranging the individual from the internality of the family, accustom him more and more to public life, because criticism of this is the
only thing which can prevent the cynicism of private life, the half-ness of
knowledge and will, and the spirit of caste, which has so extensively
prevailed. The individual shall be educated into a self-consciousness of the
essential equality and freedom of all men, so that he shall recognize and
acknowledge himself in each one and in all. But this essential and solid
unity of all men shall not evaporate into the insipidity of a humanity without distinctions, but instead it shall realize the form of a determinate
individuality and nationality, and shall enlighten the idiosyncrasy of its
nation into a broad humanity. The unrestricted striving after Beauty,
Truth, and Freedom, actually through its own strength and immediately,
not merely mediately through ecclesiastical consecration, will become Religion.*

*The Education of the State must rise to a preparation for the unfettered
activity of self-conscious Humanity.*

THE SCIENCE OF EDUCATION.

A PARAPHRASE OF DR. KARL ROSEN-
KRANZ'S
PAEDAGOGIK ALS SYSTEM.

BY ANNA C. BRACKETT.

ST. LOUIS:
G. I. JONES AND COMPANY.
1878.

Entered according to Act of Congress, in the year 1878, by
WILLIAM T. HARRIS,
In the office of the Librarian of Congress, at Washington.

PREFACE.

The translation of "Pedagogics as a System" was prepared and published five years ago. The wide demand for it that has made itself known since that time, especially in normal schools, has proved the value of such works in the domain of education. At the same time, the difficulty the students have always found in its use — a difficulty inseparable from any translation of a German metaphysical treatise — has led us to the conviction that a paraphrase into a more easily understood form is a necessity, if the thought of Rosenkranz is to be appropriated by the very class who are most in need of it. As was remarked in the preface to the translation, we have in English no other work of similar size which contains so much that is valuable to those engaged in the work of education. It is no compendium of rules or formulas, but rather a systematic, logical treatment of the subject, in which the attention is, as it were, concentrated upon the whole problem of education, while that problem is allowed to work itself out before us. To paraphrase the text — or, rather, to translate it from the metaphysical language in which it at present appears into a language more easy of comprehension — without losing the real significance of the statements, is the task which is here undertaken. Free illustrations and suggestions have been interwoven to give point and application to the thoughts and principles stated. This translation, or paraphrase, follows the paragraphs of the original and of the first translation. The analysis of the whole work, as it appeared in the original translation, is appended at the end of the "Introduction," as a guide to the student.

THE SCIENCE OF EDUCATION.

INTRODUCTION.

140

1. The science of Pedagogics may be called a secondary science, inasmuch as it derives its principles from others. In this respect it differs from Mathematics, which is independent. As it concerns the development of the human intelligence, it must wait upon Psychology for an understanding of that upon which it is to operate, and, as its means are to be sciences and arts, it must wait upon them for a knowledge of its materials. The science of Medicine, in like manner, is dependent on the sciences of Biology, Chemistry, Physics, etc. Moreover, as Medicine may have to deal with a healthy or unhealthy body, and may have it for its province to preserve or restore health, to assist a natural process (as in the case of a broken bone), or to destroy an unnatural one (as in the case of the removal of a tumor), the same variety of work is imposed upon Education. 1

2. Since the rules of Pedagogics must be extremely flexible, so that they may be adapted to the great variety of minds, and since an infinite variety of circumstances may arise in their application, we find, as we should expect, in all educational literature room for widely differing opinions and the wildest theories; these numerous theories, each of which 6 may have a strong influence for a season, only to be overthrown and replaced by others. 2 It must be acknowledged that educational literature, as such, is not of a high order. It has its cant like religious literature. Many of its faults, however, are the result of honest effort, on the part of teachers, to remedy existing defects, and the authors are, therefore, not harshly to be blamed. It is also to be remembered that the habit of giving reproof and advice is one fastened in them by the daily necessity of their professional work. 3

3. As the position of the teacher has ceased to be undervalued, there has been an additional impetus given to self-glorification on his part, and this also — in connection with the fact that schools are no longer isolated as of old, but subject to constant comparison and competition — leads to much careless theorizing among its teachers, especially in the literary field.

4. Pedagogics, because it deals with the human spirit, belongs, in a general classification of the sciences, to the philosophy of spirit, and in the philosophy of spirit it must be classified under the practical, and not the merely theoretical, division. For its problem is not merely to comprehend the nature of that with which it has to deal, the human spirit — its problem is not merely to influence one mind (that of the pupil) by another (that of the teacher) — but to influence it in such a way as to produce the mental freedom of the pupil. The problem is, therefore, not so much to obtain performed works as to excite mental activity. A creative process is required. The pupil is to be forced to go in certain beaten tracks, and yet he is to be so forced to go in these that he shall go of his own freewill. All teaching which does not leave the mind of the pupil free is unworthy of the name. It is true that the teacher must understand the nature of mind, as 7 he is to deal with mind, but when he has done this he has still his main principle of action unsolved; for the question is, knowing the nature of the mind, How shall he incite it to action, already predetermined in his own mind, without depriving the mind of the pupil of its own free action? How shall he restrain and guide, and yet not enslave?

If, in classifying all sciences, as suggested at the beginning of this section, we should subdivide the practical division of the Philosophy of Spirit, which might be called Ethics, one could find a place for Pedagogics under some one of the grades of Ethics. The education which the child receives through the influence of family life lies at the basis of all other teaching, and what the child learns of life, its duties, and possibilities, in its own home, forms the foundation for all after-work. On the life of the family, then, as a presupposition, all systems of Education must be built. In other words, the school must not attempt to initiate the child into the knowledge of the world — it must not assume the care of its first training; that it must leave to the family. 4 But the science of Pedagogics does not, as a science, properly concern itself with the family education, or with that point of the child's life which is dominated by the family influence. That is education, in a certain sense, without doubt, but it does not properly belong to a science of Pedagogics. But, on the other hand, it must be remembered that this science, as here expounded, presupposes a previous family life in the human being with whom it has to deal.

5. Education as a science will present the necessary and universal principles on which it is based; Education as an art will consist in the practical realization of these in the teacher's work in special places, under special circumstances, and with special pupils. In the skillful application of the principles of the science to the actual demands of the art lies the opportunity for the educator to prove himself a creative artist; and it is in the difficulty involved in this practical 8 work that the interest and charm of the educator's work consists.

The teacher must thus adapt himself to the pupil. But, in doing so, he must have a care that he do not carry this adaptation to such a degree as to imply that the pupil is not to change; and he must see to it, also, that the pupil shall always be worked upon by the matter which he is considering, and not too much by the personal influence of the teacher through whom he receives it. 5

6. The utmost care is necessary lest experiments which have proved successful in certain cases should be generalized into rules, and a formal, dead creed, so to speak, should be adopted. All professional experiences are valuable as material on which to base new conclusions and to make new plans, but only for that use. Unless the day's work is, every day, a new creation, a fatal error has been made.

7. Pedagogics as a science must consider Education —

(1) In its general idea;
(2) In its different phases;
(3) In the special systems arising from this general idea, acting under special circumstances at special times. 6

8. With regard to the First Part, we remark that by Education, in its general idea, we do not mean any mere history of Pedagogics, nor can any history of Pedagogics be substituted for a systematic exposition of the underlying idea.

9. The second division considers Education under three heads — as physical, intellectual, and moral — and forms, generally, the principal part of all pedagogical treatises.

In this part lies the greatest difficulty as to exact limitation. The ideas on these divisions are often undefined and apt to be confounded, and the detail of which they are capable is almost unlimited, for we might, under this head, speak 9 of all kinds of special schools, such as those for war, art, mining, etc.

10. In the Third Part we consider the different realizations of the one general idea of Pedagogics as it has developed itself under different circumstances and in different ages of the world.

The general idea is forced into different phases by the varying physical, intellectual, and moral conditions of men. The result is the different systems, as shown in the analysis. The general idea is one. The view of the end to be obtained determines in each case the actualization of this idea. Hence the different systems of Education are each determined by the stand-point from which the general ideal is viewed. Proceeding in this manner, it might be possible to construct a history of Pedagogics, □riori, without reference to actual history, since all the possible systems might be inferred from the possible definite number of points of view.

Each lower stand-point will lead to a higher, but it will not be lost in it. Thus, where Education, for the sake of the nation, 7 merges into the Educa-

tion based on Christianity, the form is not thereby destroyed, but, rather, in the transition first attains its full realization. The systems of Education which were based on the idea of the nation had, in the fullness of time, outgrown their own limits, and needed a new form in order to contain their own true idea. The idea of the nation, as the highest principle, gives way for that of Christianity. A new life came to the old idea in what at first seemed to be its destruction. The idea of the nation was born again, and not destroyed, in Christianity.

11. The final system, so far, is that of the present time, which thus is itself the fruit of all the past systems, as well as the seed of all systems that are to be. The science of Pedagogics, in the consideration of the system of the present, thus again finds embodied the general idea of education, and thus returns upon itself to the point from whence it set out. In the First and Second Parts there is already given the idea which dominates the system found thus necessarily existing in the present.

10

PART I. Inits General Idea.	Its Nature. Its Form. Its Limits.			
PART II. Inits Special Elements.	Physical. Intellectual. Moral.			
PART III. Inits Particular Systems.	National.	Passive.	Family Caste Monkish	China. India. Thibet.
		Active.	Military. Priestly Industrial	Persia. Egypt. Phœnicia.
		Individual.	Ythetic Practical Abstract Individual	Greece. Rome. Northern Barbarian
	Theocratic.			Jews.

Education

Monkish.

Chivalric.

Humanitarian.   For Civil   ForSpecial Jesuitic.
                Life.   Callings.   Pietistic.

                              To achie-   TheHuman
                              ve
                              an Ideal   ThePhilant
                              ofCulture. Movement.

For Free Citizensip.

FIRST PART.
The General Idea of Education.

12. A full treatment of Pedagogics must distinguish –
(1) The nature of Education;
(2) The form of Education;
(3) The limits of Education.

I. – The Nature of Education.

13. The nature of Education is determined by the nature of mind, the distinguishing mark of which is that it can be developed only from within, and by its own activity. Mind is essentially free – i.e , it has the capacity for freedom – but it cannot be said to possess freedom till it has obtained it by its own voluntary effort. Till then it cannot be truly said to be free. Education consists in enabling a human being to take possession of, and to develop himself by, his own efforts, and the work of the educator cannot be said to be done in any sense where this is not accomplished. In general, we may say that the work of education consists in leading to a full development of all the inherent powers of the mind, and that its work is done when, in this way, the mind has attained perfect freedom, or the state in which alone it can be said to be truly itself. 8

The isolated human being can never become truly man. If such human beings (like the wild girl of the forest of Ardennes) have been found, they have only proved to us that reciprocal action with our fellow beings is necessary for the development 12 of our powers. Caspar Hauser, in his subterranean prison, will serve as an example of what man would be without men. One might say that this fact is typified by the first cry of the newly-born child. It is as if the first expression of its seemingly indepen-

dent life were a cry for help from others. On the side of nature the human being is at first quite helpless.

14. Man is, therefore, the only proper object of education. It is true that we speak of the education of plants and of animals, but we instinctively apply other terms when we do so, for we say "raising" plants, and "training" animals. When we "train" or "break" an animal, it is true that we do, by pain or pleasure, lead him into an exercise of a new activity. But the difference between this and Education consists in the fact that, though he possessed capacity, yet by no amount of association with his kind would he ever have acquired this new development. It is as if we impress upon his plastic nature the imprint of our loftier nature, which imprint he takes mechanically, and does not himself recognize it as his own internal nature. We train him for our recognition, not for his own. But, on the contrary, when we educate a human being, we only excite him to create for himself, and out of himself, that for which he would most earnestly strive had he any appreciation of it beforehand, and in proportion as he does appreciate it he recognizes it joyfully as a part of himself, as his own inheritance, which he appropriates with a knowledge that it is his, or, rather, is a part of his own nature. He who speaks of "raising" human beings uses language which belongs only to the slave-dealer, to whom human beings are only cattle for labor, and whose property increases in value with the number.

Are there no school-rooms where Education has ceased to have any meaning, and where physical pain is made to produce its only possible result — a mechanical, external repetition? The school-rooms where the creative word — the only thing which can influence the mind — has ceased to be used as the means are only plantations, where human beings are degraded to the position of lower animals.

15. When we speak of the Education of the human 13 race, we mean the gradual growth of the nations of the earth, as a whole, towards the realization of self-conscious freedom. Divine Providence is the teacher here. The means by which the development is effected are the various circumstances and actions of the different races of men, and the pupils are the nations. The unfolding of this great Education is generally treated of under the head of Philosophy of History.

16. Education, however, in a more restricted sense, has to do with the shaping of the individual. Each one of us is to be educated by the laws of physical nature — by the relations into which we come with the national life, in its laws, customs, etc., and by the circumstances which daily surround us. By the force of these we find our arbitrary will hemmed in, modified, and forced to take new channels and forms. We are too often unmindful of the power with which these forces are daily and hourly educating us — i.e., calling out our possibilities into real existence. If we set up our will in opposition to either of these; if we act in opposition to the laws of nature; if we seriously offend the laws, or even the customs, of the people among whom we live; or if we despise our individual lot, we do so only to find ourselves crushed in the encounter. We only learn the impotence of the individual against these mighty powers; and that discovery is, of itself, a part of our education. It is sometimes only by such severe means that God is revealed to the man who persistently misunderstands and defies His creation. All suffering brought on ourselves by our own violation of laws, whether natural, ethical, or divine, must be, however, thus recognized as the richest blessing. We do not mean to say that it is never allowable for a man, in obedience to the highest laws of his spiritual being, to break away from the fetters of nature — to offend the ethical sense of his own people, or to struggle against the might of destiny. Reformers and martyrs would be examples of such, and our remarks above do not apply to them, but to the perverse, the frivolous, and the conceited; to those who are seeking in their action, not the undoubted will of God, but their own individual will or caprice.

17. But we generally use the word Education in a still 14 narrower sense than either of these, for we mean by it the working of one individual mind upon or within another in some definite and premeditated way, so as to fit the pupil for life generally, or for some special pursuit. For this end the educator must be relatively finished in his own education, and the pupil must possess confidence in him, or docility. He must be teachable. That the work be successful, demands the very highest degree of talent, knowledge, skill, and prudence; and any development is impossible if a well-founded authority be wanting in the educator, or docility on the part of the pupil.

Education, in this narrowest and technical sense, is an outgrowth of city or urban life. As long as men do not congregate in large cities, the three forces spoken of in 16 — i.e., the forces of nature, national customs, and circumstances — will be left to perform most of the work of Education; but, in modern city life, the great complication of events, the uncertainty in the results — though careful forethought has been used — the immense development of individuality, and the pressing need of various information, break the power of custom, and render a different method necessary. The larger the city is, the more free is the individual in it from the restraints of customs, the less subjected to curious criticism, and the more able is he to give play to his own idiosyncrasies. This, however, is a freedom which needs the counterpoise of a more exact training in conventionalities, if we would not have it dangerous. Hence the rapid multiplication of educational institutions and systems in modern times (one chief characteristic of which is the development of urban life). The ideal Telemachus of Fenelon differs very much from the real Telemachus of history. Fenelon proposed an education which trained a youth to reflect, and to guide himself by reason. The Telemachus of the heroic age followed the customs ("use and wont") of his times with na جمي obedience. The systems of Education once sufficient do not serve the needs of modern life, any more than the defenses once sufficient against hostile armies are sufficient against the new weapons adopted by modern warfare.

15

18. The problem with which modern Education has to deal may be said, in general terms, to be the development in the individual soul of the indwelling Reason, both practical (as will) and theoretical (as intellect). To make a child good is only a part of Education; we have also to develop his intelligence. The sciences of Ethics and Education are not the same. Again, we must not forget that no pupil is simply a human being, like every other human being; he is also an individual, and thus differs from every other one of the race. This is a point which must never be lost sight of by the educator. Human beings may be — nay, must be — educated in company, but they cannot be educated simply in the mass.

19. Education is to lead the pupil by a graded series of exercises, previously arranged and prescribed by the educator, to a definite end. But these exercises must take on a peculiar form for each particular pupil under the special circumstances present. Hasty and inconsiderate work may, by chance, accomplish much; but no work which is not systematic can advance and fashion him in conformity with his tenure, and such alone is to be called Education; for Education implies both a comprehension of the end to be attained and of the means necessary to compass that end.

20. Culture, however, means more and more every year; and, as the sum total of knowledge increases for mankind, it becomes necessary, in order to be a master in any one line, to devote one's self almost exclusively to that. Hence arises, for the teacher, the difficulty of preserving the unity and wholeness which are essential to a complete man. The principle of division of labor comes in. He who is a teacher by profession becomes one-sided in his views; and, as teaching divides and subdivides into specialities, this abnormal one-sideness tends more and more to appear. Here we find a parallelism in the profession of Medicine, with a corresponding danger of narrowness; for that, too, is in a process of constant specialization, and the physician who treats nervous diseases is likely to be of the opinion that all trouble arises from that part of the organism, or, at least, that all remedies should 16 be applied there. This tendency to one-sideness is inseparable from the progress of civilization and that of science and arts. It contains, nevertheless, a danger of which no teacher should be unwarned. An illustration is furnished by the microscope or telescope; a higher power of the instrument implies a narrower field of view. To concentrate our observation upon one point implies the shutting out of others This difficulty with the teacher creates one for the pupil.

In this view one might be inclined to judge that the life of the savage as compared with that of civilized man, or that of a member of a rural community as compared with that of an inhabitant of a city, were the more to be desired. The savage has his hut, his family, his cocoa-palm, his weapons, his passions; he fishes, hunts, amuses himself, adorns himself, and enjoys the consciousness that he is the center of a little world, while the denizen of a city must often acknowledge that he is, so to speak, only one wheel of a gigantic machine. Is the life of the savage, therefore, more favorable to human development? The characteristic idea of modern civilization is: The development of the individual as the end for which the State exists. The great empires of Persia, Egypt, and India, wherein the individual was of value only as he ministered to the strength of the State, have given way to the modern nations, where individual freedom is pushed so far that the State seems only an instrument for the good of the individual. From being the supreme end of the individual, the State has become the means for his advancement into freedom; and with this very exaltation of the value of the mere individual over the State, as such, there is inseparably connected the seeming destruction of the wholeness of the individual man. But the union of State and individual, which was in ancient times merely mechanical, has now become a living process, in which constant interaction gives rise to all the intellectual life of modern civilization.

21. The work of Education being thus necessarily split up, we have the distinction between general and special schools. The work of the former is to give general development — what is considered essential for all men; that of the 17 latter, to prepare for special callings. The former should furnish a basis for the latter — i.e., the College should precede the Medical School, etc., and the High School the Normal. In the United States, owing to many causes, this is unfortunately not the case.

The difference between city and country life is important here. The teacher in a country school, and, still more, the private tutor or governess, must be able to teach many more things than the teacher in a graded school in the city, or the professor in a college or university. The danger on the one side is of superficiality, on the other of narrowness.

22. The Education of any individual can be only relatively finished. His possibilities are infinite. His actual realization of those possibilities must always remain far behind. The latter can only approximate to the former. It can never reach them. The term "finishing an education" needs, therefore, some definition; for, as a technical term, it has undoubtedly a meaning. An immortal soul can never complete its development; for, in so doing, it would give the lie to its own nature. We cannot speak properly, however, of educating an idiot. Such an unfortunate has no power of generalization, and no conscious personality. We can train him mechanically, but we cannot educate him. This will help to illustrate the difference, spoken of in 14, between Education and Mechanical training.

We obtain astonishing results, it is true, in our schools for idiots, and yet we cannot fail to perceive that, after all, we have only an external result. We produce a mechanical performance of duties, and yet there seems to be no actual mental growth. It is an exogenous, and not an endogenous, growth, to use the language of Botany. 9 Continual repetition, under the most gentle patience, renders the movements easy, but, after all, they are only automatic, or what the physicians call reflex.

We have the same result produced in a less degree when we 18 attempt to teach an intelligent child something which is beyond his active comprehension. A child may be taught to do or say almost anything by patient training, but, if what he is to say is beyond the power of his mental comprehension, and hence of his active assimilation, we are only training him as we train an animal (14), and not educating him. We call such recitations parrot recitations, and, by our use of the word, express exactly in what position the pupils are placed. An idiot is only a case of permanently arrested development. What in the intelligent child is a passing phase is for the idiot a fixed state. We have idiots of all grades, as we have children of all ages.

The above observations must not be taken to mean that children should never be taught to perform operations in arithmetic which they do not, in cant phrase, "perfectly understand," or to learn poetry whose whole meaning they cannot fathom. Into this error many teachers have fallen.

There can be no more profitable study for a teacher than to visit one of these numerous idiot schools. He finds the alphabet of his professional work there. As the philologist learns of the formation and growth of language by examining, not the perfectly formed languages, but the dialects of savage tribes, so with the teacher. In like manner more insight into the philosophy of teaching and of the nature of the mind can be acquired by teaching a class of children to read than in any other grade of work.

II. — The Form of Education.

23. The general form of Education follows from the nature of mind. Mind is nothing but what it itself creates out of its own activity. It is, at first, mind as undeveloped or unconscious (in the main); but, secondly, it acquires the power of examining its own action, of considering itself as an object of attention, as if it were a quite foreign thing — i.e., it reflects (in this stage it is really ignorant that it is studying its own nature); and, finally, it becomes conscious that this, which it had been examining, and of whose existence it is conscious, is its 19 own self: It attains self-consciousness. It is through this estrangement from itself, given back to itself again and restored to unity, but it is no longer a simple, unconscious unity. In this third state only can it be said to be free — i.e., to possess itself. Education cannot create; it can only help to develop into reality the previously-existent possibility; it can only help to bring forth to light the hidden life.

24. All culture, in whatever line, must pass through these two stages of estrangement and of reunion; the reunion being not of two different things, but the recognition of itself by thought, and its acceptance of itself as itself. And the more complete is the estrangement — i.e., the more perfectly can the thought be made to view itself as a somewhat entirely foreign to itself, to look upon it as a different and independent somewhat — the more complete and perfect will be its union with and acceptance of its object as one with itself when the recognition does finally take place. Through culture we are led to this conscious possession of our own thought. Plato gives to the feeling, with which knowledge must necessarily begin, the name of wonder. But wonder is not knowledge; it is only the first step towards it. It is the half-terrified attention which the mind fixes on an object, and the half-

terror would be impossible did it not dimly forebode that it was something of its own nature at which it was looking. The child delights in stories of the far-off, the strange, and the wonderful. It is as if they hoped to find in these some solution to themselves — a solution which they have, as it were, asked in vain of familiar scenes and objects. Their craving for such is the proof of how far their nature transcends all its known conditions. They are like adventurous explorers who push out to unknown regions in hopes of finding the freedom and wealth which lies only within themselves. They want to be told about things which they never saw, such as terrible con-flagrations, banditti life, wild animals, gray old ruins, Robinson Crusoes on far-off, happy islands. They are irresistibly attracted by whatever is highly colored and dazzlingly lighted. The child prefers the story of Sinbad the Sailor to any tales of his own home and nation, because mind has this necessity 20 of getting, as it were, outside of itself so as to obtain a view of itself. As the child grows to youth he is, from the same reasons, desirous of traveling.

25. Work may be defined as the activity of the mind in a conscious con-centration on, and absorption in, some object, with the purpose of ac-quiring or producing it. Play is the activity of the mind which gives itself up to surrounding objects according to its own caprice, without any thought as to results. The Educator gives out work to the pupil, but he leaves him to himself in his play.

26. It is necessary to draw a sharp line between work and play. If the Educator has not respect for work as an activity of great weight and im-portance, he not only spoils the relish of the pupil for play, which loses all its charm of freedom when not set off by its antithesis of earnest labor, but he undermines in the pupil's mind all respect for any real existence. On the other hand, he who does not give to the child space, time, and opportu-nity for play prevents the originality of his pupil from free development through the exercise of his creative ingenuity. Play sends the child back to his work refreshed, because in it he loses himself without constraint and according to his own fancy, while in work he is required to yield himself up in a manner prescribed for him by another.

Let the teacher watch his pupils while at play if he would discover their individual peculiarities, for it is then that they unconsciously betray their real propensities. This antithesis of work and play runs through the entire life, the form only of play varying with years and occupations. To do what we please, as we please, and when we please, not for any reason, but just because we please, remains play always. Children in their sports like nothing better than to counterfeit what is to be the earnest work of their after-lives. The little girl plays with her dolls, and the boy plays he is a soldier and goes to mimic wars.

It is, of course, an error to suppose that the play of a child is simply muscular. The lamb and the colt find their full enjoyment in capering aimlessly about the field. But to the child play would be incomplete which did not bring the mind 21 into action. Children derive little enjoyment from purely muscular exercise. They must at the same time have an object requiring mental action to attain it. A number of children set simply to run up and down a field would tire of the exercise in five minutes; but put a ball amongst them and set them to a game and they will be amused by it for hours.

Exceptional mental development is always preceded, and is, indeed, produced by, an exceptional amount of exercise in the form of play on the part of the special faculties concerned. The peculiar tendencies exhibited in play are due to the large development of particular faculties, and the ultimate giant strength of a faculty is brought about by play. The genius is no doubt born, not made; but, although born, it would dwindle away in infancy were it not for the constant exercise taken in play, which is as necessary for development as food for the maintenance of life.

27. Work should never be treated as if it were play, nor play as if it were work. Those whose work is creative activity of the mind may find recreation in the details of science; and those, again, whose vocation is scientific research can find recreation in the practice of art in its different departments. What is work to one may thus be play to another. This does not, however, contradict the first statement.

28. It is the province of education so to accustom us to different conditions or ways of thinking and acting that they shall no longer seem strange or foreign to us. When these have become, as we say, "natural" to us — when we find the acquired mode of thinking or acting just what our inclination leads us to adopt unconsciously, a Habit has been formed. A habit is, then, the identity of natural inclination with the special demands of any particular doing or suffering, and it is thus the external condition of all progress. As long as we require the conscious act of our will to the performance of a deed, that deed is somewhat foreign to ourselves, and not yet a part of ourselves. The practical work of the educator may thus be said to consist in leading the mind of the pupil over certain lines of thought till it becomes "natural" or spontaneous for him to go by that road. Much time is wasted in 22 schools where the pupil's mind is not led aright at first, for then he has to unlearn habits of thought which are already formed. The work of the teacher is to impress good methods of studying and thinking upon the minds of his pupils, rather than to communicate knowledge.

29. It is, at first sight, entirely indifferent what a Habit shall relate to — i.e., the point is to get the pupil into the way of forming habits, and it is not at first of so much moment what habit is formed as that a habit is formed. But we cannot consider that there is anything morally neutral in the abstract, but only in the concrete, or in particular examples. An action may be of no moral significance to one man, and under certain circumstances, while to another man, or to the same man under different circumstances, it may have quite a different significance, or may possess an entirely opposite character. Appeal must be made, then, to the individual conscience of each one to decide what is and what is not permissible to that individual under the given circumstances. Education must make it its first aim to awaken in the pupil a sensitiveness to spiritual and ethical distinctions which knows that nothing is in its own nature morally insignificant or indifferent, but shall recognize, even in things seemingly small, a universal human significance. But, yet, in relation to the highest interests of morality or the well-being of society, the pupil must be taught to subordinate without hesitation all that relates exclusively to his own personal comfort or welfare for the well-being of his fellow-men, or for moral rectitude.

When we reflect upon habit, it at once assumes for us the character of useful or injurious. The consequences of a habit are not indifferent.

Whatever action tends as a harmonious means to the realization of our purpose is desirable or advantageous, and whatever either partially contradicts or wholly destroys it is disadvantageous. Advantage and disadvantage being, then, only relative terms, dependent upon the aim or purpose which we happen to have in view, a habit which may be advantageous to one man under certain circumstances may be disadvantageous to another man, or even to the same man, under other circumstances. 23 Education must, then, accustom the youth to consider for himself the expediency or inexpediency of any action in relation to his own vocation in life. He must not form habits which will be inexpedient with regard to that.

31. There is, however, an absolute distinction of habits as morally good and bad. From this absolute stand-point we must, after all, decide what is for us allowable or forbidden, what is expedient and what inexpedient.

32. As to its form, habit may be either passive or active. By passive habit is meant a habit of composure which surveys undisturbed whatever vicissitudes, either external or internal, may fall to our lot, and maintains itself superior to them all, never allowing its power of acting to be paralyzed by them. It is not, however, merely a stoical indifference, nor is it the composure which comes from inability to receive impressions — a sort of impassivity. It is that composure which is the highest result of power. Nor is it a selfish love of ease which intentionally withdraws itself from annoyances in order to remain undisturbed. It is not manifested because of a desire to be out of these vicissitudes. It is, while in them, to be not of them. It is the composure which does not fret itself over what it cannot change. The soul that has built for itself this stronghold of freedom within itself may vividly experience joy and sorrow, pain and pleasure, and yet serenely know that it is intrenched in walls which are inaccessible to their attacks, because it knows that it is infinitely superior to all that may chance or change. What is meant by active habit in distinction from passive habit is found in our external activity, as skill, facility, readiness of information, etc. It might be considered as the equipping of our inner selves for active contest with the external world; while passive habit is the fortifying of our inner selves against the attack of the external world. The man who possesses habit in both these forms impresses himself in many different ways on the outer world, while at the same time, and all the time, he preserves intact his personality from the constant assaults of the outer world. He handles both spear and shield.

33. All education, in whatever line, must work by forming 24 habits physical, mental, or moral. It might be said to consist in a conversion of actions which are at first voluntary, by means of repetition, into instructive actions which are performed, as we say, naturally — i.e., without any conscious volition. We teach a child to walk, or he teaches himself to walk by a constant repetition of the action of the will upon the necessary muscles; and, when the thinking brain hands over the mechanism to the trained spinal cord, the anxious, watchful look disappears from the face, and the child talks or laughs as he runs: then that part of his education is completed. Henceforth the attention that had been necessary to manage the body in walking is freed for other work. This is only an illustration, easily understood, of what takes place in all education. Mental and moral acts, thoughts, and feelings in the same way are, by repetition, converted into habits and become our nature; and character, good or bad, is only the aggregate of our habits. When we say a person has no character, we mean exactly this: that he has no fixed habits. But, as the great end of human life is freedom, he must be above even habit. He must not be wholly a machine of habits, and education must enable him to attain the power of breaking as well as of forming habits, so that he may, when desirable, substitute one habit for another. For habits may be (29), according to their nature, proper or improper, advantageous or disadvantageous, good or bad; and, according to their form, may be (32) either the acceptance of the external by the internal or the reaction of the internal upon the external. Through our freedom we must be able, not only to renounce any habit formed, but to form a new and better one. Man should be supreme above all habits, wearing them as garments which the soul puts on and off at will. It must so order them all as to secure for itself a constant progress of development into still greater freedom. In this higher view habits become thus to our sight only necessary accompaniments of imperfect freedom. Can we conceive of God, who is perfect Freedom, as having any habits? We might say that, as a means toward the ever-more decided realization of the Good, we must form a habit of voluntarily making and breaking off habits. We must characterize as bad those habits which 25 relate only to our personal convenience or enjoyment. They are often not essentially blameworthy, but there lies in them a hidden danger that they may allure us into luxury or effeminacy. It is a false and mechanical way of looking at the affair to suppose that a habit which had been formed by a certain number of repetitions can be broken off by an equal number of refusals. We can never utterly renounce a habit which we decide to be undesirable for us except through decision and firmness.

34. Education, then, must consider the preparation for authority and obedience (17); for a rational ordering of one's actions according to universal principles, and, at the same time, a preservation of individuality (18); for work and play (25); for habits of spontaneity or originality (28). To endeavor by any set rules to harmonize in the pupil these opposites will be a vain endeavor, and failure in the solution of the problem is quite possible by reason of the freedom of the pupil, of surrounding circumstances, or of mistakes on the part of the teacher, and the possibility of this negative result must, therefore, enter as an element of calculation into the work itself. All the dangers which may in any way threaten the youth must be considered in advance, and he must be fortified against them. While we should not intentionally expose the youth to temptation in order to prove his strength of resistance, neither should we, on the other hand, endeavor to seclude him from all chance of dangerous temptation. To do the former

156

would be satanic; while to do the latter would be ridiculous, useless, and in fact dangerous in the highest degree, for temptation comes more from within than from without, and any secret inclination will in some way seek, or even create, its own opportunity for gratification. The real safety from sin lies, not in seclusion of one's self from the world 10 — for all the elements of worldliness are innate in each individual — but in an occupying of the restless activity in other ways, in learning and discipline; these being varied as time goes on, according to the age and degree of proficiency. Not to crush out, but to direct, 26 the child's activity, whether physical or mental, is the key to all real success in education. The sentimentalism which has, during the last few years, in this country (the United States), tended to diminish to so great an extent the actual work to be performed by our boys and girls, has set free a dangerous amount of energy whose new direction gives cause for grave alarm. To endeavor to prevent the youth from all free and individual relations with the real world, implies a never-ending watch kept over him. The consciousness of being thus "shadowed" destroys in the youth all elasticity of spirit, all confidence, and all originality. A constant feeling of, as it were, a detective police at his side obscures all sense of independent action, systematically accustoming him to dependence. Though, as the tragic-comic story of Peter Schlemihl shows, the loss of a man's own shadow may involve him in a series of fatalities, 11 yet to be "shadowed" constantly by a companion, us in the pedagogical system of the Jesuits, undermines all naturalness. And, if we endeavor to guard too strictly against what is evil and wrong, the pupil reacts, bringing all his intelligence into the service of his craft and cunning, till the would-be educator stands aghast at the discovery of such evil-doing as he had supposed impossible under his strict supervision. Within the circle of whatever rules it may be found necessary to draw around the young there must always be left space for freedom. Pupils should always be led to see that all rules against which they fret are only of their own creation; and that as grave-stones mark the place where some one has fallen, so every law is only a record of some previous wrong-doing. The law "Thou shalt not kill" was not given till murder had been committed. In other words, the wrong deed preceded the law against it, and perfect obedience is the same as perfect freedom. No obedience except that which we gain from the pupil's own convictions has real educational significance.

35. If there appears in the youth any decided deformity opposed to the ideal which we would create in him, we should at 27 once inquire into its history and origin. The negative and positive are so closely related, and depend so intimately on each other, in our being that what appears to us to be negligence, rudeness, immorality, foolishness, or oddity may arise from some real necessity of the pupil which in its process of development has only taken a wrong direction.

36. If it should appear, on such examination, that the wrong action was the result of avoidable ignorance, of caprice, or willfulness on the part of the pupil, this calls for a simple prohibition on the part of the teacher, no reason being assigned. His authority must be sufficient for the pupil without any reason. When the fault is repeated, and the pupil is old enough to understand, then only should the grounds of the prohibition be stated with it. This should, however, be done in few words, and the educator must never allow himself to lose, in a doctrinal lecture, the idea of discipline. If he do, the pupil will soon forget that it was his own misbehavior which was the cause of all the remarks. The statement of the reason must be honest, and must be presented to the youth on the side most easy for him to appreciate. False reasons are not only morally wrong, but they lead the mind astray. We also commit a grave error when we try to unfold to the youth all the possible consequences of his wrong act, for those possible consequences are too far off to affect his mind. The long lecture wearies him, especially if it be in a stereotyped form; and with teachers who are fault-finding, and who like to hear themselves talk, this is apt to be the case. Still more unfortunate would it be if we really should affect the lively imagination of a sensitive youth by our description of the wretchedness to which his wrong-doing, if persisted in, might lead him, for then the conviction that he has already taken one step in that direction may produce in him a fear which in the future man may become terrible depression and lead to degradation.

37. If to censure we add the threat of punishment, we have then what in common language is called scolding.

If threats are made, the pupil must be made to feel that they will be faithfully executed according to the word. 28

The threat of punishment is, however, to be avoided; for circumstances may arise which will render its fulfillment not only objectionable, but wrong, and the teacher will then find himself in the position of Herod and bound "for his oath's sake" to a course of action which no longer seems the best. Even the law in affixing a penalty to definite crimes allows a certain latitude in a maximum and minimum of awarded punishment.

38. It is only after other means of reformation have been tried, and have failed, that punishment is justifiable for error, transgression, or vice. When our simple prohibition (36), the statement of our reason for the prohibiting (36), and threat of punishment (37) have all failed, then punishment comes and intentionally inflicts pain on the youth in order to force him by this last means to a realization of his wrong-doing. And here the punishment must not be given for general bad conduct or for a perverse disposition — those being vague generalities — but for a special act of wrong-doing at that time. He should not be punished because he is naturally bad or because he is generally naughty, but for this one special and particular act which he has committed. Thus the punishment will act on the general disposition, not directly, but through this particular act, as a manifestation of the disposition. Then it will not accuse the innermost nature of the culprit. This way of punishment is not only demanded by justice, but it is absolutely necessary in view of the fact of the sophistry inherent in human nature which is always busy in assigning various motives for its actions. If the child understands, then, that he is punished for that particular act which he knows himself to have committed, he cannot feel the bitter sense of injustice and misunderstanding which a punishment inflicted for general reasons, and which attributes to him a depravity of motives and intentions, so often engenders.

39. Punishment as an educational means must, nevertheless, be always essentially corrective, since it seeks always to bring the youth to a comprehension of his wrong-doing and to a positive alteration in his behavior, and, hence, has for its aim to improve him. At the same time it is a sad testimony of the insufficiency of the means which have been previously tried. 29 We should on no account aim to terrify the youth by physical force, so that to avoid that he will refrain from doing the wrong or from repeating a wrong act already done. This would lead only to terrorism, and his growing strength would soon put him beyond its power and leave him without motive for refraining from evil. Punishment may have this effect in some degree, but it should, above all, be made to impress deeply upon his mind the eternal truth that the evil deed is never allowed in God's universe to act unrestrained and according to its own will, but that the good and true is the only absolute power in the world, and that it is never at a loss to avenge any contradiction of its will and design.

It may be questioned whether the moral teaching in our schools be not too negative in its measures; whether it do not confine itself too much to forbidding the commission of the wrong deed, and spend too little force in securing the performance of the right deed. Not a simple refraining from the wrong, but an active doing of the right would be the better lesson to inculcate.

In the laws of the state the office of punishment is first to satisfy justice, 12 and only after this is done can the improvement of the criminal be considered. If government should proceed on the same basis as the educator, it would make a grave mistake, for it has to deal, not with children, but with adults, to whom it concedes the dignity of full responsibility for all their acts. It has not to consider the reasons, either psychological or ethical, which prompted the deed. The actual deed is what it has first of all to deal with, and only after that is considered and settled can it take into view any 30 mitigating circumstances connected therewith, or any peculiarity of the individual. The educator, on the other hand, has to deal with those who are immature and only growing toward responsibility. As long as they are under the care of a teacher, he is at any rate partially accountable for what they do. We must never confound the nature of punishment in the State with that of punishment as an educational means.

40. As to punishment, as with all other work in education, it can never be abstractly determined beforehand, but it must be regulated with a view to the individual pupil and his peculiar circumstances. What it shall be, and how and when administered, are problems which call for great ingenuity and tact on the part of the educator. It must never be forgotten that punishments vary in intensity at the will of the educator. He fixes the standard by which they are measured in the child's mind. Whipping is actual physical pain, and an evil in itself to the child. But there are many other punishments which involve no physical pain, and the intensity of which, as felt by the child, varies according to an artificial standard in different schools. "To sit under the clock" was a great punishment in one of our public schools — not that the seat was not perfectly comfortable, but that one was never sent there to sit unless for some grave misdemeanor. The teacher has the matter in his own hands, and it is well to remember this and to grade his punishments with much caution, so as to make all pass for their full value. In some schools even suspension is so common that it does not seem to the pupil a very terrible thing. "Familiarity breeds contempt," and frequency implies familiarity. A punishment seldom resorted to will always seem to the pupil to be severe. As we weaken, and in fact bankrupt, language by an inordinate use of superlatives, so, also, do we weaken any punishment by its frequent repetition. Economy of resources should be always practiced.

41. *In general, we might say that, for very young children, corporal punishment is most appropriate; for boys and girls, isolation; and for older youth, something which appeals to the sense of honor.*

31

42. *(1) Corporal punishment implies physical pain. Generally it consists of a whipping, and this is perfectly justifiable in case of persistent defiance of authority, of obstinate carelessness, or of malicious evil-doing, so long or so often as the higher perceptions of the offender are closed against appeal. But it must not be administered too often, or with undue severity. To resort to deprivation of food is cruel. But, while we condemn the false view of seeing in the rod the only panacea for all embarrassing questions of discipline on the teacher's part, we can have no sympathy for the sentimentality which assumes that the dignity of humanity is affected by a blow given to a child. It is wrong thus to confound self-conscious humanity with child-humanity, for to the average child himself a blow is the most natural form of retribution, and that in which all other efforts at influence at last end. The fully grown man ought, certainly, not to be flogged, for this kind of punishment places him on a level with the child; or, where it is barbarously inflicted, reduces him to the level of the brute, and thus absolutely does degrade him. In English schools the rod is said to be often used; if a pupil of the first class, who is never flogged, is put back into the second, he becomes again subject to flogging. But, even if this be necessary in the schools, it certainly has no proper place in the army and navy.*

43. *(2) To punish a pupil by isolation is to remove him temporarily from the society of his fellows. The boy or girl thus cut off from companionship, and forced to think only of himself, begins to understand how helpless he is in such a position. Time passes wearily, and he is soon eager to return to the companionship of parents, brothers and sisters, teachers and fellow-students.*

But to leave a child entirely by himself without any supervision, and perhaps in a dark room, is as wrong as to leave two or three together without supervision. It often happens when they are kept after school by themselves that they give the freest rein to their childish wantonness, and commit the wildest pranks.

44. *(3) Shutting children up in this way does not touch 32 their sense of honor, and the punishment is soon forgotten, because it relates only to certain particular phases of their behavior. But it is quite different when the pupil is isolated from his fellows on the ground that by his conduct he*

has violated the very principles which make civilized society possible, and is, therefore, no longer a proper member of it. This is a punishment which touches his sense of honor, for honor is the recognition of the individual by others as their equal, and by his error, or by his crime, he had forfeited his right to be their equal, their peer, and has thus severed himself from them.

The separation from them is thus only the external form of the real separation which he himself has brought to pass within his soul, and which his wrong-doing has only made clearly visible. This kind of punishment, thus touching the whole character of the youth and not easily forgotten, should be administered with the greatest caution lest a permanent loss of self-respect follow. When we think our wrong-doing to be eternal in its effects, we lose all power of effort for our own improvement.

This sense of honor cannot be developed so well in family life, because in the family the ties of blood make all in a certain sense equal, no matter what may be their conduct. He who has by wrong-doing severed himself from society is still a member of the family, and within its sacred circle is still beloved, though it may be with bitter tears. No matter how wrong he may have been, he still can find there the deepest sympathy, for he is still father, brother, etc. It is in the contact of one family with another that the feeling of honor is first developed, and still more in the contact of the individual with an institution which is not bound to him by any natural ties, but is an organism entirely external to him. Thus, to the child, the school and the school-classes offer a means of development which can never be found in the family.

This fact is often overlooked by those who have the charge of the education of children. No home education, no private tutorship, can take the place of the school as an educational influence. For the first time in his life the child, on being 33 sent to school, finds himself in a community where he is responsible for his own deeds, and where he has no one to shield him. The rights of others for whom he has no special affection are to be respected by him, and his own are to be defended. The knowledge gained at the school is by no means the most valuable acquisition there obtained. It must never be forgotten by the teacher that the school is an institution on an entirely different basis from the family, and that personal attachment is not the principle on which its rule can be rightly based.

45. This gradation of punishment from physical pain, up through occasional isolation, to the touching of the innermost sense of honor is very carefully to be considered, both with regard to the different ages at which they are severally appropriate and to the different discipline which they necessarily produce. Every punishment must, however, be always looked at as a means to some end, and is thus transitory in its nature. The pupil should always be conscious that it is painful to the teacher to punish him. Nothing can be more effectual as a means of cure for the wrong-doer than to perceive in the manner and tone of the voice, in the very delay with which the necessary punishment is administered, that he who punishes also suffers in order that the wrong-doer may be cured of his fault. The principle of vicarious suffering lies at the root of all spiritual healing.

III. — The Limits of Education.

46. As far as the external form of education is concerned, its limit is reached in the instrumentality of punishment in which we seek to turn the activity which has been employed in a wrong direction into its proper channel, to make the deed positive instead of negative, to substitute for the destructive deed one which shall be in harmony with the constructive forces of society. But education implies its real limits in its definition, which is to build up the individual into theoretical and practical Reason. When this work goes properly on, the authority of the educator, as authority, necessarily 34 loses, every day, some of its force, as the guiding principles come to form a part of the pupil's own character, instead of being superimposed on him from without through the mediation of the educator. What was authority becomes now advice and example; unreasoning and implicit obedience passes into gratitude and affection. The pupil wears off the rough edges of his crude individuality, which is transfigured, so to speak, into the universality and necessity of Reason, but without losing his identity in the process. Work becomes enjoyment, and Play is found only in a change of activity. The youth takes possession of himself, and may now be left to himself. There are two widely differing views with regard to the limits of education; one lays great stress on the powerlessness of the pupil and the great power of the teacher, and asserts that the teacher must create something out of the pupil.

This view is often seen to have undesirable results, where large numbers are to be educated together. It assumes that each pupil is only "a sample of the lot" on whom the teacher is to affix his stamp, as if they were different pieces of goods from some factory. Thus individuality is destroyed, and all reduced to one level, as in cloisters, barracks, and orphan asylums, where only one individual seems to exist. Sometimes it takes the form of a theory which holds that one can at will flog anything into or out of a pupil. This may be called a superstitious belief in the power of education. The opposite extreme may be found in that system which advocates a "severe letting alone," asserting that individuality is unconquerable, and that often the most careful and circumspect education fails of reaching its aim because the inherent nature of the youth has fought against it with such force as to render abortive all opposing efforts. This idea of Pedagogy produces a sort of indifference about means and ends which would leave each individuality to grow as its own instinct and the chance influences of the world might direct. The latter view would, of course, preclude the possibility of any science of education, and make the youth only the sport of blind fate. The comparative power of inherited tendencies and of educational appliances is, however, one which every educator should carefully 35 study. Much careless generalization has been made on this topic, and opinion is too often based upon some one instance where accurate observation of methods and influences have been wanting.

47. Education has necessarily a definite subjective limit in the individuality of the youth, for it can develop in him only that which exists in him as a possibility. It can lead and assist, but it has no power to create. What nature has denied to a man education cannot give him, any more than it can on the other hand annihilate his original gifts, though it may suppress, distort, and measurably destroy them. And yet it is impossible to decide what is the real essence of a man's individuality until he has left behind him the years of growth, because it is not till then that he fully attains conscious possession of himself. Moreover, at this critical time many traits which were supposed to be characteristic may prove themselves not to be so by disappearing, while long-slumbering and unsuspected talents may crop out. Whatever has been forced upon a child, though not in harmony with his individuality, whatever has been driven into him without having been actively accepted by him, or having had a definite relation to his culture — will remain perhaps, but only as an external foreign ornament, only as a parasitic growth which weakens the force of his real nature. But we must distinguish from these little affectations which arise from a misconception of the limits of individuality that effort of imitation which children and young people often exhibit in trying to copy in their own actions those peculiarities which they observe and admire in perfectly-developed persons with whom they may come in contact. They see a reality which corresponds to their own possibility, and the presentiment of a like or a similar attainment stirs them to imitation, although this external imitation may be sometimes disagreeable or ridiculous to the lookers-on. We ought not to censure it too severely, remembering that it springs from a positive striving towards true culture, and needs only to be properly directed, and never to be roughly put down.

48. The objective limit of education consists in the means 36 which can be applied for it. That the capacity for culture should exist is the first condition of success, but it is none the less necessary that it be cultivated. But how much cultivation shall be given to it must depend in very great degree on the means which are practicable, and this will undoubtedly again depend on the worldly possessions and character of the family to which the pupil belongs. If he comes of a cultivated and refined family, he will have a great advantage at the start over his less favored comrades; and, with regard to many of the arts and sciences, this limitation of education is of great significance. But the means alone will not answer. Without natural capacity, all the educational apparatus possible is of no avail. On the other hand, real talent often accomplishes incredible feats with very limited means; and, if the way is only once open, makes of itself a center of attraction which draws to itself as with magnetic power the necessary means. Moral culture is, however, from its very nature, raised above such dependence.

If we fix our thought on the subjective limit — that of individuality (47) — we detect the ground for that indifference which lays little stress on education (46, end). If, on the other hand, we concentrate our attention on the means of culture, we shall perceive the reason of the other extreme spoken of — of that pedagogical despotism (46) which fancies that it is able to prescribe and enforce at will upon the pupil any culture whatever, without regard to his special characteristics.

49. Education comes to its absolute limit when the pupil has apprehended the problem which he is to solve, has comprehended the means which are at his disposal, and has acquired the necessary skill in using them. The true educator seeks to render himself unnecessary by the complete emancipation of the youth. He works always towards the independence of the pupil, and always with the design of withdrawing so soon as he shall have reached this stand-point, and of leaving him to the full responsibility for his own deeds. To endeavor to hold him in the position of a pupil after this time has been reached would be to contradict the very essence of education, which must find its result in the independent maturity of the youth. The inequality which formerly existed between pupil and 37 teacher is now removed, and nothing becomes more oppressive to the former than any endeavor to force upon him the authority from which, in reality, his own efforts have freed him. But the undue hastening of this emancipation is as bad an error as an effort after delay. The question as to whether a person is really ready for independent action — as to whether his education is finished — may be settled in much the same way in education as in politics. When any people has progressed so far as to put the question whether they are ready for freedom, it ceases to be a question; for, without the inner consciousness of freedom itself, the question would never have occurred to them.

50. But, although the pupil may rightly now be freed from the hands of instructors, and no longer obtain his culture through them, it is by no means to be understood that he is not to go on with the work himself. He is now to educate himself. Each must plan out for himself the ideal toward which he must daily strive. In this process of self-transformation a friend may aid by advice and example, but he cannot educate, for the act of educating necessarily implies inequality between teacher and pupil. The human necessity for companionship gives rise to societies of different kinds, in which we may, perhaps, say that there is some approach to educating their members, the necessary inequality being supplied by various grades and orders. They presuppose education in the usual sense of the word, but they wish to bring about an education in a higher sense, and, therefore, they veil the last form of their ideal in mystery and secrecy.

By the term Philister the Germans indicate the man of a civilized state who lives on, contented with himself and devoid of any impulse towards further self-culture. To one who is always aspiring after an Ideal, such a one cannot but be repulsive. But how many are they who do not, sooner or later, in mature life, crystallize, as it were, so that any active life, any new progress, is to them impossible?

38

ANALYSIS AND COMMENTARY.

1. Pedagogics is not a complete, independent science by itself. It borrows the results of other sciences [e.g., it presupposes the science of Rights, treating of the institutions of the family and civil society, as well as of the State; it presupposes the science of anthropology, in which is treated the relations of the human mind to nature. Nature conditions the development of the individual human being. But the history of the individual and the history of the race presents a continual emancipation from nature, and a continual growth into freedom, i.e., into ability to know himself and to realize himself in the world by making the matter and forces of the world his instruments and tools. Anthropology shows us how man as a natural being — i.e., as having a body — is limited. There is climate, involving heat and cold and moisture, the seasons of the year, etc.; there is organic growth, involving birth, growth, reproduction, and decay; there is race, involving the limitations of heredity; there is the telluric life of the planet and the circulation of the forces of the solar system, whence arise the processes of sleeping, waking, dreaming, and kindred phenomena; there is the emotional nature of man, involving his feelings, passions, instincts, and desires; then there are the five senses, and their conditions. Then, there is the science of phenomenology, treating of the steps by which mind rises from the stage of mere feeling and sense-perception to that of self-consciousness, i.e., to a recognition of mind as true substance, and of matter as mere phenomenon created by Mind (God). Then, there is psychology, including the treatment of the stages of activity of mind, as so-called "faculties" of the mind, e.g., attention, sense-perception, imagination, conception, understanding, judgment, reason, and the like. Psychology is generally made (by English writers) to include, also, what is here called anthropology and phenomenology. After psychology, there is the science of ethics, or of morals and customs; then, the Science of Rights, already mentioned; then, Theology, or the Science of Religion, and, after all these, there is Philosophy, or the Science of Science. Now, it is clear that the Science of Education treats of the process of development, by and through which man, as a merely 39 natural being, becomes spirit, or self-conscious mind; hence, it presupposes all the sciences named, and will be defective if it ignores nature, or mind, or any stage or process of either, especially Anthropology, Phenomenology, Psychology, Ethics, Rights, Ythetics, or Science of Art and Literature, Religion, or Philosophy].

2. The scope of pedagogics being so broad, and its presuppositions so vast, its limits are not well defined, and its treatises are very apt to lack logical sequence and conclusion; and, indeed, frequently to be mere collections of unjustified and unexplained assumptions, dogmatically set forth. Hence the low repute of pedagogical literature as a whole.

3. Moreover, education furnishes a special vocation, that of teaching. (All vocations are specializing — being cut off, as it were, from the total life of man. The "division of labor" requires that each individual shall concentrate his endeavors and be a part of the whole).

4. Pedagogics, as a special science, belongs to the collection of sciences (already described, in commenting on 1) included under the philosophy of Spirit or Mind, and more particularly to that part of it which relates to the will (ethics and science of rights, rather than to the part relating to the intellect and feeling, as anthropology, phenomerology, psychology,

æsthetics, and religion. "Theoretical" relates to the intellect, "practical" relates to the will, in this philosophy). The province of practical philosophy is the investigation of the nature of freedom, and the process of securing it by self-emancipation from nature. Pedagogics involves the conscious exertion of influence on the part of the will of the teacher upon the will of the pupil, with a purpose in view — that of inducing the pupil to form certain prescribed habits, and adopt prescribed views and inclinations. The entire science of mind (as above shown), is presupposed by the science of education, and must be kept constantly in view as a guiding light. The institution of the family (treated in practical philosophy) is the starting-point of education, and without this institution properly realized, education would find no solid foundation. The right to be educated on the part of children, and the duty to educate on the part of parents, are reciprocal; and there is no family life so poor and rudimentary that it does not furnish the most important elements of education — no matter what the subsequent influence of the school, the vocation, and the state.

5. Pedagogics as science, distinguished from the same as an art: the former containing the abstract general treatment, and the latter 40 taking into consideration all the conditions of concrete individuality, e.g., the peculiarities of the teacher and the pupil, and all the local circumstances, and the power of adaptation known as "tact."

6. The special conditions and peculiarities, considered in education as an art, may be formulated and reduced to system, but they should not be introduced as a part of the science of education.

7. Pedagogics has three parts: first, it considers the idea and nature of education, and arrives at its true definition; second, it presents and describes the special provinces into which the entire field of education is divided; third, it considers the historical evolution of education by the human race, and the individual systems of education that have arisen, flourished, and decayed, and their special functions in the life of man.

8. The scope of the first part is easy to define. The history of pedagogics, of course, contains all the ideas or definitions of the nature of education; but it must not for that reason be substituted for the scientific investigation of the nature of education, which alone should constitute this first part (and the history of education be reserved for the third part).

9. The second part includes a discussion of the threefold nature of man as body, intellect, and will. The difficulty in this part of the science is very great, because of its dependence upon other sciences (e.g., upon physiology,

anthropology, etc.), and because of the temptation to go into details (e.g., in the practical department, to consider the endless varieties of schools for arts and trades).

10. The third part contains the exposition of the various national standpoints furnished (in the history of the world) for the bases of particular systems of education. In each of these systems will be found the general idea underlying all education, but it will be found existing under special modifications, which have arisen through its application to the physical, intellectual, and ethical conditions of the people. But we can deduce the essential features of the different systems that may appear in history, for there are only a limited number of systems possible. Each lower form finds itself complemented in some higher form, and its function and purpose then become manifest. The systems of "national" education (i.e., Asiatic systems, in which the individuality of each person is swallowed up in the substantiality of the national idea — just as the individual waves get lost in the ocean on whose surface they arise) find their complete explanation in the systems of education that arise in Christianity (the preservation of human life being the object of the nation, it follows ≤1 that when realized abstractly or exclusively, it absorbs and annuls the mental independence of its subjects, and thus contradicts itself by destroying the essence of what it undertakes to preserve, i.e., life (soul, mind); but within Christianity the principle of the state is found so modified that it is consistent with the infinite, untrammelled development of the individual, intellectually and morally, and thus not only life is saved, but spiritual, free life is attainable for each and for all).

11. The history of pedagogy ends with the present system as the latest one. As science sees the future ideally contained in the present, it is bound to comprehend the latest system as a realization (though imperfect) of the ideal system of education. Hence, the system, as scientifically treated in the first part of our work, is the system with which the third part of our work ends.

12. The nature of education, its form, its limits, are now to be investigated. (13-50.)

13. The nature of education determined by the nature of Mind or Spirit, whose activity is always devoted to realizing for itself what it is potentially — to becoming conscious of its possibilities, and to getting them under the control of its will. Mind is potentially free. Education is the means by which man seeks to realize in man his possibilities (to develop the possibili-

ties of the race in each individual). Hence, education has freedom for its object.

14. Man is the only being capable of education, in the sense above defined, because the only conscious being. He must know himself ideally, and then realize his ideal self, in order to become actually free. The animals not the plants may be trained, or cultivated, but, as devoid of self-consciousness (even the highest animals not getting above impressions, not reaching ideas, not seizing general or abstract thoughts), they are not realized for themselves, but only for us. (That is, they do not know their ideal as we do.)

15. Education, taken in its widest compass, is the education of the human race by Divine Providence.

16. In a narrower sense, education is applied to the shaping of the individual, so that his caprice and arbitrariness shall give place to rational habits and views, in harmony with nature and ethical customs. He must not abuse nature, nor slight the ethical code of his people, nor despise the gifts of Providence (whether for weal or woe), unless he is willing to be crushed in the collision with these more substantial elements.

17. In the narrowest, but most usual application of the term, 42 we understand by "education" the influence of the individual upon the individual, exerted with the object of developing his powers in a conscious and methodical manner, either generally or in special directions, the educator being relatively mature, and exercising authority over the relatively immature pupil. Without authority on the one hand and obedience on the other, education would lack its ethical basis — a neglect of the will-training could not be compensated for by any amount of knowledge or smartness.

18. The general province of education includes the development of the individual into the theoretical and practical reason immanent in him. The definition which limits education to the development of the individual into ethical customs (obedience to morality, social conventionalities, and the laws of the state — Hegel's definition is here referred to: "The object of education is to make men ethical") is not comprehensive enough, because it ignores the side of the intellect, and takes note only of the will. The individual should not only be man in general (as he is through the adoption of moral and ethical forms — which are general forms, customs, or laws, and thus the forms imposed by the will of the race), but he should also be a self-conscious subject, a particular individual (man, through his intellect, exists for himself as an individual, while through his general habits and customs he loses his individuality and spontaneity).

19. Education has a definite object in view and it proceeds by grades of progress toward it. The systematic tendency is essential to all education, properly so called.

20. Division of labor has become requisite in the higher spheres of teaching. The growing multiplicity of branches of knowledge creates the necessity for the specialist as teacher. With this tendency to specialties it becomes more and more difficult to preserve what is so essential to the pupil — his rounded human culture and symmetry of development. The citizen of modern civilization sometimes appears to be an artificial product by the side of the versatility of the savage man.

21. From this necessity of the division of labor in modern times there arises the demand for two kinds of educational institutions — those devoted to general education (common schools, colleges, etc.), and special schools (for agriculture, medicine, mechanic arts, etc).

22. The infinite possibility of culture for the individual leaves, of course, his actual accomplishment a mere approximation to a complete education. Born idiots are excluded from the possibility of education, because the lack of universal ideas in their consciousness 43 precludes to that class of unfortunates anything beyond a mere mechanical training.

23. Spirit, or mind, makes its own nature; it is what it produces — a self-result. From this follows the form of education. It commences with (1) undeveloped mind — that of the infant — wherein nearly all is potential, and but little is actualized; (2) its first stage of development is self-estrangement — it is absorbed in the observation of objects around it; (3) but it discovers laws and principles (universality) in external nature, and finally identifies them with reason — it comes to recognize itself in nature — to recognize conscious mind as the creator and preserver of the external world — and thus becomes at home in nature. Education does not create, but it emancipates.

24. This process of self-estrangement and its removal belongs to all culture. The mind must fix its attention upon what is foreign to it, and penetrate its disguise. It will discover its own substance under the seeming alien being. Wonder is the accompaniment of this stage of estrangement. The love of travel and adventure arises from this basis.

25. Labor is distinguished from play: The former concentrates its energies on some object, with the purpose of making it conform to its will and purpose; play occupies itself with its object according to its caprice and arbitrariness, and has no care for the results or products of its activity; work is prescribed by authority, while play is necessarily spontaneous.

26. Work and Play: the distinction between them. In play the child feels that he has entire control over the object with which he is dealing, both in respect to its existence and the object for which it exists. His arbitrary will may change both with perfect impunity, since all depends upon his caprice; he exercises his powers in play according to his natural proclivities, and therein finds scope to develope his own individuality. In work, on the contrary, he must have respect for the object with which he deals. It must be held sacred against his caprice, must not be destroyed nor injured in any way, and its object must likewise be respected. His own personal inclinations must be entirely subordinated, and the business that he is at work upon must be carried forward in accordance with its own ends and aims, and without reference to his own feelings in the matter.

Thus work teaches the pupil the lesson of self-sacrifice (the right of superiority which the general interest possesses over the particular), while play develops his personal idiosyncrasy.

44

27. Without play, the child would become more and more a machine, and lose all freshness and spontaneity — all originality. Without work, he would develop into a monster of caprice and arbitrariness.

From the fact that man must learn to combine with man, in order that the individual may avail himself of the experience and labors of his fellow-men, self-sacrifice for the sake of combination is the great lesson of life. But as this should be voluntary self-sacrifice, education must train the child equally in the two directions of spontaneity and obedience. The educated man finds recreation in change of work.

28. Education seeks to assimilate its object — to make what was alien and strange to the pupil into something familiar and habitual to him. [The pupil is to attack, one after the other, the foreign realms in the world of nature and man, and conquer them for his own, so that he can be "at home" in them. It is the necessary condition of all growth, all culture, that one widens his own individuality by this conquest of new provinces alien to him. By this the individual transcends the narrow limits of particularity and becomes generic – the individual becomes the species. A good definition of education is this: it is the process by which the individual man elevates himself to the species.]

29. (1) Therefore, the first requirement in education is that the pupil shall acquire the habit of subordinating his likes and dislikes to the attainment of a rational object.

It is necessary that he shall acquire this indifference to his own pleasure, even by employing his powers on that which does not appeal to his interest in the remotest degree.

30. Habit soon makes us familiar with those subjects which seemed so remote from our personal interest, and they become agreeable to us. The objects, too, assume a new interest upon nearer approach, as being useful or injurious to us. That is useful which serves us as a means for the realization of a rational purpose; injurious, if it hinders such realization. It happens that objects are useful in one sense and injurious in another, and vice versa. Education must make the pupil capable of deciding on the usefulness of an object, by reference to its effect on his permanent vocation in life.

31. But good and evil are the ethical distinctions which furnish the absolute standard to which to refer the question of the usefulness of objects and actions.

32. (2) Habit is (a) passive, or (b) active. The passive habit is that which gives us the power to retain our equipoise of mind in the 45 midst of a world of changes (pleasure and pain, grief and joy, etc). The active habit gives us skill, presence of mind, tact in emergencies, etc.

33. (3) Education deals altogether with the formation of habits. For it aims to make some condition or form of activity into a second nature for the pupil. But this involves, also, the breaking up of previous habits. This power to break up habits, as well as to form them, is necessary to the freedom of the individual.

34. Education deals with these complementary relations (antitheses): (a) authority and obedience; (b) rationality (general forms) and individuality; (c) work and play; (d) habit (general custom) and spontaneity. The development and reconciliation of these opposite sides in the pupil's character, so that they become his second nature, removes the phase of constraint which at first accompanies the formal inculcation of rules, and the performance of prescribed tasks. The freedom of the pupil is the ultimate object to be kept in view, but a too early use of freedom may work injury to the pupil. To remove a pupil from all temptation would be to remove possibilities of growth in strength to resist it; on the other hand, to expose him needlessly to temptation is fiendish.

35. Deformities of character in the pupil should be carefully traced back to their origin, so that they may be explained by their history. Only by comprehending the historic growth of an organic defect are we able to prescribe the best remedies.

36. If the negative behavior of the pupil (his bad behavior) results from ignorance due to his own neglect, or to his wilfulness, it should be met directly by an act of authority on the part of the teacher (and without an appeal to reason). An appeal should be made to the understanding of the pupil only when he is somewhat mature, or shows by his repetition of the offence that his proclivity is deep-seated, and requires an array of all good influences to reinforce his feeble resolutions to amend.

37. Reproof, accompanied by threats of punishment, is apt to degenerate into scolding.

38. After the failure of other means, punishment should be resorted to. Inasmuch as the punishment should be for the purpose of making the pupil realize that it is the consequence of his deed returning on himself, it should always be administered for some particular act of his, and this should be specified. The "overt act" is the only thing which a man can be held accountable for in a court of justice; although it is true that the harboring 46 of evil thoughts or intentions is a sin, yet it is not a crime until realized in an overt act.

40. Punishment should be regulated, not by abstract rules, but in view of the particular case and its attending circumstances.

41. Sex and age of pupil should be regarded in prescribing the mode and degree of punishment. Corporal punishment is best for pupils who are very immature in mind; when they are more developed they may be punished by any imposed restraint upon their free wills which will isolate them from the ordinary routine followed by their fellow-pupils. (Deprivation of the right to do as others do is a wholesome species of punishment for those old or mature enough to feel its effects, for it tends to secure respect for the regular tasks by elevating them to the rank of rights and privileges.) For young men and women, the punishment should be of a kind that is based on a sense of honor.

42. (1) Corporal punishment should be properly administered by means of the rod, subduing wilful defiance by the application of force.

48. (2) Isolation makes the pupil realize a sense of his dependence upon human society, and upon the expression of this dependence by co□□ation in the common tasks. Pupils should not be shut up in a dark room, nor removed from the personal supervision of the teacher. (To shut up two or more in a room without supervision is not isolation, but association; only it is association for mischief, and not for study.)

44. (3) Punishment based on the sense of honor may or may not be based on isolation. It implies a state of maturity on the part of the pupil. Through his offence the pupil has destroyed his equality with his fellows, and has in reality, in his inmost nature, isolated himself from them. Corporal punishment is external, but it may be accompanied with a keen sense of dishonor. Isolation, also, may, to a pupil, who is sensitive to honor, be a severe blow to self-respect. But a punishment founded entirely on the sense of honor would be wholly internal, and have no external discomfort attached to it.

45. The necessity of carefully adapting the punishment to the age and maturity of the pupil, renders it the most difficult part of the teacher's duties. It is essential that the air and manner of the teacher who punishes should be that of one who acts from a sense of painful duty, and not from any delight in being the cause of suffering. Not personal likes and dislikes, but the rational necessity which 47 is over teacher and pupil alike, causes the infliction of pain on the pupil.

46. Punishment is the final topic to be considered under the head of "Form of Education."

In the act of punishment the teacher abandons the legitimate province of education, which seeks to make the pupil rational or obedient to what is reasonable, as a habit, and from his own free will. The pupil is punished in order that he may be made to conform to the rational, by the application of constraint. Another will is substituted for the pupil's, and good behavior is produced, but not by the pupil's free act. While education finds a negative limit in punishment, it finds a positive limit in the accomplishment of its legitimate object, which is the emancipation of the pupil from the state of imbecility, as regards mental and moral self-control, into the ability to direct himself rationally, When the pupil has acquired the discipline which enables him to direct his studies properly, and to control his inclinations in such a manner as to pursue his work regularly, the teacher is no longer needed for him — he becomes his own teacher.

There may be two extreme views on this subject — the one tending towards the negative extreme of requiring the teacher to do everything for the pupil, substituting his will for that of the pupil, and the other view tending to the positive extreme, and leaving everything to the pupil, even before his will is trained into habits of self-control, or his mind provided with the necessary elementary branches requisite for the prosecution of further study.

47. (1) The subjective limit of education (on the negative side) is to be found in the individuality of the pupil — the limit to his natural capacity.

48. (2) The objective limit to education lies in the amount of time that the person may devote to his training. It, therefore, depends largely upon wealth, or other fortunate circumstances.

49. (3) The absolute limit of education is the positive limit (see 46), beyond which the youth passes into freedom from the school, as a necessary instrumentality for further culture.

50. The pre-arranged pattern-making work of the school is now done, but self-education may and should go on indefinitely, and will go on if the education of the school has really arrived at its "absolute" limit — i.e., has fitted the pupil for self-education. Emancipation from the school does not emancipate one from learning through his fellow-men. Man's spiritual life is one depending upon co□□ation with his fellow-men. Each must avail himself of the 48 experience of his fellow-men, and in turn communicate his own experience to the common fund of the race. Thus each lives the life of the whole, and all live for each. School-education gives the pupil the instrumentalities with which to enable him to participate in this fund of experience — this common life of the race. After school-education comes the still more valuable education, which, however, without the school, would be in a great measure impossible.

ERRATA.

26. Last two paragraphs should be within quotation marks, being from an English author.

29. The second and third paragraphs belong to 30. — the numbering being omitted.

33. Line four — "instructive" should be "intuitive."

49

SECOND PART.
The Special Elements of Education.

51. Education is the development of the theoretical and practical Reason which is inborn in the human being. Its end is to be accomplished by the labor which transforms a condition, existent at first only as an ideal, into a fixed habit, and changes the natural individuality into a glorified humanity. When the youth stands, so to speak, on his own feet, he is emancipated from education, and education then finds its limit. The special elements which may be said to make up education are the life, the cognition, and the will of man. Without the first, the real nature of the soul can never be made really to appear; without cognition, he can have no genuine will — i.e., one of which he is conscious; and without will, no self-assurance, either of life or of cognition. It must not be forgotten that these three so-called elements are not to be held apart in the active work of education; for they are inseparable and continually interwoven the one with the other. But none the less do they determine their respective consequences, and sometimes one, sometimes another has the supremacy. In infancy, up to the fifth or sixth year, the physical development, or mere living, is the main consideration; the next period, that of childhood, is the time of acquiring knowledge, in which the child takes possession of the theory of the world as it is handed down — a tradition of the past, such as man has made it through his experience and insight; and finally, the period of youth must pave the way to a practical activity, the character of which the self-determination of the will must decide.

52. We may, then, divide the elements of Pedagogics into 50 three sections: (1) the physical, (2) the intellectual, (3) the practical. (The words "orthobiotics," "didactics," and "pragmatics" might be used to characterize them.)

Ythetic training is only an element of the intellectual, as social, moral, and religious training are elements of the practical. But because these latter elements relate to external things (affairs of the world), the name pragmatics, is appropriate. In so far as education touches on the principles which underlie ethics, politics, and religion, it concurs with those sciences, but it is distinguished from them in the capacity which it imparts for solving the problems presented by the others.

The scientific order of topics must be established through the fact that the earlier, as the more abstract, constitute the condition of their presupposed end and aim, and the later because the more concrete constitute the ground of the former, and consequently their final cause, or the end for which they exist; just as in human beings, life in the order of time comes before cognition, and cognition before will, although life really presupposes cognition, and cognition will.

FIRST DIVISION.

PHYSICAL EDUCATION, OR ORTHOBIOTICS.

53. Only when we rightly comprehend the process of life may we know how to live aright. Life, the "circle of eternal change," is constantly transforming the inorganic into the organic, and after using it, returning it again to the realm of the inorganic. Whatever it does not assimilate of that which it has taken in simply as a stimulant, and whatever has become dead, it separates from itself and rejects. The organism is in perfect health when it accomplishes this double task of organizing and disorganizing. On the comprehension of this single fact all laws of physical health or of hygiene are based. This idea of the essence of life is expressed by Goethe in his Faust, where he sees the golden buckets perpetually rising 51 and sinking. 13 When the equilibrium of the upward and downward motion is disturbed, we have disease. When the motion ceases we have death, in which the whole organism becomes inorganic, and the "dust returns to dust."

54. It follows from this that not only in the organism as a whole, but in every organ, and every part of every organ, this restless change of the inorganic to the organic is going on. Every cell has its own history, and this history is only the same as that of the whole of which it forms a part. Activity is then not inimical to the organism, but is the appointed means by which the progressive and retrogressive metamorphoses must be carried out. In order that the process may go on harmoniously, or, in other words, that the body may be healthy, the whole organism, and every part of it in

178

its own way, must have its period of productive activity and then also its period of rest in which it finds renewal of strength for another period of activity. Thus we have waking and sleep, inspiration and expiration of air. Periodicity is the law of life. When we understand the relative antagonism (their stage of tension) of the different organs, and their cycles of activity, we shall hold the secret of the constant self-renewal of life. This thought finds expression in the old fairy stories of "The Search after the Fountain of Youth." And the figure of the fountain, with its rising and falling waters, doubtless finds its origin in the dim comprehension of the endless double movement, or periodicity of life.

55. When to any organ, or to the whole organism, not sufficient time is allowed for it to withdraw into itself and to repair waste, we are conscious of fatigue. While the other organs all rest, however, one special organ may, as if separated from them, sustain a long-continued effort of activity even to the point of fatigue, without injury — as, e.g., the lungs in talking while all the other members are at rest. But, on the other hand, it is not well to talk and run at the same time.

52

The idea that the body may be preserved in a healthy state longer by sparing it — i.e., by inactivity — is an error which springs from a false and mechanical conception of life. It is just as foolish to imagine that health depends on the abundance and excellence of food, for without the power of assimilating the food taken, nourishment of whatever kind does more harm than good; all real strength develops from activity alone.

56. Physical education, according as it relates to the repairing, the muscular, or the emotional activities, is divided into (1) diatetics, (2) gymnastics, (3) sexual education. In the direct activity of life these all interact with each other, but for our purposes we are obliged to speak of them as if they worked independently. Moreover, in the development of the human being, they come into maturity of development in a certain order: nutrition, muscular growth, sexual maturity. But Pedagogics can treat of these only as they are found in the infant, the child, and the youth; for with the arrival of mature life, education is over.

First Chapter.
Diatetics.

57. By diatetics we mean the art of repairing the constant waste of the system, and, in childhood, of also building it up to its full form and size.

Since in reality each organism has its own way of doing this, the diatetical practice must vary somewhat with sex, age, temperament, occupation, and circumstances. The science of Pedagogics has then, in this department, only to enunciate general principles. If we go into details, we fall into triviality. Nothing can be of more importance for the whole life than the way in which the physical education is managed in the very first stages of development. So generally is this fact accepted, that almost every nation has its own distinct system, which has been carefully elaborated. Many of these systems, no doubt, are characterized by gross errors, and widely differ as to time, place, and character, and yet they all have a justification for their peculiar form.

53

58. The best food for the infant in the first months of its life is its mother's milk. The employment of another nurse, if a general custom, as in France, is highly objectionable, since with the milk the child is likely to imbibe to some extent his physical and ethical nature. The milk of an animal can never supply the place to a child of that of its own mother. In Walter Scott's story of The Fair Maid of Perth, Eachim is represented as timorous by nature, having been nourished by a white doe after the death of his mother.

59. When the teeth make their appearance, it is a sign that the child is ready for solid food; and yet, till the second teeth appear, light, half-solid food and vegetables should constitute the principal part of the diet.

60. When the second teeth have come, then the organism demands both vegetable and animal food. Too much meat is, doubtless, harmful. But it is an error to suppose that man was intended to eat vegetables alone, and that, as some have said, the adoption of animal food is a sign of his degeneracy.

The Hindoos, who live principally on a vegetable diet, are not at all, as has been asserted, a mild and gentle race. A glance into their stories, especially their erotic poetry, proves them to be quite as passionate as any other people.

61. Man is an omnivorous being. Children have, therefore, a natural desire to taste of every thing. With them, eating and drinking have still a poetic side, and there is a pleasure in them which is not wholly the mere pleasure of taste. Their proclivity to taste of every thing should not, there-

fore, be harshly censured, unless it is associated with disobedience, or pursued in a clandestine manner, or when it betrays cunning and greediness.

62. Children need much sleep, because they are growing and changing so fast. In later years, waking and sleeping must be regulated, and yet not too exactly.

63. The clothing of children should follow the form of the body, and should be large enough to give them free room for the unfettered movement of every limb in play.

The Germans do more rationally for children in the matter of sleep and of dress than in that of food, which they often 54 make too rich, and accompany with coffee, tea, etc. The clothing should be not only suitable in shape and size, it must also be made of simple and inexpensive material, so that the child may not be hampered in his play by the constant anxiety that a spot or a rent may cause fault to be found with him. If we foster in the child's mind too much thought about his clothes, we tend to produce either a narrow-mindedness, which treats affairs of the moment with too much respect and concerns itself with little things, or an empty vanity. Vanity is often produced by dressing children in a manner that attracts attention. (No one can fail to remark the peculiar healthful gayety of German children, and to contrast it with the different appearance of American children. It is undoubtedly true that the climate has much to do with this result, but it is also true that we may learn much from that nation in our way of treating children. Already we import their children's story-books, to the infinite delight of the little ones, and copies of their children's pictures are appropriated constantly by our children's magazines and picture-books. It is to be greatly desired that we should adopt the very sensible custom which prevails in Germany, of giving to each child its own little bed to sleep in, no matter how many may be required; and, in general, we shall not go far astray if we follow the Germans in their treatment of their happy children.)

64. Cleanliness is a virtue to which children should be trained, not only for the sake of their physical health, but also because it has a decided moral influence. Cleanliness will not have things deprived of their distinctive and individual character, and become again a part of original chaos. It is only a form of order which remands all things, dirt included, to their own places, and will not endure to have things mixed and confused. All adaptation in dress comes from this same principle. When every thing is in its proper place, all dressing will be suitable to the occasion and to the wearer, and the era of good taste in dress will have come. Dirt itself, as Lord Palmers-

ton so wittily said, is nothing but "matter out of place." Cleanliness would hold every individual thing strictly to its differences from other things, and for the reason that it 55 makes pure air, cleanliness of his own body, of his clothing, and of all his surroundings really necessary to man, it develops in him the feeling for the proper limitations of all existent things. (Emerson says: "Therefore is space and therefore is time, that men may know that things are not huddled and lumped, but sundered and divisible." He might have said, "Therefore is cleanliness.")

Second Chapter.
Gymnastics.

65. Gymnastics is the art of cultivating in a rational manner the muscular system. The activity of the voluntary muscles, which are under the control of the brain, in distinction from the involuntary, which are under the control of the spinal cord, renders possible the connection of man with the external world, and acts in a reflex manner back upon the involuntary or automatic muscles for the purposes of repair and sensation. Because the activity of muscle-fibre consists in the change from contraction to expansion, and the reverse, gymnastics must use a constant change of movements which shall not only make tense, but relax the muscles that are to be exercised.

66. The gymnastic art among any people will always bear a certain relation to its art of war. So long as fighting consists mainly of personal, hand-to-hand encounters of two combatants, so long will gymnastics turn its chief effort towards the development of the greatest possible amount of individual strength and dexterity. But after the invention of fire-arms of long range has changed the whole idea of war, the individual becomes only one member of a body, the army, the division, or the regiment, and emerges from this position into his individuality again only occasionally, as in sharpshooting, in the onset, or in the retreat. Modern gymnastics, as an art, can never be the same as the ancient art, for this very reason: that because of the loss of the individual man in the general mass of combatants, the matter 56 of personal bravery is not of so much importance as formerly. The same essential difference between ancient and modern gymnastics, would result from the subjective, or internal character of the modern spirit. It is impossible for us, in modern times, to devote so much thought to the care of the body and to the reverential admiration of its beauty as did the Greeks.

The Turners' Unions and Turners' Halls in Germany belonged to the period of intense political enthusiasm in the German youth, and had a political significance. Now they have come back again to their place as an instrument of education, and seem in great cities to be of much importance. In mountainous countries, and in country life generally, a definite gymnastic drill is of much less importance, for much and varied exercise is of necessity a constant part of the daily life of every one.

The constant opportunity and the impulse to recreation helps in the same direction. In cities, on the contrary, there is not free space enough either in houses or yards for children to romp to their heart's and body's content. For this reason a gymnasium is here useful, so that they may have companionship in their plays. For girls this exercise is less necessary. Dancing may take its place, and systematic exercise should be used only where there is a tendency to some weakness or deformity. They are not to become Amazons. On the other hand, boys need the feeling of comradeship. It is true they find this in some measure in school, but they are not there perfectly on an equality, because the standing is determined to some extent by his intellectual ability. The academic youth cannot hope to win any great preëmnence in the gymnastic hall, and running, climbing, leaping, and lifting do not interest him very much as he grows older. He takes a far more lively interest in exercises which have a military character. In Germany the gymnastic art is very closely united with the art of war.

(The German idea of a woman's whole duty — to knit, to sew, and to obey implicitly — is perhaps accountable for what Rosenkranz here says of exercise as regards girls. We, however 57 , who know that the most frequent direct cause of debility and suffering in our young women is simply and solely a want of muscular strength, may be pardoned for dissenting from his opinion, and for suggesting that dancing is not a sufficient equivalent for the more violent games of their brothers. We do not fear to render them Amazons by giving them more genuine and systematic exercise, both physically and intellectually.)

67. The main idea of gymnastics, and indeed of all exercise, is to give the mind control over its natural impulses, to make it master of the body which it inhabits, and of itself. Strength and dexterity must combine to give us a sense of mastership. Strength by itself produces the athlete, dexterity by itself the acrobat. Pedagogics must avoid both these extremes. Neither must it base its teaching of gymnastics on the idea of utility — as, e.g., that man might save his life by swimming, should he fall into the water, and hence swimming should be taught, etc.

The main thought must be always to enable the soul to take full and perfect possession of the organism, so as not to have the body form a limit or fetter to its action in its dealings with the external world. We are to give it a perfect instrument in the body, in so far as our care may do so. Then we are to teach it to use that instrument, and exercise it in that use till it is complete master thereof.

(What is said about the impropriety of making athletes and acrobats may with justice be also applied to what is called "vocal gymnastics;" whence it comes that we have too often vocal athletes and acrobats in our graduates, and few readers who can read at sight, without difficulty or hesitation, and with appreciation or enjoyment, one page of good English.)

68. There are all grades of gymnastic exercises, from the simple to the most complex, constituting a system. At first sight, there seems to be so much arbitrariness in these things that it is always very satisfactory to the mind to detect some rational system in them. Thus we have movements (a) of the lower extremities, (b) of the upper, (c) of the 58 whole body, with corresponding movements, alternately, of the upper and of the lower extremities. We thus have leg, arm, and trunk movements.

69. (1) The first set of movements, those of the legs and feet, are of prime importance, because upon them depends the carriage of the whole body. They are (a) walking, (b) running, (c) leaping; and each of these, also, may have varieties. We may have high and low leaping, and running may be distinguished as to whether it is to be a short and rapid, or a slow and long-continued movement. We may also walk on stilts, or run on skates. We may leap with a pole, or without one. Dancing is only an artistic and graceful combination of these movements.

70. (2) The second set comprises the arm movements, which are about the same as the preceding, being (a) lifting, (b) swinging; (c) throwing. The use of horizontal poles and bars, as well as climbing and dragging, belong to lifting. Under throwing, come quoit and ball-playing and bowling. These movements are distinguished from each other not only quantitatively, but qualitatively; as, for instance, running is not merely rapid walking; it is a different kind of movement from walking, as the position of the extended and contracted muscles is different.

71. (3) The third set of exercises, those of the trunk, differ from the other two, which should precede it, in that they bring the body into contact with an object in itself capable of active resistance, which it has to subdue. This object may be an element (water), an animal, or a human being; and thus we have (a) swimming, (b) riding, (c) fighting in single combat. In swimming we have the elastic fluid, water, to overcome by means of arm and leg movements. This may be made very difficult by a strong current, or by rough water, and yet we always have here to strive against an inanimate object. On the contrary, in horseback riding we have to deal with something that has a self of its own, and the contest challenges not our strength alone, but also our skill and courage. The motion is therefore very complex, and the rider must be able to exercise either or all of these qualities at need. But his 59 attention must not be wholly given to his horse, for he has to observe also the road, and indeed every thing around him. One of the greatest advantages of horseback riding to the overworked student or the business man lies doubtlessly in the mental effort. It is impossible for him to go on revolving in his mind the problems or the thoughts which have so wearied or perplexed him. His whole attention is incessantly demanded for the management of his horse, for the observation of the road, which changes its character with every step, and with the objects, far or near, which are likely to attract the attention of the animal he rides. Much good, doubtless, results from the exercise of the muscles of the trunk, which are not in any other motion called into such active play, but much also from the unavoidable distraction of the mind from the ordinary routine of thought, which is the thing most needed. When the object which we are to subdue, instead of being an animal, is a man like ourselves, as in single combat, we have exercise both of body and mind pushed to its highest power. We have then to oppose an intelligence which is equal to our own, and no longer the intelligence of an unreasoning animal. Single combat is the truly chivalrous exercise; and this also, as in the old chivalry time, may be combined with horsemanship.

In single combat we find also a qualitative distinction, and this of three kinds: (a) boxing and wrestling, (b) fighting with canes or clubs, and (c) rapier and sword fencing. The Greeks carried wrestling to its highest pitch of excellence. Among the British, a nation of sailors, boxing is still retained as a national custom. Fencing with a cane or stick is much in use among the French artisan class. The cane is a sort of refined club. When the sword or rapier makes its appearance, we come to mortal combat. The southern European excels in the use of the rapier; the Germans in that of the sword. The appearance of the pistol marks the degeneracy of the art of single combat, as it makes the weak man equal to the strong, and there is therefore no more incentive to train the body to strength in order to overcome an enemy. (The trained intelligence, the quick eye, the steady hand, the wary thought to perceive and to take advantage of an opportunity — these 60 are the qualities which the invention of gunpowder set up above strength and brute force. The Greek nation, and we may say Greek mythology and art, would have been impossible with gunpowder; the American nation impossible without it.)

Third Chapter.
Sexual Education.

[This chapter is designed for parents rather than for teachers, and is hence not paraphrased here. A few observations are, however, in place.] Great care is necessary at the period of youth that a rational system of food and exercise be maintained. But the general fault is in the omission of this care in preceding years. One cannot neglect due precautions for many years, and then hope to repair the damage caused, by extreme care for one or two years.

Special care is necessary that the brain be not overworked in early years, and a morbid excitation of the whole nervous system thereby induced. We desire to repress any tendency to the rapid development of the nervous system. Above all, is the reading of the child to be carefully watched and guarded. Nothing can be worse food for a child than what are called sensational romances. That the reading of such tends to enfeeble and enervate the whole thinking power is a fact which properly belongs to the intellectual side of our question not yet reached, and may be here merely mentioned. But the effect on the physical condition of the youth, of such carelessly written sensational stories, mostly of the French type, and full of sensuous, if not sensual suggestions, is a point not often enough considered. The teacher cannot, perhaps, except indirectly, prevent the reading of such trash at home. But every influence which he can bring to bear towards the formation of a purer and more correct taste, he should never omit. Where there is a public library in the town, he should make himself acquainted with its contents, and give the children direct help in their selection of books.

61

This is an external means. But he should never forget that every influence which he can bring to bear in his daily work to make science pleasant and attractive, and every lesson which he gives in the use of pure, correct English, free from exaggeration, from slang, and from mannerism, goes far to render such miserable and pernicious trash distasteful even to the child himself.

Every example of thorough work, every pleasure that comes from the solving of a problem or the acquisition of a new fact, is so much fortification against the advances of the enemy; while all shallow half work, all pretence or show tend to create an appetite in the child's mind which shall demand such food.

The true teacher should always have in his mind these far-away and subtle effects of his teaching; not present good or pleasure either for himself or his pupil, but the far-off good — the distant development. That idea would free him from the notion, too common in our day, that the success or failure of his efforts is to be tested by any adroitly contrived system of examinations; or still worse, exhibitions. His success can alone be tested by the future lives of his pupils — by their love for, or dislike of, new knowledge. His success will be marked by their active growth through all their lives; his failure, by their early arrested development.

62

AN OUTLINE OF EDUCATIONAL PSYCHOLOGY.

BY WM. T. HARRIS.

[TO BE USED AS AN INTRODUCTION TO PARAGRAPHS 81 TO 102 OF ROSENKRANZ'S PEDAGOGICS.]

I.

What beings can be educated; the plant has reaction against its surroundings in the form of nutrition; the animal has reaction in the form of nutrition and feeling; Aristotle calls the life of the plant the "nutritive soul," and the life of the animal the "sensitive soul."

The life of the plant is a continual reproduction of new individuals — a process of going out of one individual into another — so that the particular individual loses its identity, although the identity of the species is preserved.

That which is dependent upon external circumstances, and is only a circumstance itself, is not capable of education. Only a "self" can be educated; and a "self" is a conscious unity — a "self-activity," a being which is through itself, and not one that is made by surrounding conditions.

Again, in order that a being possess a capacity for education, it must have the ability to realize within itself what belongs to its species or race.

If an acorn could develop itself so that it could realize, not only its own possibility as an oak, but its entire species, and all the varieties of oaks within itself, and without losing its particular individuality, it would possess the capacity for education. But an acorn, in reality, cannot develop its possibility without the destruction of its own individuality. The acorn vanishes in the oak tree, and the crop of acorns which succeeds is not again the same acorn, except in kind or species. "The species lives, but the individual dies," in the vegetable world.

So it is in the animal world. The brute lives his particular life, unable to develop within himself the form of his entire species, and 63 still less the form of all animal life. And yet the animal possesses self-activity in the powers of locomotion, sense-perception, feeling, emotion, and other elementary shapes. Both animal and plant react against surroundings, and possess more or less power to assimilate what is foreign to them. The plant takes moisture and elementary inorganic substances, and converts them into nutrition wherewith to build its cellular growth. The animal has not only this power of nutrition, which assimilates its surroundings, but also the power of feeling, which is a wonderful faculty. Feeling reproduces within the organism of the animal the external condition; it is an ideal reproduction of the surroundings. The environment of the plant may be seized upon and appropriated in the form of sap, or in the form of carbonic acid, for the nourishment of that plant; but there is no ideal reproduction of the environment in the form of feeling, as in the animal.

In the activity of feeling, the animal transcends his material, corporeal limits — lives beyond his mere body, and participates in the existence of all nature. He reproduces within himself the external. Such being the nature of the activity of feeling, which forms the distinguishing attribute that divides animals from plants, the question meets us at the outset, "Why is not the animal capable of education? Why can he not realize within himself his entire species or race, as man can?"

In order to settle this fundamental question, we must study carefully the scope and limits of this activity, which we have termed "Feeling," and which is known under many names — as, sensation, sensibility, sensitivity, sense-perception, intuition, and others.

Education aims to develop the mind as intellect and will. It must know what it is to develop, and learn to distinguish higher or more complete stages of intellect and will from those which are rudimentary.

Again, the discussion of mind begins properly with the first or most un-developed manifestation — at the stage where it is common to brutes and human beings. Hence we may begin our study of educational psychology at this point where the distinction between animal and plant appears, and where the question of the capacity for education arises.

When we understand the relation of feeling or sensibility to the higher manifestations of mind, we shall see in what consists a capacity for educa-tion, and we shall learn many essentials in regard to the matter and me-thod, the what and the how of education.

A general survey of the world discovers that there is inter-action 64 among its parts. This is the verdict of science, as the systematic form of human experience. In the form of gravitation we understand that each body depends upon every other body, and the annihilation of a particle of matter in a body would cause a change in that body which would affect every other body in the physical universe. Even gravitation, therefore, is a manifestati-on of the whole universe in each part of it, although it is not a manifestati-on which exists for that part, because the part does not know it.

There are other forms wherein the whole manifests itself in each part of it — as, for example, in the phenomena of light, heat, and possibly in mag-netism and electricity. These forms of manifestation of the external world upon an individual object are destructive to the individuality of the object. If the nature of a thing is stamped upon it from without, it is an element only, and not a self; it is dependent, and belongs to that on which it de-pends. It does not possess itself, but belongs to that which makes it, and which gives evidence of ownership by continually modifying it.

But the plant, as we just now said, has some degree of self-activity, and is not altogether made by the totality of external conditions. The growth of the plant is through assimilation of external substances. It reacts against its surroundings and digests them, and grows through the nutrition thus formed.

All beings that cannot react against surroundings and modify them, lack individuality. Individuality begins with this power of reaction and modifi-cation of external surroundings. Even the power of cohesion is a rudimen-tary form of reaction and of special individuality.

In the case of the plant, the reaction is real, but not also ideal. The plant acts upon its food, and digests it, or assimilates it, and imposes its form on that which it draws within its organism. It does not, however, reproduce within itself the externality as that external exists for itself. It does not form within itself an idea, or even a feeling of that which is external to it. Its participation in the external world is only that of real modification of it or through it; either the plant digests the external, or the external limits it, and prevents its growth, so that where one begins the other ceases. Hence it is that the elements — the matter of which the plant is composed, that which it has assimilated even — still retain a large degree of foreign power or force — a large degree of externality which the plant has not been able to annul or to digest. The plant-activity subdues its food, changes its shape and its place, subordinates it to its use; but what the matter brings with it, and still 65 retains of the world beyond the plant, does not exist for the plant; the plant cannot read or interpret the rest of the universe from that small portion of it which it has taken up within its own organism. And yet the history of the universe is impressed on each particle of matter, as well within the plant as outside of it, and it could be understood were there capacities for recognizing it.

The reaction of the life of the plant upon the external world is not sufficient to constitute a fixed, abiding individuality. With each accretion there is some change of particular individuality. Every growth to a plant is by the sprouting out of new individuals — new plants — a ceaseless multiplication of individuals, and not the preservation of the same individual. The species is preserved, but not the particular individual. Each limb, each twig, even each leaf is a new individual, which grows out from the previous growth as the first sprout grew from the seed. Each part furnishes a soil for the next. When a plant no longer sends out new individuals, we say it is dead. The life of the plant is only a life of nutrition.

Aristotle called vegetable life "the nutritive soul," and the life of the animal the "feeling," or sensitive soul. Nutrition is only an activity of preservation of the general form in new individuals, it is only the life of the species, and not the life of the permanent individual.

Therefore we see that in the vegetable world we do not possess a being that can be educated — for no individual of it can realize within itself the species; its realization of the species is a continual process of going out of itself in new individuals, but no activity of return to itself, so as to preserve the identity of an individual.

190

II.

Feeling is a unity of the parts of an organism everywhere present in it; feeling is also an ideal reproduction of the external surroundings; feeling is therefore a synthesis of the internal and external. Aristotle joins locomotion and desire to feeling, as correlates; how desire is a more explicit recognition of the unity of the external and internal than the first form of feeling is; feeling reproduces the external without destroying its externality, while nutrition receives the external only after it has destroyed its individuality and assimilated it; desire is the side of feeling that unfolds into will.

With feeling or sensibility we come to a being that reacts on the external world in a far higher manner, and realizes a more wonderful form of individuality.

The animal possesses, in common with the plant, a process of assimilation and nutrition. Moreover, he possesses a capacity to feel. Through feeling, or sensation, all of the parts of his extended organism are united in one centre. He is one individual, and not a bundle 66 of separate individuals, as a plant is. With feeling, likewise, are joined locomotion and desire. For these are counterparts of feeling. He feels — i.e., lives as one indivisible unity throughout his organism and controls it, and moves the parts of his body. Desire is more than mere feeling. Mere feeling alone is the perception of the external within the being, hence an ideal reproduction of the external world. In feeling, the animal exists not only within himself, but also passes over his limit, and has for object the reality of the external world that limits him. Hence it is the perception of his finiteness — his limits are his defects, his needs, wants, inadequateness — his separation from the world as a whole. In feeling, the animal perceives his separation from the rest of the world, and also his union with it. Feeling expands into desire when the external world, or some portion of it, is seen as ideally belonging to the limited unity of the animal being. It is beyond the limit, and ought to be assimilated within the limited individuality of the animal.

Mere feeling, when attentively considered, is found to contain these wonderful features of self-activity: it reproduces for itself the external world that limits it; it makes for itself an ideal object, which includes its own self and its not-self at the same time. It is a higher form than mere nutrition; for nutrition destroys the nature of such externality as it receives into itself, while feeling preserves the external in its foreign individuality.

But through feeling the animal ascends to desire, and sees the independent externality as an object for its acquisition, and through locomotion it is enabled to seize and appropriate it in a degree which the plant did not possess.

III.

The various forms of feeling — its specialization: (a) touch, the feeling of mere limits, the indifferent external independence of the organism and its surroundings; (b) taste, feeling of the external object when it is undergoing dissolution by assimilation; (c) smell, the feeling of chemical dissolution in general; (d) hearing, the feeling of the resistance of bodies against attacks: sound being vibration caused by elastic reaction against attacks on cohesion; (e) seeing, the feeling of objects in their independence, without dissolution or attack; plant life, nutrition, a process in which the individuality is not preserved either in time or in space; animal life, as feeling, preserves its individuality as regards space, but not as regards time.

Having noted these important characteristics of the lower orders of life, and found that reaction from the part against the whole — from the internal against the external — belongs to plant life and animal life, we may now briefly mention the ways in which feeling is particularized. In the lower animals it is only the feeling of touch; in 67 higher organisms it becomes also localized as seeing, hearing, taste, and smell. These forms of sense-perception constitute a scale (as it were) of feeling. With touch, there is reproduction of externality, but the ideality of the reproduction is not so complete as in the other forms. With taste, the feeling cognizes the external object as undergoing dissolution, and assimilation within its own organism. We taste only what we are beginning to destroy by the first process of assimilation — that of eating. In smell, we perceive chemical dissolution of bodies. In seeing and hearing, we have the forms of ideal sensibility. Hearing perceives the attack made on the individuality of an external thing, and its reaction in vibrations, which reveal to us its internal nature — its cohesion, etc. In seeing, we have the highest form of sense-perception as the perception of things in their external independence — not as being destroyed chemically, like the objects of taste and smell; not as being attacked and resisting, like the objects which are known through the ear; not as mere limits to our organism, as in the sense of touch.

Sense-perception, as the developed realization of the activity of feeling, belongs to the animal creation, including man as an animal.

192

We have not yet, therefore, answered the question of capacity for education, so far as it concerns a discrimination between man and the brute. We have only arrived at the conclusion that the vegetable world does not possess the capacity for education, because its individual specimens are no complete individuals, but only transitory phases manifesting the species by continual reproduction of new individuals which are as incomplete as the old ones. Plant life does not possess that self-activity which returns into itself in the same individual — if we may so express it; it goes out of one individual into another perpetually. Its identity is that of the species, but not of the individual.

How is it with the animal — with the being which possesses sensibility, or feeling? This question recurs. In feeling there is a reaction, just as in the plant. This reaction is, however, in an ideal form — the reproduction of the external without assimilation of it — and especially is this the case in the sense of sight, though it is true of all forms of sensation to a less degree.

But all forms of sensibility are limited and special; they refer only to the present, in its forms of here and now. The animal cannot feel what is not here and now. Even seeing is limited to what is present before it. When we reflect upon the significance of this limitation of sense-perception, we shall find that we need some higher form of self-activity still before we can realize the species in the individual 68 i.e., before we can obtain the true individual — the permanent individuality.

The defect in plant life was, that there was neither identity of individuality in space nor identify in time. The growth of the plant destroyed the individuality of the seed with which we began, so that it was evanescent in time; it served only as the starting-point for new individualities, which likewise, in turn, served again the same purpose; and so its growth in space was a departure from itself as individual.

The animal is a preservation of individuality as regards space. He returns into himself in the form of feeling or sensibility; but as regards time, it is not so — feeling being limited to the present. Without a higher activity than feeling, there is no continuity of individuality in the animal any more than in the plant. Each new moment is a new beginning to a being that has feeling, but not memory.

Thus the individuality of mere feeling, although a far more perfect realization of individuality than that found in plant life, is yet, after all, not a continuous individuality for itself, but only for the species.

In spite of the ideal self-activity which appertains to feeling, even in sense-perception, only the species lives in the animal and the individual dies, unless there be higher forms of activity.

IV.

Representation is the next form above sense-perception. The lowest phase of representation is recollection, which simply repeats for itself a former sense-perception or series of sense-perceptions; in representation the mind is free as regards external impressions; it does not require the presence of the object, but recalls it without its own time and place; fancy and imagination are next higher than recollection, because the mind not only recalls images, but makes new combinations of them, or creates them altogether; attention is the appearance of the will in the intellect; with attention begins the separation of the transient from the variable in perception; memory is the highest form of representation; memory deals with general forms — not mere images of experience, but general types of objects of perception; memory, in this sense, is productive as well as reproductive; with memory arises language.

Here we pass over to the consideration of higher forms of intellect and will.

While mere sensation, as such, acts only in the presence of the object — reproducing (ideally), it is true, the external object, the faculty of representation is a higher form of self-activity (or of reaction against surrounding conditions), because it can recall, at its own pleasure, the ideal object. Here is the beginning of emancipation from the limitations of time.

69

The self-activity of representation can summon before it the object that is no longer present to it. Hence its activity is now a double one, for it can seize not only what is now and here immediately before it, but it can compare this present object with the past, and identify or distinguish between the two. Thus recollection or representation may become memory.

As memory, the mind achieves a form of activity far above that of sense-perception or mere recollection. It must be noted carefully that mere recollection or representation, although it holds fast the perception in time (making it permanent), does not necessarily constitute an activity completely emancipated from time, nor indeed very far advanced towards it. It is only the beginning of such emancipation. For mere recollection stands in the presence of the special object of sense-perception; although the object is no longer present to the senses (or to mere feeling), yet the image is present to the representative perception, and is just as much a particular here and now as the object of sense-perception. There intervenes a new activity on the part of the soul before it arrives at memory. Recollection is not memory, but it is the activity which grows into it by the aid of the activity of attention.

The special characteristics of objects of the senses are allowed to drop away, in so far as they are unessential and merely circumstantial, and gradually there arises in the mind the type — the general form — of the object perceived. This general form is the object of memory. Memory deals therefore with what is general, and a type, rather than with what is directly recollected or perceived.

The activity by which the mind ascends from sense-perception to memory is the activity of attention. Here we have the appearance of the will in intellectual activity. Attention is the control of perception by means of the will. The senses shall no longer passively receive and report what is before them, but they shall choose some definite point of observation, and neglect all the rest.

Here, in the act of attention we find abstraction, and the greater attainment of freedom by the mind. The mind abstracts its view from the many things before it, and concentrates on one point.

Educators have for many ages noted that the habit of attention is the first step in intellectual education. With it we have found the point of separation between the animal intellect and the human. Not attention simply — like that with which the cat watches by the hole of a mouse — but attention which arrives at results of abstraction, is the distinguishing characteristic of educative beings.

Attention abstracts from some things before it and concentrates 70 on others. Through attention grows the capacity to discriminate between the special, particular object and its general type. Generalization arises, but not what is usually called generalization — only a more elementary form of it. Memory, as the highest form of representation — distinguishing it from mere recollection, which reproduces only what has been perceived — such memory deals with the general forms of objects, their continuity in time. Such activity of memory, therefore, does not reproduce mere images, but only the concepts or general ideas of things, and therefore it belongs to the stage of mind that uses language.

V.

Language marks the arrival at the stage of thought — at the stage of the perception of universals — hence at the possibility of education; language fixes the general types which the productive memory forms; each one of these types, indicated by a word, stands for a possible infinite of sense-perceptions or recollections; the word tree stands for all the trees that exist, and for all that have existed or will exist. Animals do not create for themselves a new world of general types, but deal only with the first world of particular objects; hence they are lost in the variety and multiplicity of continuous succession and difference. Man's sense-perception is with memory; hence always a recognition of the object as not wholly new, but only as an example of what he is mostly familiar with. Intellectual education has for its object the cultivation of reflection; reflection is the Platonic "Reminiscence," which retraces the unconscious processes of thought

Language is the means of distinguishing between the brute and the human — between the animal soul, which has continuity only in the species (which pervades its being in the form of instinct), and the human, soul, which is immortal, and possessed of a capacity to be educated.

There is no language until the mind can perceive general types of existence; mere proper names nor mere exclamations or cries do not constitute language. All words that belong to language are significative — they "express" or "mean" something — hence they are conventional symbols, and not mere individual designations. Language arises only through common consent, and is not an invention of one individual. It is a product of individuals acting together as a community, and hence implies the ascent of the individual into the species. Unless an individual could ascend into the species he could not understand language. To know words and their meaning is an activity of divine significance; it denotes the formation of universals in the mind — the ascent above the here and now of the senses, and above the representation of mere images, to the activity which grasps together the general conception of objects, and thus reaches beyond what is transient and variable.

71

Doubtless the nobler species of animals possess not only sense-perception, but a considerable degree of the power of representation. They are not only able to recollect, but to imagine or fancy to some extent, as is evidenced by their dreams. But that animals do not generalize sufficiently to form for themselves a new objective world of types and general concepts, we have a sufficient evidence in the fact that they do not use words, or invent conventional symbols. With the activity of the symbol-making form of representation, which we have named Memory, and whose evidence is the invention and use of language, the true form of individuality is attained, and each individual human being, as mind, may be said to be the entire species. Inasmuch as he can form universals in his mind, he can realize the most abstract thought; and he is conscious. Consciousness begins when one can seize the pure universal in the presence of immediate objects here and now.

The sense-perception of the mere animal, therefore, differs from that of the human being in this: —

The human being knows himself as subject that sees the object, while the animal sees the object, but does not separate himself, as universal, from the special act of seeing. To know that I am I, is to know the most general of objects, and to carry out abstraction to its very last degree; and yet this is what all human beings do, young or old, savage or civilized. The savage invents and uses language — an act of the species, but which the species cannot do without the participation of the individual.

It should be carefully noted that this activity of generalization which produces language, and characterizes the human from the brute, is not the generalization of the activity of thought, so-called.

It is the preparation for thought. These general types of things are the things which thought deals with. Thought does not deal with mere immediate objects of the senses; it deals rather with the objects which are indicated by words — i.e., general objects.

Some writers would have us suppose that we do not arrive at general notions except by the process of classification and abstraction, in the mechanical manner that they lay down for this purpose. The fact is that the mind has arrived at these general ideas in the process of learning language. In infancy, most children have learned such words as is, existence, being, nothing, motion, cause, change, I, you, he, etc., etc.

But the point is not the mere arrival at these ideas. Education does not concern itself with that; it does not concern itself with 72 children who have not yet learned to talk — that is left for the nursery.

It is the process of becoming conscious of these ideas by reflection, with which we have to concern ourselves in education. Reflection is everywhere the object of education. Even when the school undertakes to teach pupils the correct method of observation — how to use the senses, as in "object-lessons" — it all means reflective observation, conscious use of the senses; it would put this in the place of the na‌جمي spontaneity which characterizes the first stages of sense-perception.

We must not underrate these precepts of pedagogy because we find that they are not what it claims for them — i.e., they are not methods of first discovery, and of arrival at principles, but only methods of reflection, and of recognizing what we have already learned. We see that Plato's "Reminiscence" was a true form of statement for the perception of truths of reflection. The first knowing is utterly unconscious of its own method; the second or scientific form of knowing, which education develops, is a knowing in which the mind knows its method. Hence it is a knowing which knows its own necessity and universality.

VI.

Education presupposes the stage of mind reached in productive memory; it deals with reflection; four stages of reflection: (a) sensuous ideas perceive things; (b) abstract ideas perceive forces or elements of a process; (c) concrete idea perceives one process, a pantheistic first principle, persistent force; (d) absolute idea perceives a conscious first principle, absolute person.

We have considered in our psychological study thus far the forms of life and cognition, contrasting the phase of nutrition with that of feeling, or sensibility. We have seen the various forms of feeling in sense-perception, and the various forms of representation as the second phase of intellectual activity — the forms of recollection, fancy, imagination, attention, and memory. We draw the line between the animals capable of education and those not capable of it, at the point of memory defined — not as recollection, but as the faculty of general ideas or conceptions, to which the significant words of language correspond.

With the arrival at language, we arrive at education in the human sense of the term; with the arrival at language, we arrive at the view of the world at which thought as a mental process begins. As sense-perception has before it a world of present objects, so thought has 73 before it a world of general concepts, which language has defined and fixed.

It is true that few persons are aware that language stands for a world of general ideas, and that reflection has to do with this world of universals. Hence it is, too, that so much of the so-called science of education is very *crude and impractical. Much of it is materialistic, and does not recognize the self-activity of mind; but makes it out to be a correlation of physical energies – derived from the transmutation of food by the process of digestion, and then by the brain converted into thought.*

Let us consider now the psychology of thinking, or reflection, and at first in its most inadequate forms. As a human process, the knowing is always a knowing by universals – a re-cognition, and not simple apprehension, such as the animals, or such as beings have that do not use language. The process of development of stages of thought begins with sensuous ideas, which perceive mere individual, concrete, real objects, as it supposes. In conceiving these, it uses language and thinks general ideas, but it does not know it, nor is it conscious of the relations involved in such objects. This is the first stage of reflection. The world exists for it as an innumerable congeries of things, each one independent of the other, and possessing self-existence. It is the stand-point from which atomism would be adopted as the philosophic system. Ask it what the ultimate principle of existence is, and it would reply, "Atoms."

But this view of the world is a very unstable one, and requires very little reflection to overturn it, and bring one to the next basis – that of abstract ideas. When the mind looks carefully at the world of things, it finds that there is dependence and interdependence. Each object is related to something else, and changes when that changes. Each object is a part of a process that is going on. The process produced it, and the process will destroy it – nay, it is destroying it now, while we look at it. We find, therefore, that things are not the true beings which we thought them to be, but processes are the reality. Science takes this attitude, and studies out the history of each thing in its rise and its disappearance, and it calls this history the truth. This stage of thinking does not believe in atoms or in things; it believes in forces and processes – "abstract ideas" – because they are negative, and cannot be seen by the senses. This is the dynamic stand-point in philosophy.

Reflection knows that these abstract ideas possess more truth, more reality, than the "things" of sense-perception; the force is more 74 real than the thing, because it outlasts a thing, – it causes things to originate, and to change, and disappear.

This stage of abstract ideas or of negative powers or forces finally becomes convinced of the essential unity of all processes and of all forces; it sets up the doctrine of the correlation of forces, and believes that persistent force is the ultimate truth, the fundamental reality of the world. This we may call a concrete idea, for it sets up a principle which is the origin of all things and forces, and also the destroyer of all things, and hence more real than the world of things and forces; and because this idea, when carefully thought out, proves to be the idea of self-determination — self-activity.

Persistent force, as taught us by the scientific men of our day, is the sole ultimate principle, and as such it gives rise to all existence by its self-activity, for there is nothing else for it to act upon. It causes all origins, all changes, and all evanescence. It gives rise to the particular forces — heat, light, electricity, magnetism, etc. — which in their turn cause the evanescent forms which sense-perception sees as "things."

We have described three phases: —

I. Sensuous Ideas perceive "things."
II. Abstract Ideas perceive "forces."
III. Concrete Idea perceives "persistent force."

In this progress from one phase of reflection to another, the intellect advances to a deeper and truer reality 14 at each step.

75

Sense-ideas which look upon the world as a world of independent objects, do not cognize the world truly. The next step, abstract ideas, cognizes the world as a process of forces, and "things" are seen to be mere temporary equilibria in the interaction of forces; "each thing is a bundle of forces." But the concrete idea of the Persistent force sees a deeper and more permanent reality underlying particular forces. It is one ultimate force. In it all multiplicity of existences has vanished, and yet it is the source of all particular existence.

This view of the world, on the stand-point of concrete idea, is pantheistic. It makes out a one supreme principle which originates and destroys all particular existences, all finite beings. It is the stand-point of Orientalism, or of the Asiatic thought. Buddhism and Brahminism have reached it, and not transcended it. It is a necessary stage of reflection in the mind, just as much as the stand-point of the first stage of reflection, which regards the world as composed of a multiplicity of independent things; or the stand-point of the second stage of reflection, which looks upon the world as a collection of relative existences in a state of process.

The final stand-point of the intellect is that in which it perceives the highest principle to be a self-determining or self-active Being, self-conscious, and creator of a world which manifests him. A logical investigation of the principle of "persistent force" would prove that this principle of Personal Being is presupposed as its true form. Since the "persistent force" is the sole and ultimate reality, it originates all other reality only by self-activity, and thus is self-determined. Self-determination implies self-consciousness as the true form of its existence.

These four forms of thinking, which we have arbitrarily called sensuous, abstract, concrete, and absolute ideas, correspond to four views of the world: (1) as a congeries of independent things; (2) as a play of forces; (3) as the evanescent appearance of a negative essential power; (4) as the creation of a Personal Creator, who makes it the theatre of the development of conscious beings in his image. Each step upward in ideas arrives at a more adequate idea of the true reality. Force is more real than thing; persistent force than particular forces; Absolute Person is more real than the force or forces which he creates.

76

This form of thinking is the only form which is consistent with the theory of education. Each individual should ascend by education into participation — conscious participation — in the life of the species. Institutions — family, society, state, church — all are instrumentalities by which the humble individual may avail himself of the help of the race, and live over in himself its life. The highest stage of thinking is the stage of insight. It sees the world as explained by the principle of Absolute Person. It finds the world of institutions a world in harmony with such a principle.

1 The parallelism between these two sciences, Medicine and Education, is an obvious point, which every student will do well to consider.

2 This will again remind the student of the theories of treatment in medicine in diseases which, in the seventeenth century, were treated only by bleeding and emetics, are now treated by nourishing food, and no medicines, etc.

3 The teacher will do well to consider the probable result of the constant association with mental inferiors entailed by his work, and also to consider what counter-irritant is to be applied to balance, in his character, this unavoidable tendency.

4 The age at which the child should be subject to the training of school life, or Education, properly so-called, must vary with different races, nations, and different children.

5 The best educator is he who makes his pupils independent of himself. This implies on the teacher's part an ability to lose himself in his work, and a desire for the real growth of the pupil, independent of any personal fame of his own — a disinterestedness which places education on a level with the noblest occupations of man.

6 See analysis.

7 Asiatic systems of Education have this basis (see 178 of the original).

8 The definition of freedom here implied is this: Mind is free when it knows itself and wills its own laws.

9 Perhaps, however slow the growth, there is real progress in liberating the imprisoned soul (?)

10 "When me they fly, I am the wings." — Emerson.

11 The story of Peter Schlemihl, by Chamisso, may be read in the English translation published in "Hedge's German Prose Writers."

12 That is, punishment is retributive and not corrective. Justice requires that each man shall have the fruits of his own deeds; in this it assumes that each and every man is free and self-determined. It proposes to treat each man as free, and as the rightful owner of his deed and its consequences. If he does a deed which is destructive to human rights, it shall destroy his rights and deprive him of property, personal freedom, or even of life. But corrective punishment assumes immaturity of development and consequent lack of freedom. It belongs to the period of nurture, and not to the period of maturity. The tendency in our schools is, however, to displace the forms of mere corrective punishment (corporal chastisement), and to substitute for them forms founded on retribution — e.g., deprivation of privileges. See secs. 42 and 43.

13 Faust; Part I., Scene I. "How all weaves itself into the Whole! Each works and lives in the other! How the heavenly influences ascend and descend, and reach each other the golden buckets!"

14 Hume, in his famous sketch of the Human Understanding, makes all the perceptions of the human mind resolve themselves into two distinct kinds: impressions and ideas. "The difference between them consists in the degrees of force and liveliness with which they strike upon the mind, and make their way into our thought and consciousness. Those perceptions which enter with the most force and violence we may name impressions, and under this name include all our sensations, passions, and emotions, as they make their first appearance in the soul. By ideas, I mean the faint images of these in thinking and reasoning." "The identity which we ascribe to the mind of man is only a fictitious one."

From this we see that his stand-point is that of ' sensuous ideas," the first stage of reflection. The second or third stage of reflection, if consistent, would not admit the reality to be the object of sense-impressions, and the abstract ideas to be only "faint images." One who holds, like Herbert Spencer, that persistent force is the ultimate reality — "the sole truth, which transcends experience by underlying it" — ought to hold that the generalization which reaches the idea of unity of force is the truest and most adequate of thoughts. And yet Herbert Spencer holds substantially the doctrine of Hume, in the words: "We must predicate nothing of objects too great or too multitudinous to be mentally represented, or we must make our predications by means of extremely inadequate representations of such objects — mere symbols of them." (Page 27 of "First Principles.")